Bottle of Beef, Book 3:

The Two Become One

By

Paul Tompkins

© Bottle of Beef, 2021. All Rights Reserved.

Unreal people are fiction, real people are not as depicted. Use at your own risk, Bottle of Beef is not responsible for anything you do after reading this book.

They call me Bridbrad McStabbinstuff. By "they" I mean Bottle, Bottle is the only one who calls me that. I actually don't mind, it's pretty funny. I am the Public Relations Department here at Bottle of Beef. You might remember me from such books as Bottle of Beef: The Media Empire of Doom. I played the small but rewarding part of Narry the Narrator in that book, and I'm also the de facto photographer. Now, I'm the substitute writing writer when Bottle isn't feeling it. It started out as Bottle pretending to speak for his audience, but he got to the point where he was chewing a hole in the middle of the candle so it could burn on all three ends and eventually he had to outsource that job. Luckily, we aren't getting much mail, so I have lots of free time.

If you are new here, then welcome to the third book. It's not mandatory, but our humble little empire actually has a long and winding back story, chronicled in A Year in the Life of Bottle the Curmudgeon, and Bottle of Beef: The Media Empire of Doom. Long story longer, as Bottle likes to say, we're a little imaginary art collective specializing in terrible music, amateurish visual art, and esoteric literature, mostly music reviews that veer off into socio-political commentary like a drunk driver on his/her way from a wedding to her/his own funeral. We're also imaginary, and that can be difficult to understand. A lot of people know that reality and the way we describe reality are actually different things. What most people don't understand is that there are people like Bottle, born inside the Matrix, he calls himself an Imagineer. I'm not an Imagineer, and neither is Gladys or Skip. We were once real people. We had lives, we had friends, we walked around and went grocery shopping, and all those normal people things other people do. However, we all suffered some relatively unimportant calamities in real life, and ended up here. Waifs and strays of rainy days, as Gladys likes to say. Bottle would probably smirk and refer to the Escalator of Doom. The important metaphor at play is that when you hit rock bottom you have to have something to do. Lots of people unfortunately fail and go nowhere, many find that they knew what they wanted to do all along and it merely required losing all the pointless ceremony that was holding them back, but a few of us needed the colorfully colloquial cattle-prod to the scrotum. Whether by fate or by happenstance, we crossed paths with Bottle and he without thinking said "here, do this, this is helpful." If there were such a thing as the inverse of a motivational speaker, Bottle would be that thing. Strangely enough, it seems to work for some of us. I for one haven't exploded.

So, welcome. Kick your shoes off, find a comfortable chair, and enjoy this third and final installment of the Saga of Beef. There will be turbulence, your stewardess might vomit, but I'm confident we'll land at whatever airport the underpaid and sleep-deprived air traffic controller told Kareem Abdul-Jabaar was ready for landing. I checked the passenger list and Ted Striker got marooned in Minnesota. I also checked the menu, and the only available foodstuffs are deer jerky and radishes, so we shouldn't have to worry about food poisoning. Prison rules: do your own time, and we'll have a function waiting for you when you get out. Bottle, that's your cue…

Yes – Fragile

I've been on an extended break. No particular reason, I just wasn't feeling it. I have a new record coming in the mail next week, but I got impatient and bought a few old ones today. It's an interesting collection, for sure.

In honor of feeling quite fragile after my second dose of corona virus vaccine, yes, you guessed who right, it's Yes's Fragile. Even better, in honor of acquiring a new keyboardist who wasn't afraid of a little Moog, Yes made a Richard Wright style not a Pink Floyd album. Every member has a solo track, but the rest are group jams. They were crunched for money after buying Wakeman new gear, so they put the whole thing together quick as an experiment.

Rick Wakeman was actually offered a spot in Yes and David Bowie's band on the same day, but in the end he decided he didn't want to play David Bowie songs every day for the next however many years.

Fragile isn't a concept per se, more like a conglomeration of coincidental feelings about the band. As for it merely being a technical show-off album with no overarching theme or shape, bollocks. The band was fragile (they fired their keyboardist for being a Luddite, remember?), they were about to get quite famous because the preceding tour went really well, the artist took it literal and painted a fragile planet breaking up as a wooden spaceship flies overhead, and the pieces are lovely (unlike anything on those two underwhelmingly Syd-less Pink Floyd albums).

Wakeman hated his extracts of the third movement from Brahms' 4th Symphony, but he wasn't yet free from his solo contract that forbade him from writing new material. The band itself had just paid off their previous manager so he couldn't steal 5% of their future royalties for no effort. Bruford had never composed anything before. All in all, I'd say this is about as good a "we don't know what we're doing" album as anyone could make.

I still feel like garbage, but this album certainly isn't. Flighty and spastic, sure, but I'd choose playful and unpredictable. Now, if you'll excuse me, I'm going to curl up under a fuzzy warm blanket and sleep until I feel better. Maybe we'll do another one tomorrow.

Red Rider – Don't Fight It

[Yawn] Welp, 11 hours of sleep seemed to do the trick. What's next for an album? The American version of Red Rider's first album, Don't Fight It? Ok, I won't.

Did he seriously just pronounce Somalia like it rhymes with Jambalaya? Yes, multiple times. Alright, I know I've experienced Red Rider backward, 3, 2, 1, what the hell am I listening to?

This is the weirdest conglomeration of New Wave, 80s Apartment Rock, and Alternative Arizona Troubadour (think Dead Hot Workshop or Gin Blossoms). I know I said you can taste the neon rainbow, but even that doesn't do it justice. It's like the Miami Vice version of Jewell of the Nile inside Toto's Africa. One minute they're on a yacht, then they're at a corporate $1,000 a plate fundraiser dinner, then their Jeep is stuck in a mud pit for no reason. We could have just skipped the entire Sandra saga from the last book, and only listened to the title track.

Why did they shuffle the playlist and leave out Talking to Myself? Someone must have thought it made more sense this way. I guess the concept is that love is a wild ride in a flying car. "Iron in your soul" appears in multiple songs, but I have a hard time believing that's a familiar idiom, even in Canada.

I guess, if you forced me to sum it all up, it's Billy Joel's Uptown Girl, but he definitely feels like he can't keep up. He just wants to unwind after a week of being a corporate zombie. I don't dislike it at all, but it's definitely strange, and undeniably 80s.

Trillion

Wowzers, have I got an obscure album tonight. Even more obscure than Starcastle, if you can believe it. Here's the self-titled debut by Trillion. Snow-leopard Cerberus doesn't lie, this is weird prog from Chicago, Illinois.

Prog Rock has always been one of those give it a decade genres, but Trillion got 1 album and no proper follow-up. They fired their singer then drifted off on various side paths. Patrick Leonard had the most prolific career, co-writing and arranging most of Madonna's biggest early hits. This album, though, is high-octane glam with enough twists and turns to make you deeply regret eating all that deep-fried carnival food before strapping into the Tilt-o-Whirl.

Let's talk about obscurity. It's a ridiculous concept, considering 100% of all bands start out as obscure. In fact, it's statistically bizarre to be famous. The industry cheats by spending millions of millions of dollars manufacturing that recognition, pretending that you should think their bands are already famous, or merely hiding the fact that the new guys are actually the kids and friends of already famous people with a built-in fan base. It's the farm team approach to big business. In short, mainstream music is a byproduct of business, not the other way around. Unlike Steve Albini, or Sylvia Massey, or even Todd Rundgren, most big label affiliated producers are in it for the money and the things you can get away with when you have it. The individual members of Trillion were way more interested in their individual careers than this particular band, and they all succeeded in that respect.

Does that make the sentiment of Hold Out ironic? Probably. Regardless, this album definitely deserves its inclusion on the list of highly underappreciated American Prog albums. It sounds a whole lot like Boston on more than two occasions, but it sounds like every other Prog-Rock band too, so who cares?

I guess what I'm trying to say is that if you like over the top, glamy 70s rock with random excursions into folk and disco, then check out this album barely anybody remembers. It's quite enjoyable.

Kansas – Vinyl Confessions

I needed to hear Vinyl Confessions for myself. Now that I have, I am completely convinced that Kerry Livgren was completely bat-shit insane. Hear me out, this is an important part of my much larger collection of containers with cow parts in them.

First, let's go back to Flyleaf. I pointed out that that was a Jesus album that didn't actually have anything to do with actual Jesus. Guess what, neither does this Kansas album that Steve Walsh preemptively opted out of, and after which Robby Steinhardt said "yeah, me neither."

Now, Christianity at large might have been totally different in the 70s, but to me it's no better or worse than any other religion. Critics hated this album and the next one (and multiple band members quit) because they were "overtly Christian" and they might as well be Foreigner albums, but critics didn't like Kansas before these albums either. No Kansas album ever got great reviews in its first decade. I've said it multiple times, everyone was really tired of waiting for Kerry to write Dust in the Wind, and man were they upset when he kept writing stuff after that.

Next, I can't remind you enough that the major religious texts were not Kerry's first choice when it comes to resurrected middle-eastern hippies. He much preferred the space-alien version for quite a long time, until someone more convincing than him won a backseat bus argument.

Last, whether Kerry knew it or not, he wasn't actually complaining about the lack of Jesus. Every single sentiment he expressed in song was about some real-life, mundane aspect of American socio-political buffoonery. Hey loser, get a job (but not one that I have to participate in paying you to do). Everybody was tired of his half concocted cult ramblings and they didn't want to churn out Pop Rock for pennies. They were fine floating through the sea of uncertainty as Kansas the Prog-Rock band, but they really didn't want to bring supernatural deities and organized religion into the equation.

    Now to recap, yes, Christians found specific things to like very much about this album, but the metaphors are much more approachable than that. You can wholeheartedly agree even if you are an unrepentant godless heathen like me. Obviously, the breakable things will fly if you don't want Kansas and Foreigner to be the same band, but I've pointed that out so many times you should all be fine with it by now.

    Vinyl Confessions and Drastic Measures are totally great 80s Hard Rock albums that Kansas as a band wasn't at all happy they made. If Seeds of Change was how Kerry was treating his actual friends behind the scenes, then yeah I would have quit too.

    M: What's your point, Bottle?
    B: You mean you didn't know? This is what selling out by pandering to an emerging market looks like. "Christian music" was literally becoming big business at that exact moment. I'm a big fan of coincidence, but you're seriously stretching my suspension of disbelief if you're telling me nobody knew what was happening. Intentional or not, this was intentional, and it boiled down to money. Maybe Kerry really didn't think that way, but some of us heathens have principles, you know?

    Plus, why can't Christians like Prog Kansas? Is it 'cause Lucky Charms are made by satanic leprechauns? It is, isn't it? Enjoying the adventure is evil. Sadly, the real irony seems to be that organized religion is as corrupt as anything. Like everything else we rant and fight about, it's the hierarchy of power that corrupts. The moment you confuse your person with your function you flip right around and become a hypocrite. Kansas didn't morph and fall apart because Kerry and Dave converted to Christianity, they fell apart because he started acting like they weren't good enough.

Supertramp – Crime of the Century

It was like the crime of the century how dirty this copy of Supertramp's Crime of the Century was. Still scratchy and in need of a deep clean, but it's at least listenable after a quick Dawn bath. This is their third album after a lineup change and no longer being supported by a Dutch millionaire. They lived and made demos of 42 songs at a farmhouse in Dorset, and picked 8 for the album.

It's not a concept, it's named after the final track, but there is a definite theme of being alone in your own insecurities, afraid of the wider world and what everybody else is thinking.

Their first two albums were panned for containing too much self indulgent instrumental music. That's nonsense in my book, but this is definitely a stellar album. I love Supertramp regardless, but there's an almost "psychological thriller" aura to the album. The band all felt like this was their creative peak, but they hadn't written Breakfast in America yet, so....

The clash between Richard and Roger was always the focus of the band. Rick was the working-class Blues and Jazz kid who happened to have a financial backer, Roger was the prep-school Pop insider. They eventually grew apart and found writing together difficult, plus Roger didn't like Rick's wife's Sharon Osbourne impression (she was their manager), so he quit.

The thing about Supertramp I love is that what they're really saying is that life would be fantastic if we didn't have to go through all the competition and antagonism. What's wrong with being a dreamer? What's wrong with working hard to achieve those dreams? Why does everybody want to tear each other down? The answer is that we are our own villains.

Marianne Faithful – Broken English

Comeback albums. Back in Black and Californication spring to my mind, but everybody probably has a Tom Hanks movie of their own. You know what's not on any of them? Marianne Faithfull's Broken English. It's a doozie of an album though.

She was a 60s pop idol, like Eric Burdon and Dio. She came from the Rolling Stones camp, she was Jagger's girlfriend, but she had a legitimate career with crossover hits. The drugs, however, took their toll. She got noticeably raspy, and eventually anorexic, homeless, and heroin addicted. The preceding two albums were Folk Rock that nobody liked, she hired an aspiring producer who convinced her to go full on New Wave Synth Punk by hiring Steve Winwood to keyboard all over it, and it's quite a shock to the system.

If Lord Sutch is my spirit animal, then this is definitely the Bottle of Beef soundtrack. It's not a concept album, but very clearly the concept is "you wanna know what I think? Never mind the bullocks, here's a little slice of real for you to choke down."

This is a complicated album, and it is raw. It tackles the structural schism head on: the continuing saga of WWII, surviving that trip to the bottom of the barrel, being fed into the middle-class machine, and cutting through the BS of the facade like a hot knife through a birthday cake. It's the kind of album that needs an "I've seen a lotta things" voice like Marianne's to drive home. All that said, it's easy to interpret wrong. In fact, how you interpret it says a whole lot more about your own bias than anything else, because not very many people survive to talk about it. Not many people step outside the war and see it as the pointlessly childish game it really is. Neither side of the fight is good, and everybody suffers for it. What *are* you fighting and dying for? Why do we instill guilt and fear into our children? Why can't you see that you are still peasants in the eyes of the elite? Why *did* you do it, and why do we keep doing it to each other?

Impressive comeback, to say the least.

El-P – Cancer 4 Cure

I knew what this album review would be before I even finished ordering it: what's my album collection have to say about Brooklyn?

Well, the Beastie Boys say we can't sleep 'til we get there and have a fight or possibly play baseball with 3rd Bass, you can dial a 900 number to hear They Might Be Giants songs, Biohazard says be careful walking to the subway 'cause you might get shot, or possibly undead if Type O Negative's posse of vampires gets to you first, and now El Producto tells me there's drones flying everywhere.

Google maps has some pictures of the pretty landmarks. It has its own bridge to Manhattan. Queens and the rest of Long Island to the east, where the Good Rats and Aesop Rock used to live.

What I didn't know was how well it would culminate the random string of albums from the weekend. Too well, it turns out, but we're here to review an album not psychoanalyze myself. Turns out we'll hear El-P psychoanalyze himself, his occupation, and his city. My brain feels like the glass shards on the cover, I'm sure this will help.

Calling this album cynically paranoid is putting it mildly, but it's an album about living through it, choosing to live through it, refusing to back down and hide from living through it, being the cancer for which death is the cure, with some bravado and dick jokes along the way, of course.

As William S. Burroughs so succinctly puts it: this is war to extermination. All things must end, and these are stories about experiencing that end and living through it.

The bird with a halo came from a drawing on a toy wooden airplane made by Alexander Calder (the drawing, not the toy airplane). Here it's recreated in glass shards. The album itself is dedicated to Camu Tao, who died of lung cancer in 2008. Camu also influenced Aesop Rock's Impossible Kid, all three were good friends and band mates. Cancer 4 Cure is the first album El-P made after putting his label Definitive Jux on hiatus (he stepped down as artistic director in 2010 and it's a tombstone in the UMG graveyard now).

Musically speaking, this is deep, dark electronic beatwork, borderline Jungle and Rave, interstellar synth noise, strange samples, and bizarre live instruments. A paranoid sci-fi acid trip through the interstellar ghetto is what it sounds like.

Storywise, there're some real doozies that you just have to hear for yourself, like Upstairs Neighbor and Tougher Colder Killer. It's a complicated album, but it boils down to choosing to consciously live it. No offense, but Brooklyn sounds terrifying, with or without the drone attack.

Mastodon – Crack the Skye

Whoa whoa whoa whoa, we haven't listened to my favorite Mastodon album? Really? Oh, yeah, I know why. A) I never have much to say about stuff I really like, II) there's that highly uncomfortable issue of Brann's sister's less than intentional suicide (Brann himself is pretty sure she didn't realize the handful of pills would actually kill her), and Triangle) it's the Mastodon version of Rasputin. My wicked Caddyshack slice would have us debating that nasty bit of history where Lenin did a really bad job of reading Marx and somehow ended up being Jaime Lannister. I have in fact visited Lenin's Mausoleum in Red Square, I rode an overnight train from Moscow to St. Petersburg, I have actual Russian street art I watched that guy paint and patiently waited for it to dry, and bought my dad a bottle of Stolichnaya at the duty free shop on the way home.

So yeah, we'll just avoid all that and point out how frustrating it was to read 900,000 pages of Song of Ice and Fire, just to be angry when HBO out-paced George "Reading Rainbow" Martin's ability to finish writing the damned thing.

Spoiler alert, in the books Tyrion kills Tywin, but somehow that wasn't how the TV version went, and I for one gave up the ability to care anymore. Crap, now we're in murky Pearl Jam Ten territory, and some topics are just off limits.

This is their Aether album. It's specifically influenced by In the Court of the Crimson King and Animals (King Crimson and Pink Floyd), Tsarist Russia, and Stephen Hawking. Doubt me? Here is the honest to actual nonsense concept, copy and pasted for you to just try to comprehend:

"There is a paraplegic and the only way that he can go anywhere is if he astral travels. He goes out of his body, into outer space and a bit like Icarus, he goes too close to the sun, burning off the golden umbilical cord that is attached to his solar plexus. So he is in outer space and he is lost, he gets sucked into a wormhole, he ends up in the spirit realm and he talks to spirits telling them that he is not really dead. So they send him to the Russian cult, they use him in a divination and they find out his problem. They decide they are going to help him. They put his soul inside Rasputin's body. Rasputin goes to usurp the czar and he is murdered. The two souls fly out of Rasputin's body through the crack in the sky(e) and Rasputin is the wise man that is trying to lead the child home to his body because his parents have discovered him by now and think that he is dead. Rasputin needs to get him back into his body before it's too late. But they end up running into the Devil along the way and the Devil tries to steal their souls and bring them down…there are some obstacles along the way."

Self explanatory, really. If I had a favorite album of all time this would probably be it. I don't, but if I did, it probably would be.

Deltron 3030

The number of holes I dug today is ridiculously around a hundred. My whole body hurts. Rum and coke number two is gently fizzing, and my copy of Deltron 3030 is rotating. Glorious.

Once upon a time, Ice Cube turned to his cousin and queried "Del, what the hell is a Funkee Homosapien?" Del probably had some crazy answer for him, but the real answer is that Del is *the* Funkee Homosapien. As a kid he was super into computers and writing poetry, and when he heard Grandmaster Flash he said "that [snap], that's the kind of poetry I want to write." He thinks rap is a legitimate art form, and he is prolific, to put it mildly. He formed this super group with Dan Tha Automator and Kid Koala. He wrote the entire concept album in less than 2 weeks. It's the story of a former mech warrior in the year 3030 who rap battles to defeat the corporate overlords who made rap illegal, but gets captured and has his memory erased.

"Conscious Hip-Hop" might not be a familiar subgenre to you. It's a positive art-form focused on inspiring its audience to be aware of the world happening around them. This album is fantastic, it's a sci-fi comic book in the form of a hip-hop album.

Now, from time to time, I implore you to actually go listen to an album, and this is one album you should absolutely hear at least once. I think I can safely say that this is one of the greatest albums of all time. Even if you think you hate rap, you can't deny the following imperative: upgrade your gray matter, 'cause one day it may matter. Seriously, this is phenomenal. There's a set up for the movie Strange Brew. I made a Bob and Doug McKenzie joke once, making fun of

K-tel, I think. Track 15 is called "The News (a wholly owned subsidiary of Microsoft Inc.). I'd call this a Golden Age style album. I'd also point out that Del has been doing this since the 80s, this is what I was talking about in my review of Massive Attack. Gangsta rap is one small segment of the art form. It's an important part obviously, but there's a much wider world of less commercially accessible amazingness.

Seriously, go find Deltron 3030 on youtube or in person and love it as much as I do. It's so much fun. Cheers.

Christmas in April

S: Pssst. Pssssssst. Oi! Bottle!

B: Yes?

S: It's mid April.

B: So?

S: You told me to remind you, remember?

B: Did I? Whoa, watch where you're pointing those eyebrows. Gimme a second...carry the one...flip it and reverse it... oh, yeah! We're supposed to find out if that Christmas album by The Vandals works out of context. Fire up the old yuletube log.

Believe it or not, The Vandals have the same problem as Kansas. Remember how critics hated Kansas for being Kansas, but hated them even more when they started being Foreigner instead? Well, for some reason that I can't understand, critics don't like The Vandals because they keep making music that focuses on juvenile humor. Guys, that's what this band is, that's their box of raisins. If you don't like it, stop reviewing their albums. If your review is "I don't like The Vandals," then my response is "why did you interrupt what I was doing to tell me that?" Not in the incredulous sense, in the literal "tell me why" sense. Did they personally rob your house, are you just being a jerk, do you actually believe that killing people is the only way to solve problems?

Merry Christmas, here's some machine gun fire and police sirens. First track is amazing. You could choose to interpret it as sarcasm or not, but either way they are pointing out the absurdity of the entire situation. If you really think that way, which admit it some of you do, then you'll probably be offended. Why? You don't care what The Vandals think, you asked Santa for a gun so you can shoot them if they get near your house. Juvenile or not, the whole thing is Absurd.

I don't mean no disrespect because he's old and mean, but why do we keep inviting Grandpa to Christmas when he doesn't know my name and hits me with his cane for no reason? I love Grandpa, but he legitimately wants to make us miserable. I bought you a Christmas present, but you didn't buy me one. Screw you.

I could keep going, but yeah this album is awesome. I don't even think it's particularly juvenile. Every song is a playfully obnoxious look at the absurdity of not being honest about anything. Christmas doesn't magically make everything better.

Honestly, this album is amazing. These are incredibly complex situations, viewed from a high level of self-deprecating objectivity. This album is actually highly intellectual, and it points out the sheer insanity of defining the entire value of human life around one imaginary bipolar cataclysm in late December.

Yep, this album is at least 1,000 times better outside of its context. You're totally allowed to hate The Vandals, but I can't imagine why you would put that much effort into it, especially considering Oi to the World! is a fantastic album, and they are an amazingly underappreciated Punk band.

The Rocketeer

I'm in a weird mood. Let's listen to the score for the movie The Rocketeer. You've heard a lot of James Horner's music, but I thankfully don't remember this movie. I remember that Jennifer Connelly is in it.

One thing I can tell you is this is exceedingly sappy, decidedly American Classical music. Like, even Copland and Groffé would make the "why's there Elmer's Glue in my mouth" face. It's very "Back to the Future Part III" to my mind. Sure there's mystery and romance and adventure, but in a nauseating way.

Horner, like John Williams, had a tendency to straddle the "borrowing" fence a little to conspicuously for the legal teams of many estates, and reused his own themes enough for movie critics to notice, but we all know where commie Indonesian lady Bottle's feelings tend to land in that game of lawn darts: I didn't ask for the stuff you did to get stuck in my brain, and it's not like I just photocopied your piece and handed it to Disney.

Regardless, there's some period low-proof white people jazz, some nostalgic 1800s wild-west cowboy music, and Nazis, 'cause they're an annoyingly omnipresent thing.

On a serious note, he does some really cool "noise work" and plays around with the placement of instruments in the intense passages. I don't care for his wide open pastoral major schlock, but his dramatic minor passages are pretty great. The primary theme gets old, but I remember it being an overly sappy movie anyway, so at least it's appropriate. Not a terrible listen, but not one I'll be reaching for again any decade soon. Haven't seen the movie a second time in the last 30 years either, so at least I'm consistent.

Well, that was something. What should we listen to tomorrow?

P.S. for those of you thinking I might be ragging on Horner too much, I adore his score for Wrath of Khan, so there.

Shostakovich #5

Today we'll listen to Bernstein's 1979 Tokyo recording of Shostakovich #5. Is it proof of the rehabilitating force of the Communist Party, or the Happy Happy, Joy Joy segment of Ren & Stimpy? That, of course, depends on you. Our old friend Structuralism says it means all the meanings it is capable of meaning. Well, unless you're lying and it didn't actually mean what you said it meant for you. I know that's confusing, but remember that Shostakovich said whatever Shostakovich thought Stalin thought Shostakovich should be thinking and the actual truth of anything is completely absent.

At least *we* can all agree what constitutes unpremeditated murder again. Good. He didn't set out to murder George Floyd, but we all watched him murder George Floyd.

Nirvana – In Utero

I've mentioned In Utero a couple times, so you already know A) it's the "adult" part of the Nirvana chronology and B) it's not supposed to be trendy mainstream music. It is, by most any standards for music or lyrics, disgusting. I love it.

There are lots of back and forth and contradictory stories about the whole process and their relationship with Albini, who I believe called them "REM with stomp boxes," but I think it boils down to three things: 1) Steve Albini didn't want anything to do with anyone who wasn't an actual member of Nirvana, 2) Nirvana hated Nevermind and being famous, and 3) Albini characterized every band he worked with as "losers at the mercy of their label."

Regardless of what anyone says about it, these are songs about what it was like to be Kurt Cobain, and he clearly didn't enjoy being him. The finished product has a lot of tweaking that Albini wasn't happy about, but it sure sounds like he just pointed a bunch of microphones at their gear. I personally love the way it sounds.

No Good Deed Goes Unpunished

Alright crew. It's time to fix this thing for real. The Governor of Georgia thinks DST shortens the actual amount of night time, the guy who loaded mulch into my car decided I get black instead of brown, it's sleeting in April, some people still think killing each other is the best way to stop people from killing each other, and I don't have any more bottles. Believe me, it hurts to exert this much authority, but...

Skip. Make the first book look like the second book. 11pt Palatino, odd pages in the top right corner, quadruple check the final PDF for pagination errors.

Compy. There's still false references in the first index, and the second index doesn't exist yet.

Sandra. First cover is fine, second cover gets a red and yellow color scheme, 'cause somewhere out there there's a Russian mouse who will get the Use Your Illusion reference and giggle.

Bridbrad. Stop pretending you aren't the narrator/writing writer of all this cosmic space fantasy war silliness.

GREGORY. Stop screeching for however long this takes. Hopefully only a couple weeks, but no promises.

Carl. Reset all the mousetraps.

Gladys! Flip on the "work happens" sign.

Did I miss anyone? Oh yeah, me. When it's all said and done, I'm gonna fork over the dough for proper ISBNs and make this double headed monster distributable to the world at large.

What's our motto? "We're all dead on the inside, tee hee." Inflate the pig! Do do it! Release the beavers! Where's my coffee cup? Space cadets, I mean discorporate corporate functions, go!

Slowly the light filtered into Bottle's eyeballs. Too bright, too bright, he thought. Normally, Bottle would slowly will his appendages into action and reach the ceremonial putting on of the pants, but something was different this time.

Why bother? It's all still going to keep getting worse. There isn't a second direction for the escalator to travel, and there's nowhere to go if there were.

As he slowly acclimated to the light, Bottle made the face of someone recognizing the pointlessly familiar situation they found themselves experiencing again for the umpteenth time without a discernible reason to explain it. "Checklist time: White room, check. Black curtains, check. Sappy soft rock... no? Uh oh. Not good. Alright, I'm awake. What?"

Staring up into the vagueness, a circle of gray blobs intruded on his vision like that terrible nightmare where you wake up in a 1800s operating theater. Bottle licked his lips and smacked around to get the saliva flowing again.

B: What are you auditing?

A: There is nothing to audit. You have, as you say, poked a hole between the imaginable and the unimaginable, and we are for lack of a better term bored.

B: Schwa? You're not real.

A: But we are now imaginable, and therefore, we must have a function. We must be your enemy, we must be that unseen force that prevents you from exerting free will.

B: Guys, that's dumb. The universe doesn't run on me being mad at you. You don't have to do anything. Doing more isn't the solution to most problems. Sometimes you have to do less, choose to stop sort of thing. Be bored. You never were my enemy, so why would that be your function? Imagine something different.

A: We cannot imagine for ourselves. We live outside of the imaginable.

B: Yes, I know, and I poked the hole, so you're in my head. But you aren't real, you weren't real in the first place. Even Sandra understands that you can't actually invent something from nothing. The magic broom lives in my other office. You can't come into the bunker because there's no you to come in.

A: We must exist to be here.

B: No, no, no, and let me check just to be sure... ah, yes, NO! I, Bottle, am imagining you, the unimaginably discorporate personification of incorporation. You are not a corporation of Corporations, you are the empty shell that incorporates generic want. You aren't gods, you are not authority, you are the conglomeration of unconsequent wants. You might possibly be the inverse of gods, but that's complicated.

A: Tell us.

B: Why? It won't help. You aren't real, you don't exist, you can't exist. Sure, someone can pretend to be one of you, but you aren't in control, they make it up as they go. You might look at it and think "hey, that's an impersonation of me!," but there's no you to think that.

A: Then why are we here with you? We must exist.

B: Guys, you're killing me here. I'm not a bridge to the unimaginable, I'm not a function, I'm not in charge of anything, I don't make the rules, I just point out that there aren't any rules before you invent them, but inventing them has consequences. It's imaginary, you're part of the part on the other side that can't be imagined. I can imagine what you're doing, but even I can't actually imagine you. You're gray blobs. You exist behind the behind the scenes, and the rabbit hole in front of you is infinite.

 A: Then why are we here? Why were we invented?

 B: You aren't. You weren't.

 A: But we are legion.

 B: So? It's not my fault that people decide there has to be a reason, or that that reason has to be the solution to a non-existent problem, definitely not my fault they imagine that someone made them do it. I'm like a bug zapper in a world with no bugs, only the idea that bugs should exist. You're the reason the bugs don't exist. You guys like money, right?

 A: Money is auditable.

 B: So, yes. Ok. Say I want a whatsamawhosit, but they don't exist. If they did exist, I'd be willing to pay 5 dollars for it. There are things that sort of seem like a $5 whatsamawhosit that cost $20, but I know they aren't real whatsamawhosits, so they aren't worth more than $0. With me so far?

 A: Yes, that is all perfectly auditable.

 B: Well, you're the reason why the actual $5 dollar whatsamawhosit doesn't exist.

 A: That is nonsense.

 B: No argument from me, guys. Nonsense it is. Nevertheless, here we are inside that Cream song. I didn't bring me here, and I didn't decide to use trains as a metaphor. Stop being the reason we can't have nice things. I'm going back to sleep. I don't care what you guys do, just don't bring me back here 'cause you're bored. If you need some raisins, try just being prepared to audit whatever might need to be audited should it occur. Until then, be bored. We'll collectively think of something eventually. Maybe try figuring out what bizarre malfunction is causing Elon Musk to be preemptively sad for all the people who will die along his quest to be the guy who funded humans traveling to Mars. One of you things exists because of that mental paradox, audit yourselves until you find it.

 A: Oh, you mean Narzon? Yes, we are deeply troubled by her. She shouldn't have a name or be a she. Perhaps you are correct. We shall wait and see. Thank you.

 B: Did I help? Nevermind, don't care, just let me sleep.

 But Bottle did not get to sleep. Instead, he spontaneously awoke to find himself fully panted and already in the middle of unboldening Skip's accidental boldification of the index page numbers.

 B: Damnit, Bridbrad! Stop trying to be creative. You have no idea how hard it is to concentrate with you scribbling away up there!

System of a Down – Mezmerize/Hypnotize
 Everybody brought their helmets? Ok, here's the dooziest of doozies in my album collection:
 I can't count all the times I haven't reviewed System Of A Down's Mezmerize/Hypnotize. At least once in every major story arc, but probably more than that. How do you review it? How, Skip, how? It's worse than Year of the Black Rainbow or Automata. They hate LA, they hate war, they hate right-wing 'Merica, they hate the genocide of their people, and rightfully so on all those counts.
 On the other hand, they are like one of the biggest illusion bands ever. I don't mean they are fake or worthy of derision, I just mean that their decade and a half of inactivity is purely about money and "creative differences." They still play big shows, they all want to make more music, just not each others' music, and they can't agree on how to pay each other. That all sounds suspiciously like they aren't actually friends anymore, more like childish grown-ups knife fighting near the tire swing, but what do I know?

There is awesome stuff on these last two albums, but there is also pointless silliness. I'm all for silly, if there's a point. I guess one part of the problem is that while listening to them, I often start to wonder why they bothered. These things are surprisingly short, but also surprisingly fragmented and the kind of unfinished I would normally reserve for a critique of Paul McCartney's less than thorough audio efforts. That's my question, why bother?

The answer is that they still care. They don't want to put out crap just to sell albums, but they also don't want to walk away. Believe it or not, that's the same situation as Metallica and Sir Paul himself (though he was always happy to put out garbage albums, so whatever). Welcome to Corporate America, you own a brand. As a way of life, I think we all know that's a pretty meaningless version. That's reality, you can't be both a real person and a fictional celebrity at the same time.

Why don't presidents fight the war? Why are all these complicated geo-political power dynamics harassing me when I'm just sitting in my car waiting for my girl? Why do we keep living in this violent pornography? Penis penis penis penis vagina, that's a song, right? Remember those shiny happy people in that REM song? Were Tibetans protesting because protesting is fashionable? Do I have to go find and reread my copy of Collingwood's The Idea of History? I could, I know roughly where it is in the attic, but let's just bumble forward all willy-nilly like I'm wont to do.

Things that happened aren't History, with a capitalized but not mandatorily aspirate H (you can glottal stop if you want to, according to Men Without Ats). No, History is what you tell yourself it was like to live through those events, a self examination of situational empathy. That could go well, or not well at all, but in the end your version of the story is only as good as your ability to be a functional human with an imagination. I'm sure he had more subtle and nuanced points than that, but I am Bottle, hear me apologetically paraphrase.

The political history of China and Tibet is not my forte, so it goes right in the folder with Ireland. What I can tell you, is I generally tend to think that the people who decided to kill a bunch of other people are guilty of some form of being wrong, whence my tendency to dad-declare that you're both wrong, go somewhere else so I don't have to listen to it anymore.

Speaking of getting off my lawn, the upside to all of this is that these are fairly honest albums. By that, I mean they don't have that passive-aggressive delusion that everything would be great if it weren't for all the terrible other people ruining my master plan. Instead, it's more like "look, this is garbage, sure, but the parts I really do like wouldn't exist either, so I can't exactly say flush it all down the toilet. Am I alone in here? Yep, wish I hadn't heroined up those hypodermics after all. Help."

If we look at the band as a group of people who really don't want to be a cult, then I get it. Too bad being a big headliningly famous brand is its own kind of cult.

So maybe we listen to it as grown-ups pointing out that they are still children. No, I mean that's part of it, but not the whole shebang. For starters, we have this unspoken dark mysticism thing lurking under the surface. Something about the corporate social machine is fundamentally wrong, but all you can do is pop the largest couple zits and be depressed.

Maybe we try a completely new thing. We tried fighting the diseased programming of centuries, but that just brought even worse people out into the melee. Tucker Carlson thinks he's a Liberal who gets mad sometimes. Maybe that's true, he's certainly insane enough to plausibly be that deluded. It's interesting to remember that today's Republican Party is the offshoot of the Democratic-Republican Party, that's why they constantly forget that they agree about 85% of the time.

The Democrat side at least once in a while points out that there're millions of people who totally don't agree with either of them. RINO is one of those terms where the people who use it the most are tragic victims of their own dramatic irony. It's funny how people who vociferously proclaim liberty so often hide behind the liability shelter of incorporation and pray for a dictator when their beloved free market chooses to get rid of them. Most people want more wind and solar energy, but somehow that's unfair to the guys who profit from oil we don't want to buy or burn anymore? You do realize that "the free market" and "the tyranny of the majority" are structurally the same thing, right? No? You didn't? Well, they are. Market economics is literally the tyranny of the majority.

The guys in SOAD have net-worths around 20 million, but I've tried to explain why that's meaningless in a variety of ways. All that means is that that would be Serj or Daron's initial asking price if they were willing to sell you all their assets (cars, houses, song rights, musical instruments, etc.). What do any of them actually do in day to day life? Practice? Make phone calls? Speak at fundraiser dinners? Buy more hockey jerseys?

What was even my point? Have we even listened to it yet? Crap, no we haven't. Better do that. Funny story, I apparently had the discs switched. Let's try that again, shall we?

Welcome to the soldier side (life is war, in case you didn't get that memo). Oh, wow, I haven't listened to it in a while, and I forgot how great it starts out. It sounds amazing. It's ridiculous, and laugh out loud crazy, but the vocal equality of Serj and Daron is amazing. Serj is Serj (amazing), but Daron as an equal duet partner raises it to a whole new level. There are a few moments of "yes, we totally know the lyrics don't make sense," but the contextualization helps some. They tend to be representations of insane, erratic behavior. It helps if you remember that each song is about one thing, each exists inside a metaphor. Sometimes that metaphor is explicit, sometimes it's a philosophical perspective.

In the thank you section, Daron puts a Charles Manson quote. I get it, but that doesn't change the fact that I had to turn my hand upside down and press my thumb against my left eyeball. I assume you have some understanding of the complex meaning of that weird human body language.

I forgot how amazing the choruses are. These are mostly pop songs, by the way. Amazing dropped-c (I think, I didn't look it up to verify) riffs, exotic melodies, but pop songs. Also, these are proper half-hour albums. Daron really did play in a celebrity baseball game with Tony Danza and Frankie Avalon. And, actually that gets us to the real heart of what's going on. This is System Of A Down, you know, Armenian-Americans playing Alternative Metal about how America is so totally a nonsense, coked-up, Fascist country, and freakin' proud of it for some insane reason (it's probably the cocaine talking).

You could write an 800 page book just trying to contextualize these two albums. Early Offspring level irony, deep socio-political criticism. Actually, I bet I know the real secret: you can't do anything else after something like this. It's literally everything. I know that feeling. Hell, we're going through the last few interesting things I couldn't figure out how to weave into my two books about albums. This is literally all of them.

The middle of Hypnotize (the second of the pair) is where it all starts to go haywire for me. The title track is amazing, big hit, already referenced. It points out the sheer insanity of trying to reconcile actual reality with the ponderous weight of the political world even Atlas couldn't shoulder.

It's all an anti-TV statement. More specifically, there's the reality you walk around in, and the reality TV tells you

you didn't notice while you were foolishly out walking around.

From track 6 on, I lose it. I can't keep it all straight. It's wonderful, but I can't hold it all in my head. You win, guys. You broke me. 2020 15 years ahead of schedule. Ok Computer and Steppenwolf's Monster are the only more prescient albums I can think of at the moment.

Actually, I've never tried to listen to the second album all by itself. Maybe remind me to try it in a couple months. As it stands though, I'm at Holy Mountains and I'm done. I can't hold any more. It's a bit like Meatloaf's Bat Out Of Hell in that it's just too much, but it's totally different in the sense that I can't turn it off. I wish I could, Vicinity of Obscenity is just too goddamed much. Thumb in eyeball again. Absolutely insane, and completely terrifying.

As a listening experience, this is comparable to Ok Computer, The Black Parade, and The Downward Spiral. It has a lot more intentional humor, certainly, but it's all-consumingly intense, not least because Soldier Side is the absolute loudest thing on the entire album, possibly the universe, I think the whole thing is actually supposed to give you brain damage.

In fact, listening to these two albums in their entirety might actually be the opposite of cathartic. I love 'em, but wowzers that's a struggle and a half of an art experience.

Moody Blues – Seventh Sojourn

I'm exhausted. What a stupid week. It's times like these my brain sends up bizarre thoughts, like "get the python wrapper for jack audio server running on windows so you can use your midi controller to do bizarre things." So, I did. I guess if we're doing weird stuff I might as well mention that I've been ignoring Seventh Sojourn for ages. You see, I'm not a singer in a Rock and Roll band, and The Moody Blues are way more sappy Pop Folk than I want them to be. Tonight though, it's pretty nice lullaby music. Interesting fact, it's their 8th album. Not much better at counting than Steppenwolf, but Octo-meander doesn't quite have the same mystical vibe to it.

Actually, it's quite lovely, but it sure doesn't feel like 1972. It feels like mid-tier 60s pop, to be honest, but then again I do live in a land of make believe. Regardless, I actually love the concept. It's socio-political commentary, but capped off by that Steve Miller-esque sentiment: "what do I know? I'm just a dude who enjoys letting his mind wander. We really should try being free again sometime."

Yeah, the weird, spooky parts really hit the spot today. It's not a flashy album, but the compositions are fantastic. There are definitely places where the execution just doesn't work and it sounds like a dull shade of desert beige, but that ending is superb. If there were one album that deserved a re-recording with better equipment and fresh ears, this would be a serious contender. It's never gonna have a place in my top 100, but still a strong showing from the Blue Mood Group.

Red Hot Chili Peppers – Californication

Tonight, we tackle Californication. No, not the weird David Duchovny series, the Red Hot Chili Peppers album. Spoiler alert, it's Anthony Kiedis's version of The Fine Art of Surfacing. The Amateur Internet Interpretation squad does a fairly good job for a change, but only because the topics are well understood. See, AK uses a lot of oblique references in his lyrics, but we have a clear ledger of chronological happenings for comparison. Essentially, we know who and what he's talking about, so it's easy to play connect the dots. What people tend to forget is that this is RHCP version 4.0. If RHCP were a Linux flavor, this one would be called "Andy Albatross."

Right from the start, though, there's an interpretational trap, and a lot of people completely ignore the fact that the title actually has 2 meanings. First, the portmanteau is obvious: California + Fornication. Second, the suffix "-ication" tends to imply the process of becoming (scarification = becoming scarred, stratification = the accumulation of strata, etc.). They both work together to create the concept of being indoctrinated into the self-indulgent hedonistic fantasy of celebrity that California markets to the world. As Axl might say, it's an illusion. Luckily, RHCP didn't work too hard for their illusions, just to throw them all away. That's not to say it's bad, it's just that it's 1999, and somehow John Frusciante is not only not dead, but back in the band. Obviously, he left for a second time in the future, but right now we're supposedly listening to the "mature" RHCP right in the middle of Alternative Rock's second hot minute in the mainstream. It's downright somber at times. Mostly that's down to John who was now living his third life as the Grover Cleveland of RHCP guitarists. Actually, he came back a 3rd time in 2019, but that's not the point. The point is that he inherited Hillel Slovak's Funk-Punk position, freaked out and somehow survived his speedball free-fall into the abyss, and came back as what he really is, an Experimental Rock guitarist reinheriting Dave Navarro's shift to harder Rock and Metal, before quitting again to go back to his objectively bizarre solo material.

All that said, this is still very much a RHCP album, chock full of sexual innuendo, pop culture references, and fuzzed up Flea basslines. We should press play.

Oh yeah, I forgot, this thing is Rick Rubin loud. We'll just turn the main volume down to 78% or so. Some glorious noise rock, space funk, even the slow pieces are really pretty. Lyrically it's all over the place, but it really boils down to stories of losing your way on the quest for the Hollywood version of the American Dream. Not sure how that song about his fling with Sporty Spice fits into that, but that's summer time backward, I guess.

The point is that the Hollywood version isn't real. Reality is much dirtier, more heartbreaking, nothing goes as planned. Christgau's one star write-off is more vulgar than the actual album, or any of their others. Sex isn't offensive in and of itself. As for the whole thing not being juvenile macho funk-hop, it's totally here, just not the whole thing or singles material. As an album by a super-famous Rock band at the end of the computer-code century, this is pretty exciting and adventurous.

Obviously, we have to go back and hear Blood Sugar Sex Magik at some point. For the moment though, let's all agree to take a break from the fantasy version of what life should be like, and go get lost in the actual world full of actual people who realize you can't avoid the closing credits forever. Let's go get lost, let's go get lost....

Guns 'N Roses – Appetite for Destruction

B: Avast, there aqua C-foam green! You trying to sideswipe me?

C: What are you talking about? We were at that fancy fake French department store getting new input devices for Skip and you told me to run two aisles over and see if there was anything that resembled music worth paying full price. I grabbed two without thinking, like you like.

B: Alright, then. It's Mother's Day, but I'm not your mom, so we'll just let the subconscious RHCP chemtrails float on the breeze.

C: Again, what are you talking about?

B: Ok, I'll spell it out this one time. Mother's Milk was Frusciante's first RHCP album, I reviewed Californication last night because I just happened to be editing the Station to Station review when that lyric from the title track compulsioned me into it like Bowie's friends had to do to him, offhandedly mentioning Axl Rose in the process, every single one of those people hated the Corporate Marketing version of LA so much they tried to off themselves with cocaine and/or heroin, but somehow managed to be repeatedly resurrected, then here it is actual Mother's Day and you've given me 1) Appetite for Destruction, and 2) a now band desperately trying to resurrect the hard side of 70s rock, and we can't neglect to note the subtle unspoken antithesis between Anthony and Axl who loved and hated Kurt Cobain respectively. That's a hard pill of coincidences to swallow, even for a trained subconscious spelunker such as myself.

    C: Wowzers, when you put it like that, I guess it is pretty astonishing. Still, not on purpose, I swear. I could just as easily have picked Fugees' famous second album, The Score.

    B: I've been known to swear one or two times, two times too, when the occasion warrants. I might just have to go back later this week and buy that one myself. Oh well, if you aren't killing me softly, then I guess it's on with the show...

    You know where you are? You're in the bunker, baby. You're gonna listen to Guns 'N Roses and Greta Van Fleet with me.

    Just like Gin Blossoms, it took an entire year and heavy radio rotation for G'nR's major label debut to start flying off the shelves. Even the quickest glance at the Billboard #1s from 1987 will tell you trash rock was so far down in the underground even the Ninja Turtles didn't give these sewer rats a second glance. Walk Like an Egyptian was the best performing single of the entire year, but we're talking Bad, Madonna, Whitney Houston, George Michael, Belinda Carlisle, Bon Jovi's first time to crack the charts. 88's a slightly different story, but it's the closest thing G'nR has to a power ballad that's making it into drive time (Sweet Child 'o Mine sandwiched between George Michael and Bobby McFerrin in September). They definitely had a fan base, but by Warner standards this was a band with barely a cult following until Kurt brought everybody into the spotlight with him, whether they liked him or not.

Now, the question you're probably asking in your head is "Bottle, aren't you like diametrically opposed to Axl? He's a sexist homophobe diva with a history of drug abuse and fighting everyone about everything."

He's a person. A vociferously opinionated person, sure, but he takes full responsibility for the consequences of his actions. I agree with several of his many opinions, the same way I agree with several of Bob Geldoff's opinions. I'm not so sure Axl is as offensive a personality as Bob-o. You are free to have whatever opinion you want to have, but don't expect to get a pass if you act out the nastier ones in public. He vocally called out Trump's irresponsible shenanigans, he's lost a lot of friends along the way, he's well aware that people can and do disagree with him, and I'm certain I pointed out that he knows full well how terrible some of the things he did are. He actually asked them not to induct him into the Rock and Roll Hall of Fame. Rather than secretly ask security to escort people out of venues, he'd call them out on stage for being violent or obnoxious. People died at Guns 'N Roses shows and he found that completely horrible and unacceptable. He also lost a lot of lawsuits against him, and they had the perpetual riot problems at cancelled shows (some totally his own fault, some not his fault at all). I think the important perspective is that Axl was a "charismatic" personality, and that can either be good or terrible. Axl got a lot of the terrible side, more than most you might say.

As for the things he said that offended people, he gave probably the only legitimate apology anyone could give: he was raised in a religiously conservative Indiana town with a good lookin' momma who never was around. No, sorry, that's not right, oh yeah, he had a major dose of culture shock when he got to LA. Given his less than wholesome upbringing (documented elsewhere) he very much wished to insult specific muggers and sexual abusers without realizing that the words he used had much larger racist and homophobic implications which he did not intend to promote. To put that in Bottle terminology, he said "I'm sorry I said those shitty things, I didn't fully realize just how shitty they were at the time I said them." Also notice that he didn't try to backtrack from the consequences of having said them, he acknowledged the offense they caused. Regardless, now we listen.

Oh yeah, just fantastic trash rock. This is a fantastic album. It's crude, nasty, and dangerous, which is important because it's specifically written from the perspective of living at the bottom of the sleeze pit that is LA. Welcome to the jungle, we're not the nice guys. This is a "here's what it's really like, you won't survive it unless you're just as nasty" album.

The difference is he's not defending it, and he's not defending his part in it. He's saying he's merely one piece of trash in the heap, how you deal with that is your own problem.

Or, you really can read the album as Axl's actual culture shock. This is what happened when he bought into that Californication timeshare sales pitch. It's easy to forget where you're going, sometimes it's harder to leave. What's the mirror version of Sex, Drugs, and Rock and Roll? The offender's list, addiction, and being dead. Axl says the first one is the illusion, the second one is reality, and I don't disbelieve him. He's always been pointing out that the world he lived in is terrible, but everybody had that Neil Young reverse psychology reaction to it. Christgau hints at it in his actual review of Chinese Democracy. People interpreted Axl all wrong and it took everyone actually not caring what he had to say anymore for his real intent to finally hit home. I didn't like Chinese Democracy, but maybe I should give it another chance at some point. Regardless, I don't think I'm the one misunderstanding Appetite for Destruction. We're the biggest dirt bags we know is a pretty coherent concept in my book.

Bottle Plays Flag Football with Copyright

1

Here's a fun idea: let's tackle the problem of copyright. But first, facebook tells me that pages with reviews get more traffic. Let's find out. I double dog dare any of you to write a fictitious review of my fictional media empire. You could tell a story about a phone conversation you had with one of my minions. You could make up a story about buying an album and we sent you the wrong album but it turned out way better than the one you actually wanted. Good review, bad review, doesn't matter, if I laugh you did a great job. Now back to the thing.

Copyright laws and lawsuits are currently nonsense. I talked about it in my second book, but we're gonna go all out for this project; really understand the stupid.

2

We'll start this whole thing with one of the biggest myths about copyright. That myth is essentially this: copyright protects an artist from having their work stolen.

First of all, the legal concept of copyright is necessitated by the fact that it can and will be stolen. Your work will be stolen, used without your permission, it will inspire derivative works, if it's really great people will want it freely accessible to all humanity. That's how human ideas work.

The first important concept to nail down is that art and commercialism are fundamentally opposed to each other. We're right at the edge of a much larger problem with business in general, so we have to be careful. We need to understand what the actual thing is. The actual thing is a tangible product, capable of being mass produced for public dissemination.

Let's say you drew a picture of a tree. You own the right to control the replication and distribution of mechanical copies of that picture. You don't own the tree, you don't own the idea of drawing that tree, you own your physical drawing of the tree, and you have the right to decide what happens with that drawing now that it exists. You can light it on fire, you can make copies of it, you can sell it to someone, you can sell the copies to someone. No one else has the right to do that unless you give them explicit permission to do so. They do it anyway, and they make a billion dollars. Copyright gives you the ability to sue them for breaking the rules of the game, and lets you forcibly recover the profits you are entitled to make (unless you sold them to someone else), minus the actual costs of producing and distributing those copies. The legal system essentially punishes those who tried to go around your rights to negotiate compensation.

    Music is a little bit tougher, because there are way more parts. Books are a similar problem. The issue is that you can't copyright an idea, only your specific implementation of the idea.

    Now, the really important question: who is going to steal your work and duplicate it for profit? This might hurt a little, but the answer is a business, a legitimate business, that magically virtuous unicorn of free-market capitalism. Think about it. If that guy on the corner of 3rd St. they call "Nitro" can make and distribute your album of pop punk songs for 3-million in profit, then I'll eat my own feces.

    For a band, a record deal explains how, when, and how much that label is going to pay you for the rights to distribute your music for profit, their profit not yours. You're basically a homeless guy negotiating with a 12th-floor executive. That contract is pure garbage no matter what you think it says. Mostly it says here's your loan, good luck paying it back, wink.

    I'm off on a tangent, but it's important. Also keep in mind, lawyers don't know how your lawsuit will actually turn out either. Also also keep in mind, trials are the last resort, after all negotiation has failed to produce an acceptable compromise.

3

Copyright lawsuits are primarily about plagiarism and forgery that represent theft of revenue. We have a clear understanding that publishing someone else's work for profit without permission is unethical, we understand that similar products can be made from wildly different procedures, and we argue about cases in the murky gray area between the two.

Trademarks and patents are somewhat easier to conceptualize. With trademark, the problem is marketplace confusion, the co-opting of a familiar logo or design to trick consumers into thinking that they are buying from one company when they are not; identity theft, essentially. Similarly, patents protect inventors from the unfair advantage that large companies with vast resources have in developing an idea into a marketable product. Copyright is again a middle ground where the infringement both damages an existing revenue stream and creates some ambiguity regarding authenticity.

Evolving legal systems are completely ill equipped to deal with these problems, and that means that the whole process takes multiple rounds of appeals and debates. It also sadly means that the fields of Musicology and Music Theory get pulled into a courtroom setting and the farcical mish-mash of composition vs. statistics gets vomited into the ether, making the problem even worse in the future.

My point is that when music is involved these lawsuits aren't about music, they are actually about economics. It's not about music, it's about money, specifically who owns the right to profit from selling a particular musical idea. In the end, it all traces back to Structuralism, the clash between the abstract Language, and the novel or unique usage of that language inside a community.

4

Next we'll look at some actual cases and outline clear examples of copyright infringement. Not necessarily court cases, but instances where two artists have a legitimate dispute and are too broke/childish to make some deal to solve the problem.

Let's look at the extreme hypothetical cases. Now, this is an honest abstraction, meaning nobody is actually lying about their own actions or intentions. Probably the best example of deliberate infringement is the bass line from Under Pressure. Whoever produced Ice Ice Baby thought "that's a great bass line, I'll use that for the beat." Adding or subtracting an anacrusis (I can't remember which one they did and I don't like either song so I'm not going to go find out) doesn't change the fact that they intentionally used the bass line from a Queen/Bowie collab as the basis of a shitty Pop-Rap song. The fact that I know all the words doesn't make it not shitty. Their defense in court was "but we changed a note!" I think we can all agree that one guy took someone else's recognizable musical idea and used it as the basis for his own track.

Whether you like it or not, that's copyright infringement. For the record, I don't personally think that particular case is a good legal precedent. Ice Ice Baby is unarguably a derivative work, but the idea that Vanilla Ice and Murcury/Bowie are somehow competing for revenue from the same audience is farcical at best. I will concede that from a legal standpoint you can't argue your way out of the obvious infringement, and the ruling couldn't go any other way; they should have settled out of court.

What about Robin Thicke's Blurred Lines? The contention in that case was that Pharrell Williams "reverse engineered" a Marvin Gaye song. He did, but not by explicitly plagiarizing. His verdict was more a result of perjury than anything; he lied about the fact that he actually does that a lot.

Katy Perry rightfully won her appeal of the "ostinato" lawsuit because you can't copyright using the same 8 notes. I haven't looked into the original lawsuit filed by Flame, but I don't need to look into it to know I would have appealed that verdict just like Katy's lawyers did. It was a nonsense lawsuit.

Let's look at one of my own (not an actual lawsuit, but a case of using someone else's music to build my own piece of music). GREGORY sampled 3 pieces of music for a track on his only EP. As his publisher, I accept full responsibility for that. I don't leave my artists hanging out to dry. He took a drum sample from a Spoon song, and two samples from Steven Stark. Me being me, I called it Aboard the SS Spoon. The whole EP is a joke about an imaginary anthropomorphic skeleton being a pirate. What would happen if my friend Steven complained? I'd say "sorry, how much money will it take to make you not mad anymore?" What would happen if Spoon sent me a "cease and desist" letter? Nothing. What if they wanted royalties? I'd say "you can have 100% of the $0.00 I've made from that track." Moment of truth, what would happen if I woke up tomorrow morning and a million people had downloaded GREGORY's EP for a very generous $4? I'd be privately emailing Steven and Spoon's management to ask how they'd like me to send them some of it. I'm not a douche bag. I'm a nobody with integrity and respect, they are part of a trillion-dollar racket.

That's probably enough for now, we'll continue later when I think up more to say.

5

I mentioned Structuralism, and now is a good time to consider how language itself plays into our perception of intellectual property rights.

For our purposes, we'll say that Language is a set of symbols and rules people use to communicate, and it is to some degree continually evolving. We must take for granted that no one person can own the use of a language. Language can be constructed, regulated, suppressed, etc., but only through the communal process of multiple people using that language to communicate with each other. I cannot change a language by force, any more than others can change my internal network of meaning; the language itself evolves only when others observe, absorb, and adopt new words, ideas, etc. into their own lexicons.

An author can certainly claim ownership over a book, and the uniquely identifiable ways that book presents its ideas, but not the ideas themselves, not the metaphors, not the common idioms and sentiments that belong to the Language as it is practiced. Likewise for music, one cannot claim ownership of a harmonic progression, an abstract sequence of notes, a rhythmic pattern. This feature of language, the clash between Language itself and language usage, is the source of argument about authorship and identity.

Let's look at an example of how a clash like this happens and how it can be resolved. Paul Gallico wrote a book called The Snow Goose. The band Camel wanted to make that book into an album, but Paul said no. That's his right as the author. They eventually agreed that Camel could publish an album of instrumental music called "inspired by The Snow Goose" and everything was peachy. There are lots of reasons why Paul might have said yes or no, but probably the biggest consideration was that allowing Camel to adapt the novel into album form would significantly lower the value of selling the rights to adapt it into a movie (movie studios generally demand exclusive right). This is what I think the real purpose of copyright legislation and law should be. Yes, the primary motivation was money, but Gallico was concerned that Camel's desire to make an album from his book legitimately infringed upon his right to choose how his novel could be used as a commercial product.

Compare that scenario to the Lee Hazelwood/Dave Mustaine battle over Boots, or James Seals complaining about Type O Negative's version of Summer Breeze. It's pretty hard to claim that those cover versions could have any financial impact on the original songwriters. But, according to our laws and legislation, any suspected infringement must be legally challenged to prevent the work becoming public domain. The reason why we see so many frivolous copyright lawsuits is fairly obvious. The parties filing suit are generating little or no revenue from the original work, and winning a copyright lawsuit generates both publicity and profit far beyond compulsory licensing or negotiation. This is a misuse of the legal system.

Let's look at another high profile copyright battle, Metallia vs. Napster. The central issue of that fight was that file sharing directly damages artist revenue. Notice I said "directly." The problem with that claim is that the general public is not the consumer base of high profile artists inside the major label system. Yes, file sharing and piracy can have an impact on sales of physical media, thus indirectly damaging royalty revenue in the future, but only in relation to the consumer base who had no intention of paying for physical media in the first place. Whether or not you want to hear that new music has no correlation to whether or not you can or will buy the physical media on which it is distributed, and none of that has any bearing on whether or not any consumer will attend a concert, or buy a t-shirt, or even buy the next album. Contractually speaking, the band has been loaned a working budget to make a song or album, and the contract determines how that loan will be repaid. In short, there is no tangible theft of material or revenue from the artist by the general public. Any damage done is directly between the retail consumer and the corporate structure of the major label system; that's a problem with the way the industry in general does business. Keep in mind, I am not talking about the ethics of the situation, and I am not debating the idea that artists deserve money for their work. Instead, I question the corporate structure of the music business and its monopolization of the market.

One of the reasons that mass reproduced art is a bad commodity is that the value of art is not tied to its consumable value, but to its distributable value. There is some variation in the market for more or less likable/palatable media, but by and large albums are a niche market. You can love a band's music, but refuse to support the method or system of its distribution. This isn't fun to hear, but the giant media companies have to die. We the specialty consumers have to support small record stores and local independent musicians and producers.

Conversely, the industry has to accept that the market isn't week of release anymore. An album has to be thought of as a long term investment rather than instant merch. I like obscure 60s/70s psych and prog rock, for example. Obscure as in nobody really cared about it at the time, and few people care now.

I think we can all agree that the real purpose of copyright legislation and legal action is to prevent companies from stealing another company's product and capitalizing on their coincidental success. Exactly the kind of thing companies and corporation do all the time, Ktel, Pickwick, Roulette, foreign bootlegs, etc.

The world of Classical music has an interesting quirk of its own. Everything published before the 1920s is public domain. Companies can copyright their edition, their collection and physical publication of that notated music, musicians own the rights to their performance or recording, but the music itself is no longer protected as private property, it belongs to everyone to do with as they wish.

As I've hinted a couple times, this isn't actually about music, it's about the commodification of music and art in general. We need to look at some of the problems that the music industry has in terms of logistics, so next we'll look at the logistics of getting music from one brain to a wide variety of ears.

6

We need an outline of the logistics of mainstream commercial music. For the sake of discussion we'll distinguish between corporate and direct distribution chains. The distinction itself has nothing to do with quality, logistics, or value, only the separation of component functions. In other words, in the corporate model, no individual performs more than one component function whereas the direct model corresponds to what we call a sole proprietorship, one person performing all or most of the functions.

At the highest level, we use the familiar Production-Distribution-Consumption model. For an album, these correspond to 1) creating an album, 2) making physical copies available for retail purchase, and 3) buying and listening to that album, and each component function is performed by a separate company under the umbrella of a corporate entity or regulator. The corporation doesn't participate in the actual process, it simply determines how these components interact with each other under a single functional model.

Functions, in this sense, are not specifically what each component does, but rather the transfer between each component company. Production transfers a tangible product to distribution, distribution transfers the final consumable product to point of sale, Consumption completes the transfer of the consumable product to the paying public. Phrasing it this way eliminates some of the confusion as to where any particular person operates in this system. From start to finish, the agents interact as follows:

One company creates a performable piece of music - another company records and produces an album - another company replicates and transfers that album to stores - stores sell those copies to end users. The corporation controls how all these transactions take place, negotiating costs, managing the supply and demand, etc. They do this through legally binding contracts which explain the rules of the system and criteria for declaring those contracts void, I.e. the corporation defines the entry, operational, and exit strategies for each component of the system. From a financial standpoint, the corporation determines who is buying or selling at each stage of the process.

The music industry as a whole has a unique problem in that no one really agrees which direction this system should flow. Are bands buying access to an existing functional system, or is the system investing in music as a salable product? The answer is in general unknowable because that information is part of the private contractual agreements managed by the corporation. Similar problems can exist in other industries, but in general we assume that the revenue flows backward from the end consumer to compensate for each successive investment. This is what we assume when we talk about artist royalties and the "music business."

But, there is an alternative model, what I call the pyramid (not specifically a pyramid scheme, though that is one manifestation). In this model both the producer *and* the consumer are paying the corporation for access to the system. A band pays the system to produce a final product and the consumer pays the system for access to that product. This type of system is widespread in the music industry, and copyright litigation often feeds the machine, so to speak: the money a litigant makes from winning an infringement lawsuit not so secretly reduces or eliminates the debt owed by the artist to the corporation. In reality, it often becomes the case that an artist is competing against their own label for revenue from the same consumer base, but lacking the rights to seek other revenue sources by virtue of the contractual transfer of copyright to the corporation. These legal disputes are quite common, though rarely publicized, you just don't get anything from them like Poe and Tool's huge gaps between albums. Not a copyright problem per se, but a question of ownership that falls under works for hire by default. My point is that the whole situation is completely dysfunctional, more so that you might have imagined.

7.

What about your two books, Bottle? You do a lot of paraphrasing, quoting, making jokes, aren't you worried that someone will sue you?

Not particularly, no. One of the points of the books is that this stuff is in my head, it's part of me, it's engrained in my personality. It's also 100% fair use, critical analysis for educational purposes distilled from fully published and publicly available sources, documented, recontextualized, and under the assumption that you will go search out the material and contribute in some financially tangible form (be it buying albums, watching youtube ads, visiting websites, what have you).

It's also not derogatory in any way. If I don't like something, I try to find out why, and it almost never comes from the people making the art, it comes from me, I don't like it, I have to deal with it, bottle it up and neutralize it. We aren't talking about real people, we are talking about the public persona of fame, the illusion published by the big business of entertainment.

I'm not using the work of others for commercial financial gain, I'm talking about the process of consuming and interpreting that work in a book I wrote and published myself because it's what I do, financial gain or no. They published it for consumption, and I'm describing how I consume it. That's not only fair use, it's the intended use.

8.
What about Questlove's points, standardized sampling fees, back-room catalogue auctions, that kind of stuff?

Questlove is completely right in identifying all the exploitable loopholes, but remember we're talking about unscrupulous business practices. Both artists and rights consumers are being defrauded by "legitimate" business deals. We aren't talking person to person, we're talking about theft of publication rights. You don't have the right to publish someone else's work for your own profit. That's not up for debate. What we're trying to solve is the monopolization and exploitation of the industry itself. The real difference between Q and myself is that he lives and works inside that industry, while I do not. I can't set up a meeting to negotiate, I can't send him or anyone else a check in the mail, I can't transfer money into his paypal account, all I can do is buy a product from a major corporation who I assume has already fairly paid him for the right to manufacture and distribute that product. He and I are both describing the ways those corporations abuse and manipulate those rights in bad faith.

It wasn't Pharrell the musician paying homage to Marvin Gaye that got in trouble, it was Pharrell the producer who tried to lie about emulating Marvin Gaye to boost the popularity of a Robin Thicke single for profit who got in trouble.

Greta Van Fleet – Anthem of the Peaceful Army

Does Greta Van Fleet sound like Led Zeppelin? Do raccoons rummage through trash cans? Citadel sounded like Yes. Kansas made a Foreigner album. I legitimately couldn't tell if that new song Social Debris was Alice Cooper or Dave Mustaine until I looked it up earlier this afternoon. Josh has a super high voice, but it only resembles Robert Plant's in a superficial sense. I wouldn't confuse the two. In fact, I hear a whole lot more Budgie and The Who in their first album than anything else.

It is unapologetically 70s hard rock, but they didn't necessarily set out to be a rock band. I talked about this back with Chavelle, they're Hanson. The actual music is just what happened when these 3 brothers decided to be a band. They say it all starts out as folk songs from the futon, but I'm certainly not gonna be all "never make tired old blues rock again" like Julian Casablancas. I love this stuff. I just hope it's as wackadoodle as the sci-fi cover leads me to believe. Bring on that ironically fantastical, tree-hugging, hippy adventure through the misty mountained cosmic wilderness my inner Luddite craves.

M: Wait just a minute! You're outspokenly anti-corporate, Bottle. You're probably secretly happy those hackers created a hysterical episode of gasoline hoarding. You want to destroy the world!

B: Listen to yourself, Milton. When have I ever advocated doing terrible things to other people? Never, that's when. Both sides are equally wrong, and I refuse to participate. I'll give you the same opinion I've always given, if you have to freak out about it, then you weren't doing a good job of living in reality. Sometimes terrible things happen, and you should try to be prepared for when they do. I don't mean keeping 9 years worth of rations and ammunition in an underground bunker, I mean really thinking about what you would do if some completely logical catastrophe happened. Really understand what kinds of things you can or can't control. Differentiate between necessities and luxuries. I appreciate the luxuries, but I'm perfectly capable of chopping fire wood, walking long distance, and hunting for food. This isn't the zombie apocalypse, if all the garbage financial stupidity stopped tomorrow morning, we'd go back to worrying about things that are actually important. Now, stop trying to get me off topic, we're listening to Anthem of the Peaceful Army.

G'v'F made two EPs and generated a lot of buzz touring before this 75% newly composed debut. They walked into the studio with at least 4 times the music Van Halen had for their first album, but had the luxury of using their two weeks of studio time to write new songs on the fly. The result was a concept album about how questionable the value of modern humans is to the universe at large. Crypto-currency backed credit cards are a thing now. Humans are pretty terrible. I know, I sort of am one. Time to press the button that uses electricity generated from liquified dinosaurs to rotate this toxic plastic disc and pleasurably vibrate my eardrums.

Yeah, this is ridiculous. It's too wacky to be anything but completely sincere. I'm just as delighted by this album as I was the speech the other currently famous Greta gave. Maybe I will pony up the $35 for their follow up double album when I go back to buy The Score by Fugees.

Obetrol? The mixed-amphetamine based obesity cure-all from the 50s? Jessie's SAT study buddy? I think I speak for all the discerning drugs in music listeners with my tip of the hat to you, Mr. Greta.

Aside: Lover, Leaver is way too hot, and I really don't like how heavy I had to set the weight to get it to stop jumping out of the groove. Awesome bass throughout the whole album, but yeah, it bounces like crazy and Side A isn't gonna age well.

But back to the action. Fantastic album. Stellar from start to finish. Even the acoustic tracks rock. Weirdly pronounced words, gargling as a legitimate vocal technique, lyrical epiphanies like "the world is only what the world is made of." Check it out, you won't be sorry at all.

Fugees – The Score

One of my favorite things about The Score is that it puts you, the listener, in the actual album. You are standing there with them, hearing the conversation from all directions, they throw in those pop culture references for you to grin and nod at, you're in the movie they're making. It is a movie, it's intentionally the Tommy of hip-hop.

The first Fugees album was a flop. Strangely enough, Ruffhouse acted like that was their own fault and said here's 135k, you guys go make your own record and we'll see if it goes better before pulling the plug. So, they set up their own studio in Uncle Jean's basement and proceeded to make what almost every critic considered the best hip-hop album of the entire 1990s. Me included, this thing is fantastic.

Even less magnanimous critics were temporarily relieved that Dr. Dre didn't have anything to do with it. NWA/Death Row Dr. Dre, not Yo! MTV Raps with Ed Lover and Fab 5 Freddie Doctor Dré. I don't want you to be as confused and concerned as Enya was when Fugees wanted to sample her music. She was totally fine with it once she learned the difference (I'm lying, she sued and they ended up paying her 3-million). Fox and Gimbel weren't so amenable. They were fine with a straight up cover, but not a decomposition. Totally the right call, there. The world would be a whole lot worse without Lauryn Hill's version of Killing Me Softly With His Song.

Yes, she turned into a bit of a monster in the next decade, but this is early "she's gonna be a superstar" Lauryn, not hire 'em, steal their best riffs, fire 'em power-trip Lauryn. Before you get all cringy at my statement, remember that Lauryn's official rebuttal included calling Robert Glasper a nobody capitalizing on her name for publicity. From what I remember, his accusation was that she hired musicians under the pretense of writing and kept using their material after firing them. I'm not making a judgement on that, I'm simply pointing out that the response doesn't actually address the accusation. Also understand that she could put out a second solo album any day she feels like it. Sure, there might be nasty consequences depending on what horrible contracts are still in effect, but she doesn't need a chaperone to book studio time, or record it herself. Hell, she could freestyle acapella into her cell phone and throw up a new bandcamp page. Paypal might freak about the billions of dollars they'd have to handle if she did, but the only person holding Lauryn Hill back is Lauryn Hill. If Glasper is "entitled to his perception," then obviously there's something to be percepted, and I'm of the "you're both not being completely honest" persuasion. Regardless, this is well before the machine chewed her up and spat her out, which it goes without saying that it certainly did.

Ok, before we press play, you have to remember it's the 90s. If you're squeamish about poop, stereotypical Asian impersonation, or the word retarded, then we might have to administer my patented "am I a moron" test. It's a simple, one question test. Have you ever seriously considered pumping gasoline into a plastic bag, or putting glue in your hair? No? Ok, you're probably mature enough to handle it without freaking out.

Fugees are fascinating, all three have crazy stories I could ramble about for ages (Wyclef tried to run for president of Haiti in 2000, but couldn't because he hadn't lived in Haiti for the preceding 5 years), but I gotta stop getting so sidetracked. The album's what's important. If this isn't Golden-Age, then I don't know what is. I don't think the praise is merely white, middle-aged hacks being thankful that this one doesn't actually scare them, I think this album is an actual battle-rap masterpiece. This feels real.

I, of course, am a funny reviewer, but you need a non-joking opinion as well. For a non-snarky, historically motivated perspective about why this album is important right now, search for this excellent review by Musa Okwonga:

https://www.theringer.com/music/2021/2/12/22280168/the-fugees-the-score-diguise-resistance-as-art

Welcome back, now I have to try to tie it back into my own agenda. I had to buy this thing from Target. If that irony doesn't clench your bowels for you, then we're all doomed. I'm officially tired of novelty color-vomit records by the way, especially when the various colors have different densities and it affects playback. This one's fine, I'm just pointing out that I actually care about the music on them, not the color of the platter or hanging the jackets on my wall. I paid $34 for this, so I assume Wyclef, Lauryn, and Pras get to split upwards of 7 cents amongst their respective entourages. Yet, that's the only option I have, right? Moneywise, I choose to buy what I find valuable. In this case, thank you to Ms. Hill and her two Haitian refugee friends for inviting me to join in the resistance. I'll do what I can (mostly that involves infusing my album reviews with clever word play, alliteration, colorful metaphors, and a willingness to attentively listen to what anyone has to say).

Greta van Fleet – Battle at Garden's Gate

Oh. My. Goodness. The second Greta van Fleet album is so good. They said, ok being the new Led Zeppelin wasn't our goal at all, this time around we'll make an album about our experience touring the world. The rumors are true, there is some serious, hard-core poverty going on out there.

It would be easy to dismiss it as pandering (the lavish, textured packaging and full booklet are totally extravagant), but I reiterate my statement about the first album. These kids are so absolutely ridiculous that this simply cannot be anything but completely sincere. You couldn't fake this, no one could.

This is just an exquisite listen, which makes me sad that The Score wasn't. Much as I'm enjoying this right now, as a physical record this is 10x better quality than the repress of Fugees, and no I'm not at all happy about it. Not because one album is better or more important than the other, but because they are both monumental sophomore albums that I paid 30+ dollars to own. I've praised who knows how many physically terrible albums, but now I have to say don't buy the Target reissue of The Score. Absolutely listen to it in any format possible, but don't reward Target for selling that particular crap repress. Not fair at all, but back to GvF.

Still unapologetically 70s hard blues rock sung well above my falsetto range, but much more varied in terms of actual musical material. Man, he just lets it all out on the outro solo of Weight of Dreams. Oh good, skips at the very end. I feel a little better for that.

You know full well how tough it is for a double album to hold my complete attention, but all 4 sides of The Battle At Garden's Gate are superb. Not a dud in earshot. Will they make a third? I hope so, they're incredible.

Bottle, Bordiga

Bordiga is an absolute mess to try to actually understand, but his famous quote is quite pertinent:

The hell of Capitalism is the Firm, not the fact that the Firm has a boss.

M: There goes Bottle, quoting those evil Communists again.

B: No, no, no. I'm not quoting my hero Communism, I'm putting out an idea that I think most people don't really understand. In fact, a lot of you don't realize you actually agree, turn around and advocate for the complete opposite, then complain that things didn't go the way you thought they would.

Did you know Orwell was an ardent Democratic Socialist? I bet you didn't. He also coined the absurdist term Tory Anarchist. The point is that all the buzzwords are nonsense, he steadfastly despised Authoritarianism. So did Bordiga.

Let's tackle it. What does it mean? "The hell of Capitalism is the Firm, not the fact that the Firm has a boss." Two lowercase nouns, two capitalized nouns, and 100+ years of psychotic people arguing that their interpretation of Marx is the correct one. Feel free to jump in whenever...

So, what's a Firm? The simplest answer is that the Firm is the business entity selling their particular brand of goods and services to consumers for profit. The slightly more accurate answer is that the Firm is the business structure itself, the corporate functions that form the network of goals, rules, procedures, etc. The most realistic answer is that the Firm is the collective identity you refer to when you say "I'm the parts puller at Jimbo's Junkyard."

The question isn't what you do, the question is what does Jimbo's Junkyard do, but we have to walk through the structure to actually see it. You pull a list of parts out of old cars and Joe delivers them to customers. That's it as far as your actual work. You guys don't determine the price or collect money or anything like that, that's part of what the Firm does. On one hand, it's sort of true that Jimbo's Junkyard sells used car parts, but it's more accurate to say that the Firm acquires capital and sells the whole process to customers. They coordinate the process of acquiring old cars and selling the parts from them.

In this abstract setting, there are no laws; only actions and consequences. Either customers are happy and keep buying used car parts from Jimbo's, or they aren't and they stop. Jimbo's could find great success stealing cars and chopping them up as long as customers were still happy and paying Jimbo's for doing it. Companies still take that approach all the time. Remember, most people don't care until it affects them personally, but knowing that Jimbo's steals cars is often enough to dissuade the majority of customers from supporting that particular Firm. Regardless, the only legal mechanism we have for regulating Jimbo's activities is suing them and using force to stop it.

But what if that isn't actually Jimbo's practice? Jimbo's employs people to go out and buy old used cars, but Scooter is secretly embezzling that purchasing money and boosting cars. That's certainly not Jimbo's fault, so they fire Scooter.

The point is that nobody actually knows, and that's the hell Bordiga is talking about. It makes little difference if the Firm has a boss, owner, board of directors, what have you, the bad part is that the Firm can say whatever it wants, define its goals with the best intentions, but the Firm doesn't actually do anything. You might buy parts at Jimbo's, but if the only person you ever talk to is Frank, then the larger structure of Jimbo's is somewhat irrelevant. It is an opaque and impenetrable shell around the actual face-to-face business. What remains is to try to understand why or how or even if this is an inherent feature of Capitalism.

You're not going to like this last part. It doesn't matter what Capitalism actually is, it doesn't matter how you define it. Like a great number of ideologies, it is merely the invisible structure that absolves people from responsibility. It lets the wealthy ignore poverty, it lets greed motivate our actions without the penalty of remorse, in short it is the defense people use for taking advantage of each other instead of making an actual trade.

Regardless of what Bordiga was actually thinking at the time, what it means is that the ideology itself is antagonistic; it perpetuates itself as the solution to a problem it creates: breaking away from an established company that is failing to start a new competing company. The problem with that is the fact that the company itself doesn't actually do anything beyond defining its own internal structure, and measures its success not by its positive or negative impact, but by how much money it can make for as long as possible.

You don't have to agree with that sentiment, but it's certainly not a crazy way of describing the world. Especially if it turns out that you do agree with that sentiment.

Skip Tries to Figure things Out

E: Ok, Bottle. I've been here long enough. What are your actual political views?

B: Not applicable.

E: That can't be true. You have tons of opinions about everything. What do you actually think?

B: What's the definition of "politics" today, Compy?

C: From Oxford Languages:

Politics (noun): the activities associated with the governance of a country or other area, especially the debate or conflict among individuals or parties having or hoping to achieve power.

B: There you go. I neither have nor hope to achieve power, I don't govern anything except the conditions in my 3-foot radius of personal space, and I didn't ask to be born on this particular land mass. Yep, don't care.

E: You have to care.

B: No, I don't. I guess I do have a rule, or a guiding principle, or whatever: if you kill me, I'll be dead. Does that count?

E: ......

B: How about "I can think, or I can work, but I can't work while you keep changing what I'm supposed to think about, and I can't think if you keep changing what I'm supposed to be doing"?

E: Grrr.......

B: What answer do you want me to give you? What are we actually talking about?

S: You keep bringing up all these Marxist/Communist topics.

B: Yeah, like 3/4 of the US is already a Communist Country.

E: No, Bottle. Russia and China and North Korea and those places are Communist.

B: No, every one of those countries has Capitalist societies with varying degrees of Authoritarian governments. Stalin was a State-Capitalist. In an actual Marx-defined Communist country, every individual citizen would be self-employed within the context of "being useful."

E: No, Bottle, that's Capitalism.

B: No, Skip. I don't know what weird-ass books you've been reading, but they aren't the actual philosophical writings of philosophical thinkers. Friendliness can be just as powerful a system for bartering as money, but there's no physical representation of friendliness beyond actually being friendly.

What's the standard distinction between the two? Who owns the "means of production." I think that distinction is nonsense. It doesn't matter who "owns" the factory, what matters is who is making what trade for that factory's output. If Frank is the actual reason people buy their car parts at Jimbo's then the "Jimbo's" part is superfluous. Frank, however, makes the same measly hourly wage regardless.

Conversely, I don't show up to work every day because I enjoy it, I'm not a yay sports team kind of guy, I show up because it's the most agreeable way to get money that I can find. I don't want to need money, the State forces me to use only money.

E: Ok, I guess I don't have any idea what "the State" is.

B: It was a sketch comedy show in the 90s.

E: You are so freaking backward, Bottle.

B: Skip, we're in a Klein bottle. If you walk forward in a straight line (assuming one of your legs isn't shorter that the other) you will come back to this exact place facing the other direction. If one leg *is* shorter than the other, Jeebus only knows which direction you'll be facing when you get back. It would look like a 3-dimensional Spirograph drawing.

E: What?!

B: Ok, I know, you know how when you go to the optometrist and he swings over the phoroptor?

S: The big lens thing? Sure, why?

B: Because he doesn't have any frickin' clue how the 3 dimensions interact in your particular eyes, so he flicks random lenses in small increments in front of you to try to narrow in on your specific eye shape. At the end he just writes down what settings you thought looked best.

E: What does that have to do with Capitalism or Communism or anything?

B: The eye doctor isn't magic, he owns and operates the machine that tells him what lens prescription you need. You could go buy one if you wanted to. Hard to operate by and for yourself, but he's just selling you the process of correcting your vision for profit. Don't get me wrong, he is also legitimately making sure nothing is going terribly wrong with your eyes over time, but the actual finding your lens prescription part could be done by a 9-year-old.

S: That didn't answer my question at all.

B: Whatever it is we're talking about, you're trying to buy happiness and peace of mind. I already have that.

S: You're trying my patience Bottle. I want to know your political opinions.

B: Get rid of it. Or at the very least, stop trying to run the government like a business. Business is garbage. Marx was mostly a political anarchist, and to a large extent so am I.

People have this bizarre notion that Marx cared about government, when he didn't actually care at all. Marx cared about people, and he hated the fact that the economic elite somehow constantly morphed into authoritarian nincompoops to keep that elitism in place. I don't recognize "the government," I simply see groups of people doing things. It's helpful when they are honest about what they are actually doing.

 E: Are you trying to trick me?

 B: Whaaaa? You guys are the ones who keep asking me what to do, like I have any idea. You started it, I was just musing on a random quote I stumbled across the other morning. I thought it was interesting given the peculiarities of our enterprise.

 E: But you're just constantly bringing up Marx and Communism, and you're so backward about all of it.

 B: No, I'm not. I think I'm starting to see the problem here. Maybe I didn't do a good job of explaining it in my books. Ok, see, there're two different things going on. One is what Marx thought, the other is called Marxist Thought. Now, Marx thought all his thoughts while he was alive. A lot of people didn't like those thoughts, and most of those people ended up being really thrilled by that charmingly charismatic guy named Hitler. Now keep in mind, Hitler wasn't born until 6 years or so after Marx died, but chronological time isn't my strong suit. I'm an idea guy, and ideas don't work like that.

 Also remember that Marx grew up during what we call the Industrial Revolution (he was in his 20s at the official scholarly end of that time period). Like I mentioned a long time ago, Marx was reading first-hand news reports about our Civil War. His perspective is very different from ours, is what I'm saying.

 Marxist Thought, on the other hand, didn't start until after Marx died, so you need to keep in mind that Marx wasn't what we today would call a Marxist. Doubly confusing, Stalin wasn't by any relevant definition a Communist (Marx invented Communism from his imagination), and Marxism as manifest in Marxist Thought is more like "will the real Slim Shady please stand up" than anything Marx himself actually wrote with quill and ink. Marxist Thought is, so to Bottle speak, more of a religion than thinking.

Now, I also have to mention that Lenin wasn't very good at understanding Marx. So, when Stalin tried to govern the Soviet Union under his interpretation of Lenin's interpretation of Marx's idea of how people throughout history reacted to being repressed, he just repressed as many people as possible. I don't mean for that statement to be offensive to anyone who thought Stalin was great, I'm simply aligning myself with George Orwell's categorization of Stalin as a homicidal authoritarian nincompoop (assuming, of course, that you've read Animal Farm and 1984).

Which brings us to Socialism. Socialism doesn't have anything to do with government whatsoever. Socialism is 100% about the ownership of surplus. Anyone saying "socialism" in relation to government has no idea what they are talking about. It is the opposite of capitalism in the sense that it says surplus belongs to society at large rather than individuals as an investment. Note I said surplus. If there is no surplus production, then none of this stuff matters at all, 'cause we'll starve and/or cannibalize each other. When supply exceeds future demand, the apparent monetary value of a commodity is zero. Why do you think the lightbulb cartel invented planned obsolescence? There's a Shelby bulb still working today, right now.

Economics is about what people do with the resources available to them. If the guy who owns all the resources won't let you use them, what do you expect? Conversely, if the people who like doing things don't get anything in return, then what are you going to do, make me?

Skip, did I force you to be the editor? No, it's just that that was the only thing I could think of when you asked me what to do. You can leave any time you want. I don't have the foggiest idea *how*, but that's hardly my fault. I'm not the one who gets bored, remember? I think about stuff. If you and Compy stop handing me stuff to think about, I'll just go back to picking things up off the ground and thinking about them. That's what I do. All Marx was doing was trying to explain why he thought everything sucked, then everyone else got all "blast off, it's party time! No sleep 'til Utopia!"

E: Wow, just wow.

B: Which part? The part where everybody uses money as a universal equivalent, so obviously the apparent value of its physical manifestation converges on zero? You can't "buy" money with money, you buy money with stuff, use it to buy different stuff, and then trade that stuff for hopefully more money than you started with. The key word is "hopefully." To the best of my knowledge, no one has ever successfully legislated away hopelessness.

I don't change what I do based on what the President or Congress says/does, I simply change my plans based on what everybody else does. I can't even guess at this point, everyone's acting like lunatics.

What everybody forgets is that, Industrial Revolution aside, Marx was talking about raw materials, manufacturing, and logistics on the scale of actual individual people, and how all those industrious people combine their labours for the benefit of everyone. You can't make that happen with machine guns, it's a naturally occurring process.

All day long people scream "buy my stuff or die!," and I reply "I can't, nobody wants to pay me for the things my brain can do when it's relatively quiet, please stop yelling." Did any of that help?

E: No, not really.

B: Sorry, but you are the one who demanded an explanation. I told you I don't actually care. I'll think about it some more and try to do better next time.

A Perfect Circle – Thirteenth Step

S: Bottle, can you please focus and review an album?

B: Why? So you can feel free from pain and truth and choice and other poison devils?

S: ......!

B: Eyebrows, lady, jeez! Alright, what am I to do with all this silence? Gather 'round the package, kiddos, it's the sophomore effort from A Perfect Circle. Glad I did that recovering critic episode a while back, here's where we go after the recovery process.

Actually, the concept isn't specifically "recovery," it's being ready to recover. This is Maynard's attempt to get inside the various perspectives of "addiction" without first-hand experience. For further perspective, this is Tool's Lateralus period. You remember, you had that talk with your Shadow, now you're living the experience, sorting all the jigsaw puzzle pieces and assembling the framework, right?

This is also the new band writing for the first time. Mer De Noms was Maynard singing over Billy's already finished music. Billy wrote new music, Maynard wrote words but really wanted the music to be less "hard-rock," Danny Lohner mediated between the two (he is the actual Renholdër, by the way) then let James Iha take over touring duties (Smashing Pumpkins were smithereens by then).

Vanishing was titled that way because it was actually supposed to be on the first album, but Billy forgot that he saved it under the filename "test" and didn't find it until they were actually in the studio for this second album. I know I said he "played" on Chinese Democracy, but he was merely the ProTools operator for one of the earlier versions of the album that Axl scrapped. So confusing.

What's not confusing is how beautiful this album actually sounds. It's dedicated to Maynard's mom and dad (both deceased), and Billy and Andy Wallace recorded it. Maynard paid for it, like the executive he is.

My word, what an amazing album. If you try to compare it directly to their first, you'll almost certainly feel like this is a weird, stripped back, almost minimal version of APC, but when you get over that hump it's one of the most innovative albums I can think of; it somehow flows seamlessly from beginning to end while being totally ADD and random at every possible moment. I don't have any idea why that is, but I seriously don't hear individual songs. Obviously, I hear the songs start and end, but there aren't any conceptual breaks or episodes, it's one continuous experience. The only other album I have that reaction to is Razorblade Suitcase (maybe there are others, that's just the one that popped up in my brain). This is 50 minutes long, so it's not like there isn't ample opportunity for me to get distracted or for them to do something disruptively non-sequitur. Instead, they nailed it. And the last words of the entire album are "I choose to live." Now, if that doesn't leave you feeling empowered and a little tingly, then I don't know what to tell you.

Neil Diamond – Classics

Let's talk about this ridiculous mask mandate thing. You can read the relevant law if you want to. I did. I'm not saying that the intent is right or wrong, good or bad, I am simply trying to highlight that any supposed win for "liberty" comes at the equal expense of another's liberty. Whether you like it or not, a simple school funding bill rescinds the rights of private citizens and local, city, and business jurisdictions to mandate a relatively minor safety procedure during a public health scare, and instead consolidates that power to the level of the State of Iowa.

It amounts to taking away access to legal evaluation of citizens rights in a potential health emergency and instead declares that only the state can determine the maximum allowable safety precautions of private business. You were all for not selling cakes to homosexuals and denying marriage licenses, if memory serves.

In championing any supposed "win," you have increased the legal authority of the state of Iowa, enacted new legally binding laws governing personal relationships between citizens in place of resolving these personal disputes, and proved yet again that your "feelings" are more important than civil discussion and compromise. Add snowflakes to the list of dramatic irony terms. You have turned a simple pissing contest into an unnecessary governmental edict.

This is just my opinion, but that's the agenda that Fox News and other Conservative media outlets have been hammering since Biden officially took office. I'm not saying you can't be happy that you don't *have* to wear a mask to the grocery store, I'm saying be honest and ask whether that is worth actual governmental intervention, or whether the TV told you to feel that way. I personally think it is the actual opposite of what many people say they desire in terms of smaller, less intrusive government.

There, Skip, how's that for a political opinion?

E: I, uh, er....
B: Yep, that's the boat I row. I think I'll use my "I don't need a reason" card this turn, and we'll all just enjoy Neil Diamond's Classics in comparative silence.

Noonish Moon – Singles (American Wave)
It started as the tiniest of giggles: Hhn. Hehe. Ha ha ha. It morphed into a string of gibberish, before evolving into a bladder straining belly laugh,and careening around the corner into Cacklesville at 200 miles per hour (startling 3 cows and a woodchuck, but otherwise causing no appreciable damage to the somewhat neglected 20th-century infrastructure), and spontaneously burst into full flame-winged Phoenix flight.

It ended with Sandra slamming her fists down on the desk and exclaiming "Gentlemen! I pity any fool who interrupts me from getting through Mr. T's birthday as quickly as possible so that I can enjoy the Noonish Moon Singles collection while finishing the cover art for our soon to corporealize books this evening."

Bottle looked up and said "is it Mr. T's birthday? Awesome, I love that guy. Pretty fond of that band as well. Have fun."

And all was as well as it could possibly be.

Two, Two, Two for the Price of Two
Gzzzzzzt!

S: What was that, Bottle?
B: What was what?

Gzzzzzzzt!

S: That! That sound that sounds like a bug zapper. What did you do?
B: No idea what you're talking about, Sandra. Maybe you're just hearing the Auditors crash against the impenetrable force field that surrounds the imaginary version of reality.

Bottle and Sandra locked eyes. Slowly, Sandra's right eyebrow raised to half mast, defcon 2, the thinking woman's dilemma. She probed at her bottom lip, then smacked around a bit as though she was tasting the smell of an idea. Seemingly nonplussed, Bottle scratched lightly at the upper ridge of his ear and squinted as though he was looking off into the distant horizon, contemplating probable bifurcations in the stream of plausible futures.

With a quick crinkle of her nose, Sandra continued "why did you do that? You knew those were roughage for giraffes. You gave me a week, so I thought we would collaborate. You know full well my symbology isn't completely codified. Golf course on a spaceship was just a starting point."

B: My finger slipped.
S: Your finger slipped? Your finger just happened to slip and crash through 5 confirmation menus and a 3-digit CVV verification? Finger just happened to have a moment of clumsy and slip a second time though all of that as well?
B: Honest mistake, Sandra. I got excited and we all know I tend to take a bigger swig than advisable.
S: Head or gut?
B: Huh?
S: Head or gut, Bottle?
B: Oh, we're doing Bruce Willis movies? Ok, I'll see your Last Boyscout and raise you an I am a meat pop..."

Bottle didn't get to finish his -cicle because Sandra's tarsals t-boned both his own last boyscouts, and he fell to the ground with an unintelligible wimper. When he finally regained the majority of what consciousness was available, Sandra extended a hand and helped raise him back up into his chair.

B: I deserved that. Still, I only pulled the trigger because I liked them. I promise you'll get more say in the 3rd installment, as long as the color scheme is mostly greenish-blue. Anyway, I wasn't avoiding the choice, I was gonna choose gut.

    S: I know, it's just that the structure of it reminded me of Mr. Bungle, so I took the liberty of properly retaliating.

    B: Fair enough. Maybe we'll skip the album review tonight, and take the boys out for ice cream instead. We good?

    S: We're good. Thank you for liking the covers I made. And thank you for sticking the fork in the toaster.

    B: I do what I can. The proofs should be viewable Tuesday and then we can have a proper going away party. Well, at least until I think of the larger plot for this 3rd book. Can't seem to concentrate right this moment....

    And so, from me Bridbrad, and all of us at Bottle of Beef, mark your calendars. June is now officially Hastle a Corporate Bookseller Month. Bottle's a little busy tending to the twins, so I'll do the honors: Cheers.

Rhetorical Interlude

    All of this begs the question, why am I doing it? You might think, but Bottle, you're so anti-corporate it oozes out of your pores. You're an actual radical left anarchist railing against the exploitation of big business and now you're pretending to be a publishing company and it just doesn't make any sense.

    Well, for starters, I'm not being exploited. It's expensive, but I'm getting what I paid for. I have no expectation of selling 2 million copies of my books and retiring to a private island where the natives are my servants. I just like doing stuff, but I don't like being forced to go through pointless rituals to accomplish meaningless tasks for the benefit of others.

    What did I pay for? I paid to make my books available for anyone to purchase and enjoy, anywhere in the world.

Now, in terms of the music I publish, I don't have any need to do that. Bandcamp offers that service for free, and the compensation they and paypal take is totally fair. They both offer a useful service, and profit from delivering that service to general satisfaction for profit. Compare that to Spotify, who wrap their particular advertising marketplace in the farcical story of artists connecting to listeners (Spotify's actual business is selling advertising space in front of their user base). Plus, if you weirdos did decide you wanted CDs or just to hear it once, I have the ability to make them myself, and again Bandcamp doesn't charge me to publish them. Books, though, not so much. I certainly can't make them look and feel worthy of having on your shelf. Listening to music is mostly the same experience regardless of media format, but reading a book in your hands and staring at a computer screen (however exquisitely manufactured) are vastly different experiences. You shouldn't *have* to pay for reading my PDF files, but you definitely need to pay the workers who physically create and transport physical books.

  I'm interested in the dividing line between real and imaginary. Illusion is certainly fun as illusion (solving puzzles, being entertained by acting and fiction, etc.), but when you twist that around and start demanding that I actually believe the BS over reality for *your* benefit, I get testy. Record labels are notorious practitioners of that brand of intellectual fraud. But, no industry is immune: religion, science, government, medicine, they all have their charlatans promising magical solutions to unsolvable conundrums. There will be a 3rd book, I just can't see the forest with all these damned trees in the way.

Sting – Ten Summoner's Tales

  Alright, what kind of demons is Alf trying to summon? Skip, you might wanna unpack that one for our friends.

E: Sure, this one I get. So, yesterday you got antsy and sent Sandra's test covers out as finished pieces. You knew it was wrong, but your need to finish that project outweighed the potential consequences. You already established that eventually Sandra was going to kick you in the testicles as payback for all the friction created by officially joining our little crew, but that she had to have a good reason to actually do it and reset the karmic ledger, so to speak. Consequently, you're back to sitting with your chin in your palm contemplating what to do next, and that's a Sting album, right there. Not the Professional Wrestler, the musician. Gordon Sumner, Gordon Shumway, Ten Summoner's Tales. I think the testicle/tantric connection is happy coincidence. Did I miss anything?

B: Nope. Excellent explanation. I suppose I could add that we're dipping our toes into the wading pool of Mrs. Bottle's collection, but that has little bearing on the process itself (and we've already done it a couple times before). No agenda this time, just letting the man speak, or sing and play bass at the same time, whatever that means for you.

Yeah, you could say I'm skeptical about most everything, but there'd be nothing left if I didn't enjoy being me (liking me is totally beside the point). Are the other 9/10 sappy love songs as well? Sure, but that's not bad at all. Whooo, that's some unexpected Tele twang on track two. Sting singing country is weird, but more interesting than annoying.

Now, obviously The Police were a power trio, packed with that peculiar personality clash of big egos. Sting, Andy Summers, and Stewart Copeland are all big-time guys, just like The Doors, they were really just Cream, but this is a solo Sting sojourn about love and morality and the title is a pun on his name crossed with The Canterbury Tales character. Bowie released the first internet album, but the first thing ever properly purchased over the early internet was a copy of this CD in 1994.

Believe it or not, I'm not up on my Chaucer, and though there is surely a copy up in my attic, I'm not going up there for the sake of a Sting album. No, what makes this album interesting is that this album isn't interesting at all. This is a perfectly lovely album of perfectly lovely pop songs in every imaginable genre except Metal, but when you add it all up you get the least interesting kind of album ever documented in Bottle's Taxonomy: Ladies, what's *your* favorite Sting song?

Ew.

Red Hot Chili Peppers – Blood Sugar Sex Magik

C: Bottlebottlebottlebottle, did you hear?! Dave 1 fired Dave 2.

B: So? Don't care.

C: But he did a scandalous, naughty thing.

B: Like everybody else, all the time, everywhere? I'm still sore in delicate places over a book cover, but you don't hear me whining. Did somebody file sexual harassment or assault charges? No? Don't care.

C: But...

B: Look, you got 3 possible scenarios. 1) Dave 1 said "I'm morally appalled and I don't want you around me anymore." 2) Dave 1 thought "which will be worse for the next few years, with or without Dave 2? With. Sorry, Dave, you're fired." Or, 3) Dave 1 said "that's the last straw, Dave 2. I can't freakin' take it anymore. Get the hell out of here." Either way, my Megadeth ended with Hidden Treasures. This is between Dave and Dave, no lawsuits or criminal investigations, Bottle doesn't care. I've got a better story for tonight's album anyway...

Important distinction: sex is not in and of itself offensive, but it is also not a topic for polite conversation. Just like the acts themselves, all parties involved have to explicitly consent to talking about it. 600 something albums in, I think we can all agree that an album doesn't constitute polite conversation. I personally don't need Tipper to warn me, but you might. I warned all of you whenever I thought it prudent, didn't I?

Now, I could write thousands of different reviews for BSSM, but Dave Ellefson is the subject of today's scuttlebutt, and I know the only story that ever could possibly matter about Red Hot Chili Peppers's blockbuster Blood Sugar Sex Magik. Flea only plays bass like Flea on 1 or 2 tracks because of Kim Gordon. It's still funk obviously, but this is a straight to the point album, it's not a joke or gimmick. Yeah, his actual explanation is that he read an interview with Kim Gordon where she said she loved funk and slap bass, but she hated the way white guys had turned it into a macho frat-boy kind of thing. Flea read that and thought "oh shit, that's mostly my fault! I hope Kim hears this album as an apology, 'cause she's awesome." You know why I believe that? 'Cause Kim Gordon is awesome. She explained Thurston Moore cheating on and divorcing her by saying she still loves him very much, but he never grew out of being a chasing butterflies kind of man-child, so it's hard for her to actually be angry at him. Plus, you guys in the rest of the mainstream world are a little bit excused from understanding and appreciating just exactly how important and influential Sonic Youth actually really were. New York City, 1981. Thurston actually renamed a song to personally insult Christgau, and Kim was mad that he wouldn't give any positive support for the actual local music scene around the Village Voice office. They ended up being so popular in Europe that they didn't even need press reviews to get gigs anymore, so they just flipped him off whenever they crossed paths.

I bet you never thought an RHCP review would turn out to be about how much respect they had for Sonic Youth, huh? When it comes to Alternative anything, it's not the explosion of grungy depression-rock that started the whole thing, it's those crazy Avant Noise-Rock kids using weird tunings and screwdrivers in the 80s that paved the way. Kim Gordon expanded Flea's arsenal of bass techniques by just being her outspoken self, and Nirvana was not at all secretly Sonic Youth's little brother. Nice.

I guess there's also the Rick Rubin haunted mansion recording session thing, but that's much less interesting. Ok, it's actually super interesting. They had one more album after Mother's Milk, and decided they would go with Sony if Sony agreed to buy out their contract. That turned into a second bidding war that lasted for months. In the end Sony won, but Mo Austin from Warner Bothers called Anthony personally to say congratulations on signing with Sony, go make the amazing album we all know you're going to make. That was it, they were floored and politely asked if they could change their mind. A day or so later they were signed to Warner and this album is incredible.

At the end of the day, this is a "maturing album." Working with a producer they actually trust (even if the specific songs that result aren't their favorite), Sinead O'Connor and Nina Hagen are in Anthony's mind, Flea's thinking of what Kim said, Frusciante is trying to complement and affect the tone of the lyrical content. They're still unapologetically Red Hot Chili Peppers, but they're doing a damned good job. This really is one of the best all-around albums of all time.

Really, the only downside is it's 74 minutes long. All of those minutes are good, but it's longer than the combined Mezmerize/Hypnotize. I'm not saying it's too much or that there's any actual filler, but 17 tracks is ridiculous.

Metallica – Kill 'Em All

M: God what an awful racket.

B: Seriously, who the hell keeps inviting Milton? It's not GWAR, it's Metallica's first album. You know, I was just gonna let the lady pumping gas into a laundry basket meme go unmentioned, but yeah humans are the worst. Apocalypse now! The three horsemen and a lady one, not the Vietnam meets Heart of Darkness one based around the leak of The Pentagon Papers and Nixon's resignation. Admit it, Brando was overrated.

You're not gonna believe me but this is like lullaby music for me. Seriously, I pop in this Thrash classic and all the stress just melts out of my shoulders and I get fuzzy and calm.

Did Dave 1 write half of it? Sure sounds like it. Have the last 30 years of Hard Rock and Metal solos just been a vain attempt to emulate Kirk Hammett's Swedish Chef impersonating Eddie Van Halen impression? Certy Bergenly. Is it chocked full of poignant reminders of the fragile sacracy of life and the search for cosmic oneness? Hell no, it sounds like they are actively trying to run over your puppy with their motorcycles while also wielding chainsaws for no good reason. If this album is any indication, the reverb capabilities of Music America Recording Studio sound less like a luxury space tour of the solar system and more like the inside of a tuna can. Did they record this through the local high-school PA system? It's 1983, but it sounds like those EVH living room demos from the early 70s.

To be fair, we did just go from 1990 Rick Rubin with Warner money to a Zazula/Curico venture production, and Slayer's demos sound worse than even that Mob comp from Roulette. Zazula was a record store owner in New Jersey and one of his customers played some Metallica demos for him (acquired on vacation in San Francisco), and that was it. He created a record label just so he could fund and distribute this record. $15,000 was the advance, I think.

Metallica formed in 1981, just like Sonic Youth, and there's the secret subconscious sauce we serve and you expect on all the fine cuisine here at Bottle of Beef. Maybe that's what

I'll do. I'll just haul all the crap I make to swap meets and flea markets until I can open a record store and finally put out that Proton Funnel album like my new hero Zazula. Dream big, I say.

You know I'm just talking smack, this is a pretty historic album. The playing is phenomenal, it sounds like all the best parts of underground Metal in the early 80s, and it's pretty obvious they were going places. As a kid, I experienced Metallica backward from Master of Puppets through Ride the Lightening to Kill 'Em All (hey wait, that's what happened with Red Rider too, interesting). Anywho, I feel pretty good now. Time to check if the revised version of the first book is ready to review. Second book is totally done and ready for printing, by the way. I don't know what I did, but the first one stalled in pre-production and I had to resubmit it. Se la mort, luckily all my deadlines are self-imposed.

Dethklok – The Dethalbum

So you know how two days ago we did Kill 'Em All and I brought back the "where's my apocalypse" joke? Well, here's the text I sent Mrs. Bottle today:

They palletized, banded, corner protected, and shrink wrapped a 1lb box with 3 check valves that were backordered from a stock order we haven't actually received yet, and sent it to us on a semi. I give up. I just give up.

Bloodrocute me. I'd rather be murmaidered. I would seriously prefer devolving back into sea creatures than deal with this for the rest of eternity. Forget pumping gas into trash bags, we're like Vikings who forgot our map, started to lose hope that we'd ever find the war we were heading out to fight, but are still too proud to take the map and directions that nice witch in the woods offered to give us. Dethklok it is. The first

Dethalbum. This first album is just Brendan Small, Gene Hoglan, and Emilie Autumn.

Before Metalocalypse, Brenden Small created the cartoon Home Movies (one of my personal favorites). I mentioned Gene Hoglan when I talked about Katon de Pena, but he was in Devin Townsend's Strapping Young Lad, and is like the go to death metal session drummer. Emilie Autumn is part of the Dark Cabaret scene. Maybe we should do like a genre-mentary some time. That could be fun.

Anywho, this is a pretty stellar album. I suppose it is Symphonic Death Metal, but it's all Metal to me. Oddly, everyone's gonna knock off a star because it's parody, but are you really gonna stand there and tell me King Diamond or Dimmu Borgir don't recognize the humor element in what they do? Go watch an interview or 20 with George "Corpsegrinder" Fisher and tell me he isn't like the nicest dude on the planet. He was totally thrilled when Blizzard secretly made him a WoW character.

Now, as far as the long and prestigious history of cartoon bands goes, we'll have to refer to Bottle's Taxonomy. First you got your lower tier bands like The Archies, Josie and the Pussycats, Fat Albert's Junkyard Band, and Homer's Sadgasm and Be Sharps. They aren't low because they're bad, it's just that everybody knows them and you aren't pumping their jams at the pool party, now are you?

Next you got your weeknight headliners. Maybe obscure by mainstream standards, but who's gonna argue that Mystic Spiral from Daria, Doug's The Beets, and Love Händel aren't awesome? Before we get to the cream of the crop though, we have to call it like it is: Del The Funkee Homosapien didn't even want to do The Gorillaz, it's just that he was in the studio anyway and the previous rappers who tried did a crappy job. Regardless, we've reached the top tier and there's only room for two. Timmy and the Lords of the Underworld are arguably the better band, but who do you call if they're busy that night? Dethklok, of course. Hard to say which one is actually more brutal, but I seem to recall starting this review with an example of why we're scraping the bottom of the intelligence barrell, so go ahead and open up your briefcase of guts, build a better metal snake, face fist me, and strap me into the hatredcopter. Tomorrow better be Friday like the calendar promised is all I'm saying....

Behind the Scenes

    B: Don't be mad guys, but I kinda did an interview about our new books.

    S: You did what?!

    B: Relax. It's not gonna draw any attention to us at all. It's not like I took out an ad in Shop Saver, or Esquire, or something ridiculous. Glam Crabber Magazine had a dead page and a half, so I answered a few standard questions.

    E: I'm not familiar with Glam Crabber.

    B: No one is, it's an imaginary trade magazine for Crab fishermen who also happen to like wearing evening gowns. There's a lot of "other less relevant" former members of LUSH, because active imagination thingy.

    S: Oh, ok. I suppose if you're gonna blabvertise our book shaped things, Stormy Shipwreckson is about the least worrisome choice. Do they still put on the Tough Guys in Tiaras Summer Solstice Social?

    B: They do. Their insurance made them jettison the swimsuit competition, but somehow the bandsaw relay is perfectly fine? Beats me. Now, you guys wanna read it?

    E: I've read the damned things 20 times now, stop torturing me!

    B: Not the books, Skip, the interview.

    E: Oh. Sorry... still no. Not particularly. I'm ready to move on.

    B: Sandra?

    S: Hard pass on that one. I'm all for moving on as well.

B: Man you guys are no fun. Where's your sense of adventure? Have you been taking turns wearing GREGORY's top hat or something?

S: We're just tired, Bottle. Believe it or not, that was a lot of work, and we're still kind of afraid the whole thing will explode.

E: Plus, you'll dump the third book on us when we least expect it, and we're all terrified of what listening to the entire p(nmi)t discography is going to do to us.

B: Dude! You said it right. That's awesome. We're like a real bowling team again. The Beef Stews, or something. What's not to like?

E&S: meh.

B: Oh, I see what's going on. You got the "don't know what to do next" blues. It's only meaningful if you're trying to escape from something. Well, that's silly. Is it time to send the Cromulator out for another ridonculous retro record roundup? We could delve into the dimentia of the Musk Ox's low-orbit satellite spectacular. I can't tell you how many times I could have used high-speed internet access while macheteing my way through the rainforest, or how devestating it is to lose cell service while being chased by lions through the Okavango Delta. Meanwhile, there are drug addicts who don't want to be drug addicts anymore but can't afford full treatment because news flash they are drug addicts doing terrible things to get money to buy drugs.

See, I can just rant about anything, but GREGORY won't program some drums until I take back the hat and let him eat one of you, half the garden gnomes are moustacheless, Skip's telling me the stories don't make any sense. I'm aware, buddy, I wrote them. The Auditors think they're real, my new hero Zazula is blaming Grunge for killing Metal like that wasn't almost 30 years ago, people seem very concerned about hats all of a sudden (don't even get me started on the fact that everything's a trucker hat now), Tig Notaro (national treasure, if you ask me) was rotoscoped into a zombie movie, and everybody's just now catching up to my third life when the Initialed Instigator cranked up the cerebral jukebox to 11. It's exhausting. 14 hours of p(nmi)t and I guarantee your brain won't be able to care anymore.

What really concerns me is that Grimes watches SNL. I know I'm only 41, but my SNL was Gilda Radner and Garret Morris. I can quote gags from Laugh In, that's how old I am on the inside. Tina Fey was pretty great, but even she's all "I'm sorry I used man humor" now. You know what's never not funny? Tig Notaro moving a stool around in silence for 5 minutes while staring at you. She did an entire set without a shirt after her double mastectomy. What was I talking about? Oh yeah, you guys were whiny 'cause we finished the books and now you're all Jimi Page-ing my Lord Sutch limelight. Compy says the books will possibly be here Thursday, I used my boring old stage name for the author, both Barnes & Noble and Amazon have them listed with Bottle of Beef as the publisher, how hilarious would it be if someone from Portugal ordered them?

But before we do any of that, we're going to listen to this 2004 re-release of Doc Tate Nevaquaya's 1976 "Indian Songs from Comanche Land" because I have it, and we can. We just have to use a different computer to do it. All the linux media players are crashing today. There we go. Lovely.

Bottle's Interview

Here it is, my first interview, conducted by my long ago friend Stormy Shipwreckson. I think I did us proud.

GC: Bottle, you crusty old crawdad, it's been too long. Why don't you tell our readers a little about yourself?

B: Hello, all you glamulous crabfishers. I am known as Bottle, of the curmudgeonly Bottles. I've lived many lives, but currently I run a top secret underground media empire.

GC: I heard you did a thing.

B: I did. Several things, actually. Mostly I'm a behind the scenes kind of guy. An idea man, if you will. Tell me Stormy, are those Vince Camuto's you're wearing?

GC: I never pictured you a shoe guy, Bottle, but yes. Blue Danikas, to be precise.

B: Yeah, I'm not. I have however recently become acquainted with Sandra's preference for Freebirds. Surprisingly practical in her line of work. But enough aboot that, as my Canadian friends psychically punch me in the face, you asked me here to talk about books.

GC: So we did, so we did. What are they about?

B: 450ish pages each.

GC: Excellent. Any mention of crabs?

B: One, but the other kind, I'm afraid.

GC: I see. What can we look forward to?

B: Being finished reading them. Mostly album reviews, but I have a tendency to ramble about anything. I can be a bit much.

GC: So I remember. Swear words?

B: Absolutely. We did acquire a new editor who expurgated them from several hundred pages, but he secretly thinks I'm a Communist, and me being me....

GC: I'm blushing just thinking about it.

B: I win. But seriously, there's a lot of nautical material to be found hiding in my record collection. I mean, we're lost at sea, you guys are literally at sea most of the time. Not sure how many of you own record players, but my sense of humor is pretty salty. Plus, I got Roger's brother running around to make it interesting. A pirate's a pirate, am I right?

GC: GREGORY? Certainly not as jolly as his brother, but a charming fellow nonetheless. Well, Bottle, it has certainly been an enjoyable gam. Give my regards to the Effeminator, and may the winds blow fair.

B: I shall.

GC: One final thing, what are their titles?

B: Oh yeah, I guess I should say. Book one is A Year in the Life of Bottle the Curmudgeon, and book two is Bottle of Beef: The Media Empire of Doom. Available only on land. Sorry, I don't have carrier seagull money.

The Cars – Heartbeat City

Alright, we have to do it eventually, so I guess tonight we'll aimlessly wander the streets of Heartbeat City. Maybe we'll get mugged, that could be fun.

I'll be honest, I've never liked this album. Maybe my mind will change on this listen; it's not unprecedented. First though, we should hubcap The Cars as they are in my brain. Just about as good a self-titled debut as it's possible to make, I don't have a copy of Candy-O, Panorama is strange on purpose, I don't have Shake It Up. I have all the odd numbered Cars albums for some reason.

It's easy to pretend that the Cars is just Ric, but then you remember how much it hurt when Ben died and that Drive is arguably tied for biggest of their many hits. Christgau loved this album, but as you've no doubt noticed he and I have substantially different criteria when it comes to objectifying albums. He tends to like nonsensical collections of random songs, I tend to prefer albums that are actually good.

Interesting fact, Mutt Lange originally told Def Leppard he couldn't produce what would become Hysteria because he was working on this album. Fast forward through the multiple car crashes and learning to play the drums one-armed, and the mumps, and Def Leppard literally threw their metal fans and style in the dumpster to make a "hard rock Thriller type album." Hysteria is a significantly better album than Thriller, but the goal was to have an entire album of radio #1s without all that pesky artistry getting in the way the whole time. Sorry, was I stalling? Commence with the playlipsis...

Hello again, indeed. I did literally tie the knot on that second book, didn't I? Eerie coincidental summary of my book aside, pretty strong opener followed by farty synth bass. Nope, Looking for Love is a buried on Side B kind of song, not track 2 material. This is just the wrong direction for the album to go. U-turn for Magic though. Could have skipped the last 3 minutes altogether, if you ask me. But again, why did we drive off the cliff when the curve is clearly marked with signs and arrows and guard rails. Then we're in Stranger Eyes, for no apparent reason.

    I won't keep doing the play by play. There aren't any bad songs here, but there's no reason whatsoever why they are all here. It's exactly like Thriller, there's an awesome EP hiding in this collection of songs they picked out of a bingo/raffle tumbler. Sure that can work within the concept of naked stories in 1,000 cities (I might have that word order jumbled), but it also sounds suspiciously like "random crap." The songs aren't crap, but structurally speaking this is what an album of random crap sounds like; no continuity, no logical character unfolding, no cogent sequence of anything. I guess you could conceptualize it as a late night radio playlist, but compared to the actual albums we've listened to that use that concept, this would be a not that good version.

    They say it took Mutt 3 months to mix Hysteria, but I'd believe it more about this mongrel 'cause there's a leg sticking out of its forehead, its tail is where its left ear should be, and I'm not convinced the parent animals were compatible species in the first place. Maybe the American version of New Wave was just a little out of his comfort zone. It does sound pretty, even if it's 8 years too early for the "shuffle" button of your CD player like Fingertips from Apollo 18.

    Final verdict: I love all these songs, and I love The Cars, but this album sounds like it was meant to be shoved into a spotify or pandora or youtube playlist and never spoken of as an actual album ever again. Feel free to diagree and take a stab at explaining it to me. In the meantime, I am a bit curious what the Andy Warhol directed video for Hello Again is like. Time to fire up the youtubulator, I guess.

Join us next time when there's a high probability we listen to a terrible Paul McCartney solo album...

$45 Adventure Time

B: Alright, Cross-brace, I was wrong about wanting to listen to Macca. Corral me a collection of curiosities. I want random crap.

C: Why? You could just do that yourself.

B: Sure, I could, but you're better at it. The stuff you pick is more interesting than the stuff I pick. I don't know why, it just is. I look at the same stuff you do, but I always seem to pick the less interesting famous stuff. You come back with little gems of obscurity and weirdness.

C: Ok, I was getting bored anyway. Is there a spending limit?

B: Dunno. Anybody bought copies of our books in the last 4 days?

C: Lemme check. Oh. Uh, Bottle, you're not gonna believe this, but there're 20+ copies of those things walking around in public making friends.

B: Really? That's crazy. Flattering, but crazy. Ok, I got no argue, full 50 it is. More than two frisbees though, I always want as wide an array as accomplishable.

SWISH SWOOSH

B: That was quick. Oh, I see you scoured the used CD bin as well. Random crap indeed. Better Than Ezra, the first two Oasis albums, EL&P, Bram Tchaikovsky, the last Genesis album of the 70s, Girraffica, no sorry, I read that wrong Guiffria, and Intergalactic Touring Band. That last one's a nested bundle of random inside a one-off concept compilation, inside my instructions to be as random as possible. Well done, sir. I doff my cap at thee. Where should we start?

    C: Well, you are a strange man and there's the subtle "world having a mid-life crisis theme" to your writing, Bram Tchaikovsky's Strange Man Changed Man seems apropos.

    B: See, that's exactly why I send you Compy, I'd have thought "this looks interesting, maybe next time" and put it down in favor of a perfectly enjoyable album with nothing to talk about. As soon as you put it in my hand it makes total sense, but out there in the sea of reality I stop thinking and end up thinking "here's a thing I've heard of that probably won't be terrible." This, though, this could cause all sorts of unexpected brain damage. I'm excited. You gonna join me later for the listen, Collabatron?

    C: Maybe, no promises, I got a lot of background processes running.

    B: I hear ya. Thanks for your help.

    C: No problemo.

    B: Welp, until the rumming hour. These weeds aren't gonna whack themselves....

1 - Bram Tchaikovsky – Strange Man Changed Man

    I don't even know where to start. It's 1979, and there's a storm a brewin'. Everybody's about to hate disco, but which of the underground Rock trends is going to take its place? It turns out none of them, Synthpop will dominate the 80s in the Mainstream. One of the real contenders though is this weird thing called Power Pop. It's the name The Who gave themselves, but The Who was only one component of the cocktail we call Power Pop. If you read a lot of rock criticism you'll be completely confused because it's kind of a conglomeration of emulation: a gumbo of Beatles, Beach Boys, Who, and Byrds, like you and 3 friends are a Garage Rock band and you're not really a Punk or New Wave band, you much prefer the up-tempo sunshine and vocal harmony of 60s

Pop Rock. Critics and Rock fans automatically think you suck, and dismiss you as the bandwagoning American reaction to the British Invasion. That's really confusing for a guy like you, because you're a British 29-year-old and you thought you were just making a Rock and Roll album.

Now imagine my confusion when I put on the debut from Bram Tchaikovsky and thought "why is everyone such a moron? This is f-ing amazing!" Sure, I can hear all that stuff in there, but at the end of the day this is phenomenal. This isn't cheesy, there are no gimmicks, the rhythm guitars are smack-jangle Trash Rock, the solos are full on wailers. The only thing I can think of is that everyone hated the fact that Bram is a great singer, possibly pretending 29 is too old to form a new Rock band in the process.

Again, I have to call out Christgau because he called it a mix of old-wave and new-wave cliches. Dude, that's what Rock *is*: you pick up an electric guitar and clumsily bash your hands against it until it sounds sort of like the music in your brain. Most of that music in your brain is 10-15 years old because that's how brains work.

Luckily, in retrospect everyone gives this album 4.5 stars out of 5 (mostly because the bloated ballad Lady from the USA has no business being on this otherwise lovely album). I can see how at the time it might have come across as somewhat over-produced and pandering, all the glamour none of the danger, not to mention the confusingly implied bonfire supposedly accelerated by the can of motor oil in his hand in the photo on the back, but actually listening to it, it's really good.

Maybe it's because he was the guitarist for The Motors and the pretension of naming your new band after yourself was too much. But even there, who thought that was his real name?

So, is this the post-ironic British version of the ironic American version of the nostalgia of 60s British Pop Rock, or is this just late 70s Garage Rock from talented musicians/songwriters? Occam's Razor says it's the latter, but I stopped shaving years ago. Regardless, I found it so immensely enjoyable I flipped it back over and I'm giving it a second listen right now. Power Pop or no, this is good stuff.

Oasis and Better Than Ezra

The most confusing part of Power Pop is that it's a "make it up as we go" genre. The central theme is that critics hated "happy sounding" Rock and Roll that wasn't actually happy, more longing, pining, searching, chasing the illusion, hoping things will change with jangles on top. So, for 3 decades they just kept chucking bands that felt like that into the algae filled swimming pool. Somehow Green Day is the punk-infused version of Power Pop. Todd Rundgren? Sure. XTC? Absolutely. Gin Blossoms, Ben Folds, Cheap Trick, what is wrong with all of you? If this all reeks of the Nu-Metal incredulity I shared a while ago, then do what I do and carry an old-school clothes pin at all times. Regardless, when I think of Power Pop, I jump straight to the mid 90s version. Critically speaking, Power Pop is an American thing, but what should we call the British version? Brit...Pop...? Who's more power-pop than Oasis? Nobody, that's who. Blur is pretty Britpop, but nobody was directly comparing Blur to the Beatles, were they?

Now, you might counter-argue that Oasis is Alternative Rock, and I'd pointer-counter-argue alternative to what? Find me a song on their first two albums that isn't standard love/relationship/modern-life middle-class first-world doldrum jibber-jabber. Go ahead, I'll listen to 'em too while I wait...

... How is this any different than Bram Tchaikovsky? The guitars have nicer sounding distortion, there's a Noise Rock influence thrown in, and that's about it. It's up-tempo

Rock and Roll, Blues riffs, and the occasional boogie. It's fantastic, and I love every second of it, but they directly reference Beatles stuff, and it's a facade. Liam and Noel are about the most dysfunctionally drunk egomaniac brothers you could ever find. Worse than crazy Joe Loeffler. Even the Collyers, those kooky eccentric death-by-hoarding Manhattenite recluses, liked each other as people. So no, this isn't Alternative Rock. This is John Denver with round-framed, lilac-tinted sunglasses.

I think we need a refresher on Alternative. Luckily, Compy found some concurrent American Alternative for comparison., but back to Oasis for the moment. That first album is Definitely awesome, but Maybe a little too divorced from reality to be universally appealing. Being unapologetically British doesn't have the same flavor as the other times I mentioned that perspective. Why is that? Oh, I remember, that whole crusading, conquering, and colonizing entire continents, and cultures, but never having to apologize or feel the least bit of remorse thing. Obviously it's a bit unfair to atlas Oasis with the entirety of European History, but when you couple that kind of cultural quintessence with a veneer of "all our troubles are relatively trivial" it has a definite tang of sun-baked potato salad.

The second album is a bit better in that regard. There's a clear distinction between realities, a flavor of the unfulfilling, a recognition of incompleteness. It's still noisy jangle-pop, but there's some real human emotion to it that is somewhat missing from the first album. There's the obvious narcissistic fetishism of Wonderwall, but there's also some "don't idolize me" self-recognition to balance it.

Emotionally speaking, Morning Glory is definitely the more adventurous album. Back to back, Definitely Maybe ends up sounding like the fake travel agent kind of smiling, but Morning Glory has a more realistic FOMO quality. For the record, holy hell no, don't actually listen to the 100-minute pair back to back in one sitting like I did.

Now, is Steve Albini's categorization of Power Pop as "music for pussies" fair? No, I don't think so, you can enjoy this with or without testosterone. Besides, you probably wouldn't put Oasis anywhere near your Shellac playlist (Shellac is Albini's current band), because like I said, this isn't any kind of Alternative anything. Still, the incorporation of Noise Rock feedback and squiggly background guitar wailing gives it a burst of energy that makes the Pop part feel noticeably less uncomfortable. Plus, I think I could take Albini in a fight, but the Gallagher brothers are probably so accustomed and anesthetized to beating the crap out of each other that it's hard to imagine calling them pussies in real life and not instantly regretting it. Ok, I think we have an understanding of what Power Pop is, so let's go hear what it's not.

If you remember running through the wet grass while desperately wanting reality to not suck, then you remember Better Than Ezra's second album. I don't have that one, Compy found their major label debut, Deluxe.

Stylistically, the single most important part of Alternative Rock is the Bass Solo. That doesn't mean it's a solo solo, it means nobody else is playing for 4 or 8 bars. It can go anywhere, intro, bridge, hell you could have the chorus be a wimper and a single bass lick, it just has to say "hey, look over here, bass players are people too, and we don't have to mimic the rhythm guitar or play chord roots the whole time!"

Also note that although it's not the full "I'm not ok," there's no pizza party to look forward to after we lose in the quarter-finals. It's not in your face, but there's a whole lot of "life sucks and everyone ignores it" going on. You know why that is? Where it comes from? It's James Van Der Beek screaming "I don't want your life!" Obviously, that's a tad melodramatic, but the sentiment is real and it takes a whole lot of anger and self-confidence to give it a voice; a self-confidence that's been eroded generation by generation by the lottery myth of the American Dream, that weird idea that it's better to feed off the crumbs of false generosity than it is to do the grueling work yourself and be content.

Do my descriptions match those of the forum trolls? I doubt it. Let's peer into the imaginary 12,000 page tome that is Bottle's Taxonomy, I think the vocabulary section is somewhere in the middle... ah, here we go:

> Mainstream: mainstream music, with some obvious and/or ironic exceptions, overwhelmingly focuses on what is good, widely popular, or generically acceptable at a particular time. Criticism of mainstream culture can and does occasionally become itself mainstream, but for a significantly shorter period of time than obvious mainstream thought. We tend to call these "fads," and they tend to last anywhere from 3 to 6 years.

Flipping back a few pages:

> Alternative: whatever is unlike the concurrent mainstream at the time. Alternative music can certainly be antagonistic toward the mainstream, but more often tends to be a tangent. More of a "that's not important, this is what we should be concerned about" mentality. Alternative frequently replaces the mainstream view it criticizes, but only for a short 1-2 year time period. Alternative also tends to be a more regionally localized type of critical response to specific aspects of Mainstream. This is completely distinct from Underground, which has virtually no connection to normal daily life of the time.

So, there you have it. We might all be more confused than when we started. I think next we need to look at some truly obscure mid-80s Glam to appreciate how the macho attitudes of the 70s dissolved into the smelly, sticky hairspray fog of their own oblivion.

Guiffria

I've mentioned this before, but the 80s had the absolute most bizarre version of "romantic." It started out as the shoulder-pads and baby powder materialism of Dionne Warwick, but by the mid 80s it had morphed into this weird "I need a break from riding my motorcycle between arena gigs, c'mon babe, lay your head on my chest while I drape my leather-jacket clad arm across your shoulder as we sit on this couch in the middle of an airport hanger for no apparent reason. Welp! Time to run, those groupies over there aren't gonna have sex with themselves, see you next Tuesday. Hey, before you run off, can I borrow your hairspray?"

I'm well aware I shouldn't like it, but I love Hair Metal. I will unashamedly belt out the cheesiest power ballad you can think of with pure glee. Sure, it's total garbage, but I'm convinced it's a scientific fact that 80s Hair Metal fits into your dopamine receptors like a thing that fits perfectly into another thing (I don't know about you all reading this, but I'm starting to sound like Lewis Black and point a lot in my head). Has anyone tried playing power ballads for their patients with Tourette's, Parkinson's, Schizophrenia, and other mood disorders? Give it a try, and credit me with any tangible positive results (please don't blame me if it backfires).

Of course it's just a gimmick, that's what we're looking at, the border between sincerity and complete bold-faced lying insincerity. Whether they know it or not, critics want Power Pop to have at least a passing resemblance to Power Ballad. But what if you could almost believe it? What if there was a band so obscure but completely concocted to play cheesy love glam that you actually have to question the reality you thought you knew? Ladies and Gentleladies, I give you Guifferica. No, that's not right either. Man, that font is really hard to focus on, maybe I need my eyes checked. Guernifica? Guitarrica? Guiffria? There, yeah, that's it, Guiffria. I'm fine with using your own name, Greg, but you don't exactly have one that's easy to read. Whoa, you're the keyboard player? Man, you remind me of Gary Usher, every single thing is just subtely not right. But maybe you'll surprise me. It's happened before.

Oh, yeah, how were these guys not ginormous? It's a crime. This is amazing. The concept of their second album Silk & Steel is perfect. They put the softer, silkier songs for the ladies on Side A, and sharpen their swords for some back-alley nighttime nastiness on Side B. A split album for the split personality; that works.

Again, why the hell weren't these guys humongolossal? Ah, there it is, Ritchie Blackmore being a "how dare you upstage us" purple-people eating prima donna. Didn't help that members were in and out and cross-pollinating with Dio and Quiet Riot either. That's a shame, 'cause Hair Metal or no these guys were fantastic, and this album is just straight up fun. Fun fact, lead singer David Glen Eisley was a minor league pitcher for one of the Giants' farm teams. Now, you wanna hear some astounding guitar solos? Lanny Cordola, my friends, Lanny Cordola. Everything about this album is cream of the crop, but these guys got shafted at every possible opportunity. Hands down winner of the Bottle of Beef Most Ridiculously Underrated and Obscure Band for Absolutely No Reason Award. Not an award title that easily rolls off the tounge, but the undisputed winner is Guifflandia, so what more could you possibly want? Lazer beam sound effects? Oh, yeah, Guiffromania's got you covered there too.

I'm a sucker for synths and keyboards in general, so tomorrow I think we'll check out EL&P's 3rd album. People say it's pretty spectacular....

EL&P – Trilogy

The C-faring stranger found another Emerson, Lake, & Palmer album to add to the assortment. If you remember, my love affair with EL&P started way back in 2019 when I heard Tarkus for the first time, and I've salivated over every album I've stumbled across since then. My collection's not complete, but tonight we get to hear Trilogy. It also means we can delve a little deeper into that whole defecting from your birth-country to avoid serious tax-evasion charges thing. England's income tax system is pretty much the same as the US, it's a tiered or bracket system. Everyone pays the same amount of tax in each bracket. Also, contrary to sloppy thinking, your operational expenses get itemized and deducted from your gross income to determine your taxable income. If you made no profit, you get all the money you paid in taxes back as a refund. It's not perfect, but it's not evil either. If there weren't some mechanism for measuring economic activity, then the monetary system would be complete nonsensical gibberish.

I think the biggest misconception people have is that their taxes pay for all those evil "socialist programs" the Demoncrats invented to screw "the REAL people." That's certainly one interpretation given how people think and intentionally try to confuse each other, but from a philosophical/structural perspective it's wildly inaccurate. You have to remember that while some people run around doing whatever they feel like doing, other people are charged with trying to predict, accommodate, and compensate for that craziness. There's some real truth to the notion that a little bit of knowledge is a dangerous thing, but if you keep at it you eventually reach a plateau where you realize you're actually contributing to some of the problems you complain about.

My personal opinion is let it crash. Sure it'll suck for some people, but it already sucks for a lot of people. Very few people agree with my opinion, and even fewer will understand my metaphor, but I've given up so just let Joshua play Tic-Tac-Toe with the nuclear warheads until his neural net figures out it's pointless. I'm not happy in that head-space, but what good is lying about it?

I could keep going, but this is supposed to be an album review. The system in general does what it's supposed to do: force some of the misers to spend and some of the reckless to save. They could do that of their own volition, but they never do. Stagnation is the enemy in the eyes of the Auditors.

There is, however, a legitimate problem in the world of corporate finance. The problem is that the people with ugly ties have figured out how to take the revenue you generate and invest every penny of it in other things while sticking you, the people doing the work, with the tax burden. Music-wise, it's not the label or the manager or distributor or any of those peoples' responsibility to pay taxes on the revenue you generated in your name, it's yours. That's super easy if you actually have a few million dollars in a couple bank accounts or CDs or other low/no risk liquid assets that you'll never actually consume, but it is 100% impossible if they took your couple mil and stuck it in a hedge fund to bulk up their own portfolio while still reporting the capital gains in your name. Have you ever wondered why certain god-awful bands get all the air-play, all the press, all the TV time, all the everything for no reason when everyone absolutely hates them and there's a thousand more popular bands getting no anything? It's because the former gave their label permission to speculate with their revenue without any financial risk for doing it. 9 platinum albums later, the exec's kids are in Ivy League schools, but you're eating the cheapest peanut butter you can find with a plastic spoon wondering how you'll ever pay the 7-million in back taxes your accountant didn't pay for you at all.

EL&P, Bowie, Pink Floyd, every other famous band that complains about financial trouble they mistakenly agreed to be in, I think I even mentioned John Malkovich a year or two ago. When it comes to money, either you're paying me or

I'm paying you, and when it comes to a Major Label deal, they've got it so squirreled around that most bands are ecstatic to sign the next 12-million away to pay the measly 3-million their label turned into 9 on the side for themselves. Why did bands like Pearl Jam and Radiohead flip 'em the bird and put their albums online for "name-your-price"? Why did bands like NOFX, Squirrel Nut Zippers, Death Cab for Cutie, and Modest Mouse barely blink when they briefly blipped into the Mainstream? Because they were lucky, smart, and popular enough to be able to pay their debts and walk away.

  EL&P didn't defect because 85% of their top-tier earnings was egregious, they defected because they were tricked into giving away the profits from their own sales figures while getting scary letters and phone calls about the legitimate taxes they couldn't pay and being told that's how the game works losers, we own your copyrights, remember? The common misconception was (and still is) that the little bit of songwriter royalties they got to keep were the entire total of their taxable revenue, when in reality those royalties almost certainly fell well short of the tax burden itself, thus necessitating more and more fake generosity in the form of an advance on the next album. We call that a racket.

  No, that's not the story of every band or every label, remember that nice A&R lady who negotiated a proper deal for They Might Be Giants, or Danzig trading his coincidentally valuable label name for studio time? It is, however, the common thread in all the stories I've told about British bands under Thatcher's roof: the system and the social order are vastly more valuable than the people they encompass, and the only way to keep the machine running is to take away your ability to compete and succeed on your own merits. Publicly traded companies are the worst in that regard. Wal-Mart's job is to maximize profit for the Walton family and other shareholders for eternity. The eternity part is the only check on their actual operation, they aren't allowed to actually fail anymore. You hate Wal-Mart same as I do, but the sheer ginormity of their distribution power is enough to bankrupt every town or city in which they open a new warehouse. Wal-Mart itself has more economic power than a couple of actual State governments. The spin is that they "managed their growth well," but their actual business strategy is to strategically and systematically deflate geographic markets with sheer purchasing power to drive costs even higher for small local businesses. The average Joe simply can't afford to "shop local" without sacrificing an increasing amount of social comfort. The Bottle family stopped eating meals at restaurants years ago.

I feel like I should point out that I'm not screaming these words like a crazy person as I write them. This is my "this is reality" voice. 1.5 million people work for Wal-Mart in the US (2.2 million worldwide).

Hawaii, New Hampshire, Maine, Montana, Rhode Island, Delaware, South Dakota, North Dakota, Alaska, DC, Vermont, Wyoming. Those are the States that have less than 1.5 million residents (DC is still a state, even if it has no representation). It sounds bizarre to say Wal-Mart is 3 times more valuable than Wyoming or Vermont, doesn't it? I think that sounds insane. It's true though. More people in the US are employed by Wal-Mart than live in 12 of the 50+1 States, and that's assuming the rest of the country could absorb 100% of its peripheral influence if it ceased to exist tomorrow. I don't even want to think about the stockholders who are just pumping their dividend payout back in through the front door, so they never technically "buy" anything ever. At a payout of 2.20 per share, anyone with more than 3,000 shares is making enough to feed a family of 4 all year long. It's a generalization, but kids under 10 (and millionaires) eat free.

What does any of that have to do with 3 relatively famous English musicians forming a supergroup of insanity who were selling out 20,000 seat arenas and auditoriums on tour before they ever even set foot in a recording studio? Everything. We always have to look at both sides of the coin as it's making its ascent and descent and chaotically flipping around. From day one, critics (especially American Rock critics) wanted to paint EL&P as mindless, masturbatory, self-indulgent lunacy, but the band itself was more concerned about being type cast as a Rock band that only plays adaptations of Classical Music. Sure, that's a big part of what they do, but Greg Lake just wanted to write normal, boring, radio-friendly Pop hits for a living. He quit King Crimson to play with Emerson, and he hated everything about the Tarkus suite.

 I think the obvious point here is that nobody on the corporate inside of the industry had their hooks in EL&P, so they scrambled to capitalize as quickly and mercilessly as possible. You could call Prog a fad, it certainly fits my own definition, but it's pretty impossible to pretend it was "manufactured." This is what musicians wanted to do instead of Mainstream Pop and Arena Rock, and it caught everybody's attention, even if they weren't keen on participating in the adventure.

 I am keen on it, and this is a fantastic album. It's their 3rd studio album, there're 3 of them, and they do 3 different things. Emerson gets his crazy keyboard calisthenics workout in, Lake gets some lovely adventurish prog-folk to sing, and they do an insane version of Copland's Hoedown from Rodeo.

 Like I said, we have to keep track of which side we're looking at. From one direction, investments are a tool for building up that magic retirement number, but from the other direction you are handing your actual money to someone else to gamble rather than directly supporting your neighbors. Fine if it turns out you win, pretty devastating if you and your 4,000 neighbors don't. In general, those gamblers don't want to lose your money, but the system requires losing your money as penalty for anyone doing a bad job. Logically, they can't grow forever or we'd eventually be one nation under the Waltons. What's the exit strategy for slowly and painlessly balancing the ledger on that 200-billion and climbing? As far as I can tell there isn't one. What good is having all the money if you aren't willing to use it to make problems disappear and/or no one else can afford to buy back any of those capital assets? I think we all know I don't mean the kind of problems a $40 fishing pole or $90 car battery from Walmart can solve. It certainly is an Endless Enigma. Other endless enigmas include 1) did Storm "the pig inflator" Thorgerson actually paint this portrait? 2) are they supposed to appear conjoined like the Knights who say "Ni!"?, and finally) how terrifying would it be to stumble into the forest and confront all those EL&P clones? I just shivered a little.

Well, that was a journey. I suppose one good Prog deserves another, so join us tomorrow for a Genesis album. Should be fun.

Genesis – Duke

What's the real theme of this particular Adventure Time? Well, when it comes to assessing the validity of genre labels and the value of any particular album from them, it matters who's doing the labeling and why. Plus, I just like hating Walmart out loud. The magic part is that I didn't plan it that way, that's the story these albums tell as I pick them up. I try to make them funny or relevant, but I'm still just making it up as I go. Power Pop, Britpop, Alternative Rock, Hair Metal, Prog-Rock, and now Prog-Pop. It's the 10th Genesis album, Duke.

I'd call Duke the first proper Phil Collins's Genesis album, And Then There Were Three was merely the result of first Peter then Steve quitting. Phil's wife didn't want him to do the full tour and moved to Canada. After the 1978 tour he told the band he was moving to Canada to save his marriage, but they divorced anyway so he moved back and the trio started a new record in late 1979. Now keep in mind, this is still pre-famous Genesis, Phil's convinced they are finally about to "hit it big" like Ice Cube in his garage not wanting to be a barber for the rest of his life (a Friday reference? Bad news Bottle, it's only Wednesday). They definitely did with the next 2 albums, so Duke is the actual switcheroo, the official half prog/half pop recipe that got everybody on board. I love Invisible Touch, so let's see what Duke's all about.

  The artwork has nothing to do with the album, they just really liked Koechlin's L'Alphabet d'Albert. But, as Becky's friend points out, of course it does, of course putting Albert staring out the window on the cover becomes the titular character who we all know is Phil. It's another one of those bifurcating reality thingies I like talking about so much. Phil goes down his path where it definitely has nothing to do with whatever the band had in mind when they wrote the songs, no, not at all, not in any way, some people go down the path where that guy *is* Duke, some people hold the two ideas side by side letting whatever they know about Albert refine their understanding of the album, I only know the song Misunderstanding, so I'm new here. I'm gonna take a wild blindfolded guess and say it's a relationship metaphor: Duke and Duchess, Duke's a little bit too SQUIRREL! for Duchess's liking and now they don't pass the dutchy on the left or the right hand side 'cause she divorced him in Canada and he's recording an album with his two remaining friends in Sweden to prevent Charisma's paying for it counting as income come tax time in England. Press play...

  Holy hell-balls, now that's an intro! Yeah, that cover art is 100% the concept. I criticized Harry Connick Jr. and The Cars for a totally ridiculous track 2 slow down, but for this concept it's perfect. We're only 6 minutes in and I'm totally hooked like walleye on a minnow. Don't blow it, guys, don't blow it.

No words, Side A is phenomenal, just amazing. Seriously, this is beyond exceptional. Again, guys, don't freakin' blow it [flip] wait, mixed meters? Back to the beginning, yeah skipping beats to throw everything off kilter for the start of Side B, chef's kiss boys, magnifique. Oof, yeah, you got me right in the feels there Phil. Alone Tonight could totally have backfired, but I'm all in, you got me, you need a hug? Hyperbole, yes, go on. Oh, aw man, I'm bro crying, I feel it dude, I feel it. Whether it's real or true or not, don't care. I'm not you. But if it is true, then those are some grade-A sushi quality emotions, my man. Reprise the Guide Vocal and let the calliope cool us down before reprising the intro for the curtain call.

Bravo, guys, bravo. This is a masterpiece of an album. Seriously, if you've never listened to Duke from start to finish, then you just don't even have a clue. I mean, we started on a high note with Bram Tchaikovsky and waded through some murky territory to get here, but tomorrow's album would have to be ridiculously spectacular to top this. I don't think it's possible, honestly. There can't be a better concept album than the imaginary version of the story of the making of Duke, there just can't. I guess join us tomorrow when we find out, but I really don't think there's much point. Duke is about as good as humans could possibly make....

Intergalactic Touring Band
Speaking of Charisma...

I think of myself as an idea guy. I've invented thousands of bands, gimmicks galore, but I know my place in the upper-middle of the pantheon of pineal prestedigitation. Tonight I give you the grand prize winner of the highly coveted Bottle of Beef Holy Crap You Actually Did It award.

We've seen some great concept albums, we've seen some outstanding concept albums, fake bands making amazing albums, amazing bands making fake albums, but nothing, I mean nothing, can even hold a candle to tonight's honoree. We here at Bottle of Beef would like to present to you our dramatic interpretation of what that board meeting must have been like:

    M: Guys, we're not making any money here, and I can't help but notice the band you hired isn't recording anything at all. Time is a-ticking.

    [Humorously extended bong gurgle]

    B: ...ffffffffffffff. Damnit, Carl. I told you to close and lock the door, you're letting all the Miltons in.
    J: Well 'scuse me, Boss.
    B: Them's fightin' words, Mr. Mop. I'm barely even the boss of me, but I did sleep at a Holiday Inn Express last night. Had the weirdest dream.
    J: What's that?
    B: It's where your brain takes all the crap you experience and tries to symbolically make sense of it while your eyes are twitching, but that's not important. The Teletubby Sun Baby told me to make a concept compilation album about an epic space adventure. We're stopped for the night at some interstellar truck stop on the back end of the Gamma Quadrant, and it's karaoke night at the watering hole.

    [Another humorously long bong gurgle and exhale]

    J: I'm listening.
    B: Ok, so instead of just picking crap hits for a repub, we let Sandra go to town. The works, I'm talking a full color booklet of cartoons, stories, fake ads for futuristic cleaning products, let her go through the entire rolodex and ask anyone who answers the phone if they want to write a song from the

perspective of being the lead singer of an intergalactic touring band. Think 4 Seasons Genuine Imitation Life Gazette, but with space junk. Plenty of proofreading to keep Skipperdoodle occupied for at least a couple Tuesdays. We'll let the doofs over at Passport handle the American side, Charisma can have the UK.

J: Lemme think on that a momI'm sold. Whatcha gonna call it?

B: Intergalactic...Tour...ing...Band.

J: Winner, winner, catfish dinner. I'm hooked.

B: I know, I know, you're too kind, the applause is deafening. Happy now, Milton?

M: You're both lunatics, but I can imagine that will probably sell. I'll send Sandra the memo.

B: Good. Don't go away mad, just go away. Carl and I are very busy people. What a dweeb.

[End scene]

Rod Argent, my favorite Good Rat Peppi, Meatloaf, Arthur Brown, other less relevant characters. Rock, Prog, Soul, all the sound effects buttons, a total free-for-all. Best part? No hack-work at all. It's ridiculous, but everybody is 100% on point and totally into it, the best of everything '77 had to offer. No joke, this is my vote for best album in the universe. There's really nothing else to say, it speaks for itself. Fire up the youtubulator and point it at the Intergalactic Touring Band. You won't be sorry.

While the Bottle's away, the minions go insane

B: Guys, I'm gonna take a break.

E: Really?

B: Yes. Bottle's mom is coming to visit, and Compy somehow built an Adventure Time that ended exactly where it should. So, in honor of the serendipity, I gave the day shift the week off so I can work harder than I work at work. You'll be fine. Look for me on the evening of the 10th day, or something.

E: But what are we supposed to do?

B: Take a nap, write your own reviews, help Carl sweep, why would I care?

G: *Say hi for me!*

B: *Will do Gladys! Please don't murder any passing strangers while I'm gone!*

G: *No promises!*

B: Welp, toodles.

And with that, Bottle did a weird little dance and somersaulted into a painting on the wall while singing what I think was "Hüsker Dü, Bottle can too." In the process, a note fell out of his pocket telling me to tell you that lowercase U-umlaut is ALT+0252. Somewhat more interesting is what happened after he left.

It started with little, furtive eye movements. Compy noticed Skip would slowly raise his head up above the edge of his monitor and glance left, then right, then quickly dart under his desk and breath long labored breaths like someone who desperately wanted to hyperventilate, or at the very least pant like a dog. He nudged Sandra. "Ipskay's acting cray cray."

They watched in silence for about half an hour, during which time Skip reenacted his little pantomime 3 and a half times. The fourth was interrupted by Sanda assertively grabbing his attention by sayin "Ahem!" and twitching an eyebrow. "Knock it off, Skip, we're trying to enjoy the silence."

Then the finger drumming started. A simple tap tap at first, but it gradually morphed into the full William Tell, and abruptly stopped when Sandra's deftly hurled boot knocked the lid of Skip's laptop closed on top of his head.

S: What is your problem?

E: Have you guys noticed Bottle acting funny.

S: Bottle. Acting funny. Bottle? Our Bottle? Acting funny as opposed to the normal not funny way he acts? What?

E: Well, I mean, he's been acting weird.

S: Again, you're asking about Bottle? Short guy, says insanely ridiculous things, listens to records for fun, that's the Bottle you're asking about?

E: Is he, you know, a bit under medium rare?

S: Huh?

E: You know, a little too pink, big into the commeradery?

S: What?

E: Is Bottle a communist? I think he's a Communist.

S: Bravo, Skip. It's a new personal record, officially the stupidest thing I've heard since the last stupidest thing. Bottle reads. A lot. Possibly more than healthy, but then again he isn't technically human. Why?

E: It's just that he's constantly talking about it.

S: Yes. I think you'll find he never shuts up, but I think you'll also find that you're fixating on one little fish in the ocean that pours forth from his mouth hole. He happens to have put some thought into that topic, but as he rightly points out, he isn't the one starting that conversation. I think maybe you do need a nap. We've all been working overtime lately, and you look like you could use some fresher air. Compy, why don't you take Skip to see the trash heap. I don't think he's been down that hallway yet.

C: Sure, the Lady has lots of interesting things to say.

"Great ghastly gravy," Sandra thought. "I guess we will have to have the war again, after all. Seven more days, I just have to keep them from exploding for a week. I wonder what he's up to."

She sidled over to Compy's control center and questioned how anyone could keep track of all the open browsers, terminals, text files, and folders. It looked like a toddler's playroom, but eventually she found the Bottle monitor and scrolled his secret facebook feed. Pictures of plants, the kinds of jokes only he could tell, oh jeez he splattered blue paint all in his beard. Comrade Bottle, the hilarity. Still, she worried she wouldn't be able to hold Skip together for the whole week. Why do such nice guys get such ridiculous ideas stuck in their heads? A little brain time in the bean bag chair might help. In any case, like any other time, you often have to wait for the next adventure to begin.

The first thing she noticed when she walked into her office was the sheet of paper on her beanbag chair. She eyed it suspiciously, but eventually picked it up to read.

Hi, Sandra. Sorry for leaving you in charge of whatever nonsense happens while I'm gone. I dunno, maybe remind Skip that the whole thing boils down to 2 important concepts. 1) Do you think things happen for no apparent reason, or do you think the structure of society causes them?, and 2) is labor the basis of value, or is it something else? I doubt he'll actually explode, but either way, thanks.

Signature time, names and stuff,
    -Bottle.

The second thing she noticed was that the time vortex had stopped swirling and pulsating, and there was another note thumb-tacked to the wall.

I also took the liberty of chrono-locking the Bunker. It won't make any difference on the inside, but in the grand scheme of things it'll be like nothing actually happened. You and GREGORY will probably remember it afterward, but Skip and the others certainly won't, so don't be too hard on them. Cheers.

"Great," she thought, and flung herself backward into the beanbag chair. Just as she was starting to relax, her eyes popped back open and she asked the ceiling "are the garden gnomes sword fighting out there? Nope, don't care, officially not my problem." Then she reached over to the desk, grabbed her noise cancelling headphones, and settled in for a much needed nap.

Compy and Skip Visit the Trash Heap

C: You feeling ok, Skip?

E: Sure, why?

C: You just seem tense, man.

E: I don't know. I think the books just got to me. It's like Bottle is keeping a secret, or something. Like there's more going on than he's telling us. We black out and wake up. Some days I feel like I missed yesterday, but then the next day I know what's going to happen like a memory. It's like I have the hangover before I get drunk. That probably doesn't make any sense.

C: Oh. That's all? That's the easy part, Skip. I thought you'd been here for a while.

E: No, I think I came here right after Bottle finished the first book. No, I take that back, he finished the content of the first book, and he let me turn it into an actual book. It feels like ages ago.

C: Yeah, so you've only been here about a year. You're still new. No wonder you're acting all weird. You just gotta remember that we're inside the structure. It doesn't work the same way as real life. Real life isn't chronological.

E: Of course it is.

C: No, no, no, no, real life happens in a sequence, sure, but that sequence isn't locked into real time. Brand new things are 10 years old, the next three weeks happened while you were looking at a painting of cats playing croquet. Didn't Bottle explain all of this?

E: Sort of, I think. I wasn't really paying attention.
C: Well, there you go. That's...
E: ... my own fault.
C: Nice. Exactly. C'mon, there's someone I think you should meet.

Back and forth, up and down, around and around through B-Space they went. From the outside it looked like Compy was doing a complicated tango with a dance partner who only knew the Charleston, but eventually they stumbled into a cavernous room with what looked like a treasure horde piled 100 feet up; a gaudy, glittery volcano with a crystal swan on top.

E: What is this place?
C: Bottle calls it the trash heap, but it's really just all the good stuff they threw away while they were busy doing other stuff.
E: Who?
C: The minions. This is where they dumped all the stuff Bottle wasn't interested in at the moment.
E: Minions? I thought that was a joke.
C: Yes and no. No not real like a tree or a baseball game, but yes real in the sense that every function has to be performed. Bottle does a lot of stuff, but it's not actually Bottle doing it, if that makes sense. He just imagineers a minion who already knows how to do it, and it gets done. From the outside it looks like he just zones out and stares into space.
E: That makes no sense.
C: Agreed. Still true, though. I'll let the Lady explain.
E: What lady?
T: WHO DARE DISTURB THE SLUMBoh! Hi, Compy, lovely to see you. Who's this dashing young gentleman?
C: Hello, Lady. This is Skip. He ended up being Bottle's editor.

T: A powerful position indeed.

E: Is it? All I really do is fix the typos. Half the time I never catch 'em all.

T: Ah, so you doubt and don't believe.

E: Believe what?

T: That you invent the you you want to see.

E: Huh?

C: It's from a Helmet song.

T: Indeed. Bring a helmet. Good advice. Bottle is not as confusing or obtuse as you might think. It is an illusion. Have you tried actually listening to any of his albums?

E: Some, but I don't think I listen the same way Bottle does.

T: Few do. But when you do, remember there is no goal. There's no prize for winning. It is nothing more than an experience for you to do with as you please. You might feel completely different the next time.

E: That sounds terrible. I like things where they belong.

T: And where would that be?

E: Huh? I mean, well, you know, where they should be. Everything in its place.

T: But how could the things know their place if there is no known place for them to be?

E: Are you trying to confuse me?

T: No, I don't think so. Untrying to confuse you? Ah, yes, the other way. I'm trying to unconfused you.

E: You're as loony as the rest of them!

T: I suppose I have no argument for that. It is merely a difference of opinion. I'm sorry I couldn't help much, Compy. I fear you'll just have to let him play Tic-Tac-Toe until he figures it out. Luckily, Bottle chrono-locked the Bunker, so we'll just have to remember to be extra nice to Carl after the mess is made.

C: Oh well, thanks anyway. At least Bottle can't say we didn't try.

We join the war (already in progress)

The minutes stretched to hours, the hours lumbered by like weeks, months passed in the blink of an eye. From the outside it would look like the advice went in one ear and out the other. We, of course, know that A) you can't forget the good advice in the middle of the storm unless someone took the time to tell you in the first place, and 2nd) you went ahead and did the dumb thing anyway.

Skip sat in his command center, plotting the raid on Butterscotch Mountain. Princess Zanzibar had thwarted his every attack up to this point. His men had suffered ghastly ankle bites from those vicious garden gnomes, they ran out of pop-tart rations halfway across the River of Doom (it's wider than you thought no matter where you try to cross), and now they were marooned in the middle of Washer-Drier pass. Things looked bleak, to say the least.

What if we tried a surprise attack? Send half the platoon back around Boiler Plateau? No, that was where the Skeletonus Mousii contingent crippled our numbers last Spring.

Skip shook his head and pounded his fist on the table. There was no way out. He was doomed. DOOMED! Just then, when all hope looked as lost as half of your favorite pair of socks, Skip heard a sound. A tiny sound, but nevertheless it intrigued him. Where is it coming from? He threw open the flap of his Yurt. "Where did I get a Yurt?," he wondered out loud to the frosty air.

Tentatively, he followed the sound, an exotic scent wafted across the tundra, and soon he was floating closer and closer like a hungry cartoon wolf catching the scent of a meat pie cooling on the windowsill. Then it hit him. "Is that Astrud Gilberto?" Suddenly he found himself back in the commons, Compy and Sandra sitting with their eyes closed and their heads tilted slightly back and to the left, feet dancing out a Samba as they dreamily swiveled their chairs to and fro. Just then the DJ interrupted in his best Rico Suave impression for a brief station identification:

"You're listening to KBTL after dark. Tonight's album is a dedication from our old friend Bottle to everyone battling it out in the trenches. Don't think I'm not thinking about you, go on and let that savage beast be soothed by The Best of Astrud Gilberto. I don't have much to say, so you know that means it's lovely."

When Bottle Gets Back You're Gonna Be in Trouble (Hey la, hey la...)

E: Oof. Erg. Ah. [Stretch] I had the weirdest dream.

C: You mean the one where you raised an army of minions to storm-trooper the Land of Sugar Plums, but Princess Zanzibar annihilated your forces, and you realized you lost but ran away without properly handing your head over for enspikification like a proper loser?

E: Uh...

S: Not a dream Skip. Bottle won't be happy.

E: Ummagumma. Did I say why I did it?

S: You went off on this "Bottle's a Communist" conspiracy thing, Compy took you to see the Trash Heap, but you were too far gone at that point, so we had to just put on ear protection and let you get it out of your system.

E: Well, is he?

S: Pardon my unacceptable 90s swear words, but that's retarded. No, Bottle is not a "Communist." He'd probably be thrilled to live in a non-religiously motivated commune, but those words don't share any normal relationship to each other, except for maybe in the sense that Capitalists invariably but probably unknowingly create Communist societies under their supposedly benevolent leadership. At least I think that's how Bottle would phrase it.

E: So who are these "Auditors" he keeps mentioning? Is it a secret society like the Illuminati or the Lizard People?

C: I got this one, Sandra. No, Skip. That's nonsense. Ok, you know how every time a bell rings the copilot puts a lapel pin on a kid flying for the first time? Well, every time you blame some annoying thing on an imaginary enemy, an Auditor pops into existence on the other side. Secret cabal bent on overthrowing the Mayor of a no-name suburb? Auditors. Every stupid law, every "they're stealing our jobs!," every half-assed, lazy excuse for things not going your way? Auditors galore. They are legion. Luckily, they aren't real. Unluckily for Bottle, he has to try to figure out whether you're just being a jerk, or whether you've deluded yourself into actually believing it. If you're just being a jerk, then he can at least ignore it, but if you start demanding that he actually believe and participate in that garbage, then he has to make a contingency plan for running the hell away.

E: Is that why he's gone? He knew?

S: No, he planned this week off months ago. Complete coincidence you spazzed out. Well, I mean, he knew you were going to eventually, the timing just happened to work out perfect.

E: What do you mean I would eventually? Are you all in on it?

S: In on what? There's no secret agenda here Skip.

C: Plus, you're the only new guy. All of us knew Bottle in various other ways. We're used to it. We barely even notice.

E: How mad do you think he'll be?

S: Well, he won't be happy that you wasted all those useful minions, but probably not mad, per se. He might get frustrated if you start acting all mopey and apologetic. He might poke fun at you a little, but there's no torture prison here, Skip. I know, I drew the map as he was making it.

C: Worst case scenario, he asks the question.

E: What question?

S: Sorry, that one we can't tell you.

E: Why not?

S: Can't tell you. You'll know it if he asks. Now, please, for just a few more days, be bored. I'm sure there will be plenty more album reviews to sift through when he gets back.

Metallica – Ride the Lightening

Highly critical of those in power. Throw in a couple references to famous books, and that's Ride the Lightning. Blah, blah, whatever.

I'll take "Things A Doof Might Say for $1,000, Alex." There is so much to talk about with Metallica's second album. There's Stephen King, Hemmingway, Lovecraft, and the Bible. There's the European tour and split with Zazula. Tipper's flipping out about acknowledging that suicide exists. Everybody calls Fade to Black a power ballad, and that's just weird.

There's the fact that all the studio minions think Metallica isn't good at playing their instruments, so Cliff and the engineers are actually trying to teach Lars how to keep a consistent beat through a whole song and explaining to the confused faces the intricacies of multiple different notes happening at the same time. Not to mention that one track with a doofy chorus the Corporate guys made them write to try to get some radio play.

We all know it turned out pretty good in hindsight, but at the time it was a cacophonous disaster of insanity. I guess we'll start with the fact that their gear was stolen right before their last gig in the States and subsequent van-life tour of Europe. They had to borrow Anthrax's backup gear. They also had to actually camp at the studio because they couldn't afford hotel rooms. They slept during the day while other people recorded, and recorded at night, bashing out the whole thing in like 18 days before their first show.

Most people forget that this was still a completely independent album. Zazula/Megaforce was their distributor, but Zazula's total budget was only 20k and this went well beyond 30k, so their European label Music for Nations paid the studio costs while they essentially begged for major label support in the US. The album was released in April but it wasn't until September of '84 that Elektra finally signed them. This might seem weird to you, but you have to remember that there was no measurable market for any of this in the US. Denmark is a different story, there was a market for metal. Back in the US, though, everyone is saying "We can't put this on commercial radio, are you insane?" For some real perspective on all of that, we're talking $80,000 of 2020 money just to make it exist from a record store owner in New Jersey, and people are already complaining that it smells a bit "sell out." The band is staying in random fans' houses because they have no money. Meanwhile, Elektra re-releases it and hands them over to Mensch and Burnstein.

I know those names don't mean anything to you, but they are big names. They left their respective labels to form Q Prime with Def Leppard as their only initial client because they felt like it, and they were hard-core Accounting/A&R guys turned agents.

Metallica wanted to be Iron Butterfly heavy, not just fast as hell. They certainly succeeded on that count. It's heavy, dark, menacing, all that stuff. It's also good. It takes actual cultural artifacts and emphasizes the horrible side. This is an album explicitly about death, and even more specifically about how we fixate on actually killing each other and ourselves. It's supposed to be horrible and you're supposed to actually confront it. What you take away or get out of it is your own problem, so to speak. You know me, I like to find some essential profundity that is as challenging as it is simplistic. At the end of the day, I think we can all agree that Metallica knows what books are and how to read them.

Wow, Just Wow: JMC vs. WMG

A week ago when I was talking about EL&P I wrote the phrase "that's how the game works, losers. We own your copyrights, remember?"

Today, the story pops up that WMG literally told Jesus and Mary Chain that just because the Copyright Act of 1976 allows majority holders to nullify all grants after 35 years doesn't mean they have to, so they won't. WMG literally said "no, you can't have the rights to your recordings back." That's disgusting.

The reporting on Jesus and Mary Chain's suit against WMG is pretty terrible, so I had to actually go refresh my memory. Section 203 of the Copyright Act of 1976 specifically deals with non works for hire. It is completely within the majority owner's right to nullify all grants between 35 and 40 years with written notice and effective nullification date. However, if as their label contends these albums are declared "works for hire," then JMC has no claim to ownership of their albums at all.

What's the distinction? Simply put, did JMC sell limited rights of distribution, mechanical reproduction, etc. to the label, or were they paid for their services of creating a body of music fully owned and controlled by their label? I haven't read their contract, but Warner seems pretty confident they signed away ownership of all rights, including nullification. If it can be shown that the works in question were "for hire," then the band will lose its lawsuit because the band owns 0% of those recordings.

It's possible that public sentiment would force WMG to consider voluntarily relinquishing rights to avoid severe economic backlash, but that would be entirely out of their own generosity and concern for their bottom line. It's more likely they'd run the numbers and decide that no amount of anger will tangibly hurt their wallets, and the sad truth is Warner probably owns 100% of all rights to the albums in question.

That's disgusting.

M: Ha, Bottle, ha! Your epidermis is showing!

B: My bias? Yep, sure is, Milton. I want them to die. I want that system to crumble to dust and be replaced by something more agreeable. Pay close attention here, Milton, because this is tricky. I don't want Warner to disappear, I don't want people to lose their jobs, or be homeless. The same goes for all the major corporations, Exxon, Amazon, General Motors, you name it. They all provide useful services. Yes, even Spotify and the Police Department in your city provide a useful service that many people like and want to use (not me, but that's just my personal preference, nothing to do with the wider world). Now, tighten those ab muscles and brace for impact, because here's your sucker punch. There is no "free market," Milton. It's an illusion. It's a faceless, nameless Auditor, raging in its padded cell on the other side of the Imaginarium. It's the made-up reason we can't have nice things. It's the act of looking in the box to determine if Schroedinger murdered his imaginary cat. It's a stupid little idea that works for a while then crashes into your favorite mountain range in a fiery inferno of pointlessness.

Rhetorical question, what's a market, Milton? It's the sum total of all the past exchanges you've decided to look at. If people stop exchanging things, then there's nothing to look at tomorrow. If everyone is lying, then your observations are worthless. There's only one question that really matters, and that question is "what are we actually talking about?" What does it actually mean to talk about Foreign Trade, or Agricultural Exports? What is the point of defining an arbitrary geographical State? Why do those States have Governors? Why do we need a federal Government to keep them coordinated? Because people have everything backward.

They work as hard as they can to drive the cost of living as high as possible, then use that money to turn anything meaningful into the cheapest generic commodity it can be. The person with the most money regulates the market by only selling what makes them the most profit. Enough money and you can create a market for anything all on your own, or snuff out emerging competition by flat out buying them. Government serves no other purpose than to be the regulator, to prevent greed from ruling our lives, so electing the greediest people to tear it all down and destroy any impartiality is about as stupid an idea as I can imagine.

    People can't see the forest for the trees, they don't understand the consequences of their actions, and they have no idea which side of the equation they stand on at any given moment. Economics is a theory; a theory of life. That theory is actually very simple. You might word it differently, but the theory says that life is defined by trading what you have for what you think you want. The first rule of fight club, I mean Economics, is minimize the number of things that might prevent you from being alive tomorrow. Scare away the wildlife, build a better metal snake, convince everyone that everyone else is secretly plotting to murder them. That's the big secret, that's Bottle's skeleton in the closet, that's what Skip is freaking out about back in the Bunker. I am not afraid to die, but as annoying as I can be at times, I don't walk around giving people any reason to want to murder me. No, I'm not keen on surprise pain and suffering, I don't particularly enjoy finding new creative ways to potentially die, but I'm not afraid of it. If you're trying to kill me you'll most likely succeed. If everyone were walking around with ARs and 9s, I'd assume they were looking for any possible reason to kill each other and leave.

    If you stop eating hot dogs the terrorists win! Let 'em. But they crashed airplanes into skyscrapers! That means someone was doing a bad job of preventing it. But drugs are destroying everything. Yeah, some people would rather inject opiates in between their toes or snort Folger's Crystals than deal with the BS of actual modern life. But abortion! Yeah, some people would rather not bring a child into the life of abuse and destitution they know that child will suffer. It's a sin! That's a thing people made up to punish each other into submission. Look, you aren't giving anyone a way to get out of their terrible situation, you're telling them they deserve it as punishment for not being good enough.

Some people thrive under stress, some people crumble. Some people need psychological Rube Goldbergian contraptions to do simple things like eat food when they are hungry, some people will do anything they can to not be alive anymore. Some people refuse to participate in the simple process of trading what they have for what they want in equivalent proportions, especially when what they have is more money than they know what to do with.

At the end of the essay, you have to call it like it is. Warner Music Group only cares about maximizing the profit they make from owning the back catalogue of bands like Jesus and Mary Chain, and they'll be damned if they let anyone else, including its creators who they tricked into signing away their rights, make a penny before they do. They wish the band would just die already. That my friends is a load of horse shit that you and I, not Warner, have to shovel out of the middle of the road because A) we don't want to splash our friends on the sidewalk, and/or B) we can't afford an extra run through the car wash this week.

The myth is that America is a meritocracy, that hard work and dedication to quality equal success, but reality is the opposite when you throw money into the equation. The larger number will win most of the time. The rats rise to the top by manipulating established markets, and forcing everyday people to compete for little pieces of autonomy that the same rats also own. No, not everyone at the top is a rat, but there are rats in one or both adjacent offices. I don't know what it looks like to you, but it reminds me very much of a turtle sitting on a stack of other turtles pretending to be king of all that he sees, right up until the unassuming turtle at the bottom sneezes.

    B: You know what that means, Milton?
    M: No, what?
    B: It means my vacation is over. Back to work on Monday, making more than enough to happily live my life, but about 55% of what I need to be solvent. So to celebrate, or to punish you depending on which side of that equation you're standing on, it's time to delve into the entire p(nmi)t discography.
    M: Oh, no.
    B: Oh, very much yes. Enjoy the rest of your weekend, we've got a lot of work ahead of us.

p(nmi)t – The Discography Years, Part 1

    A long, long time ago, in a galaxy that hadn't yet experienced Trump as President, a little man decided to make as much music as possible purely for his own amusement. I've never actually met the guy, but somehow he got in touch and said "I just want to make music, but I'm broke and I don't know where to start." So I said "ok, I'm broke too, so here's what we'll do. You save whatever you can, I'll save whatever I can, and we'll just piece together a makeshift studio $100 at a time. You worry about getting it into a computer, I'll worry about how to make it listenable. We probably won't make any money, but if we do we'll just split it 50/50."
    Now, it was slow going in the beginning. Months and months would go by before he'd send some snippet to me and ask if it was any good. Normally I have more patience than a granite boulder, but he seemed to be getting really frustrated, and listening to the whining and complaining is like the most annoying thing I can think of, so I asked "who actually cares if

it's any good or not? If you think I care, you're dead wrong. Send me all of it, even the worst of the worst. If you absolutely hate it when I send it back in album form, then throw it away. If you do like it, put it on a Bandcamp page. I don't actually care." Presto differencio, the flood gates opened and it turns out he had 4 years worth of stuff hiding in there.

At first, he didn't really know what to do, so I'd just wait until I had a bunch of tracks and smash them together. Once we got going though, he'd send artwork too and say "build me something that works with that."It turned out he knew Sandra from somewhere else, so all our ideas were mingling at a party I didn't even know I was attending. I didn't even really do anything, we just all ended up in the same train car on that Tiny Universe ride at Walt Whittman World. When the stream dried up a couple years ago, I got the idea to write about stuff. I miss him and I hope he comes back, but it's not like I had a tracking device implanted under his skin or anything, so onward we go. He did at least put most of it up on his Bandcamp page, so we can all enjoy the entire collection together.

The Slumlord EP

The first thing p(nmi)t ever sent me was The Slumlord EP. Not the EP itself, the tracks. They were already titled, so all I had to do was put them in an order and give it some cover art. Bottle's taxonomy is filled with all sorts of clever ways to name things, but the standard convention for EPs is to use the title of the focal track. Slumlord stood out like, well, a stereotypically greasy slumlord. By the time we get to the second half, you can practically smell him strutting down the hallway in his sweat stained white tank top, banging on doors, and demanding rent money. Actually, in my head he looks exactly like Carl from Aqua Teen Hunger Force (no relation to my Carl whatsoever). Hyperion was a possibility, but the rest of the tracks sounded like insects and living in a run-down world, Slumlord just worked. Then I found that lovely picture of a house in Hungary, and there you go.

I suppose it's technically electronic dance music, but that's kind of like sticking a straw in your soda can. Sure, you can do it, but we all know it's completely and ridiculously unnecessary. The memo he sent with them said "here are some tracks I made with Buzz Tracker. A couple of them are pretty good."

These are all great, dude. Some of the sounds are a little gross and the bass is irreparably underpowered, I had to manually remove a lot of nasty percussive spikes to make some tracks more listenable, but it sounds like living your entire life in one of the bedrooms of that dilapidated castle and meeting with your friends at the rave dressed as a depressed vampire every night except Halloween, so who's gonna argue it isn't effective?

2012

The only response I got from the Slumlord EP was "oh, man, that's awesome. Thanks!" That was July of 2011, and I didn't hear from him again for the better part of a year. I was still working on that ridiculous Doctor Bottle thing, so it kind of took me by surprise when he dumped a bunch of stuff on me right after I moved to Iowaland.

> Hey Bottle,
>
> I was going through a bunch of old stuff I wrote and I found some finished pieces that I don't know what to do with. There's a lot of short piano pieces, and some experiments with samples, a 12-tone piece I ran through a bunch of different arpeggiators. I also have this friend who makes interesting abstract art. I don't know if you can turn it all into something or not. If not, just trash 'em. Thanks.

He was right, it was a bunch of random crap, but there was also something tangible happening there. There was the obvious collection of sample based pieces, a Flute Sonata, the 12-tone thing was super cool, and the Piano pieces. I'm inclined to believe he just selected a small square of files on what is surely the nastiest cluttered desktop in the universe, but even there, two of the pictures clearly have pianos in them. That's not abstract art, that's like Rabo Karabekian style Essentialism; complex life forms represented by the absolute minimal required geometry. Alright, you want me to build you something?

The Build Me Something Experiments.
We're jumping into our own future a little, but he had some friends and they played together off and on. The gist of the story is that they were experimenting with being a band. Their drummer wanted to play metal, but Mr. Bedroom and Bassman McRedhair were all freaked out by their drummer's other guitar playing friend, so they quit but were still all totally friends. McRedhair went on to have a prolific career in a Reggae band and started conducting musicals and now he's Artistic Overlord of his own symphony orchestra, you know like Dudamel, but cool.

Variations on a 12-tone Row.
At first I thought I might use these arpeggiations to structure a larger album, but I didn't have any idea what to stick in between, so I just added the title and published them as is. Not exciting. Fun to listen to, though. People have this strange desire to absolutely hate 12-tone music, possibly even more than Death Metal. Personally, I don't get it, homogenous dissonance is lovely.

Piano Music Volume 1.
Normally I shy away from the making music part of making music. I like the idea. I also like collections of piano miniatures. There is something immensely satisfying about a complete piece of music that fits on 1or 2 pages. This set, though, I had to actually sit down and do it. I probably could do a better version, but I also like the idea that you should make your own, so I threw in the sheet music. Sure, listen to my crappy renderings, but why not record yourself playing them for fun? Go ahead, why would I care?

Sonata for Flute and Piano.
I was about to have to do it again, publish a crappy MIDI rendering of this flute sonata. As I was making it though, it sounded more and more familiar. I've heard this piece before. Finally the sunrise happened that I went to a composers concert one time. There's an actual recording of it. It took a month of wandering through the stacks in B-space, but I eventually found it. I also found another concert with what appeared to be a brass quintet by our mysterious mail-bomber, but I'd have to wait for the potential future where he sent it to me to be sure.

Now, this isn't a standing ovation, light the roof on fire kind of flute piece, but it's pretty enjoyable in my book. In terms of writing a quirky piece using chromatic modality with the third movement equivalent of SQUIRREL!, it's quite fun. The second movement is particularly lovely, like wandering around an abandoned cathedral expecting that at any moment a ghost might cry at you.

There you have it, that was 2012. This isn't the meat and potatoes of the discography, that wouldn't begin until the orange terror started fumigating the metropolis, but it's an important basis for understanding of the future. He'll go through cycles of heavy experimental output, followed by "here's some stuff I wrote a long time ago but never recorded." There's one more of these early albums. Fair warning, he sings.

Daphne and Apollo. This is actually the second of two albums of "white guy with acoustic guitar alternative" songs. That's a hard genre to crack, in my opinion, because there's just something so inauthentic about it. I don't mean that the songs are always bad, and I don't mean that you can't do it at all, but there's this peculiarly terrible mental friction created by a dingy random guy singing songs about long lost friends and places and things. Then there's that truly bizarre moment when they pull out their own folk arrangements of Gangsta Rap. Accept it, the context of a guy alone on stage with a guitar is that he's hit rock bottom, he doesn't have any friends along for the ride, all he has left is the guitar and hitchhiking to the next bar or coffee shop to play for tips. That's the default context, you have to actually work to change it, and it's super easy to accidentally resurrect the disbelief everyone suspended. Now, it totally works for genres like Country and Screamo Folk-Metal, because that kind of down on your luck, loser looking for a new life framework is built in. Alternative, though, it either has to be obviously true or you have to method act your way to loser town to really pull it off. Don't be offended, it doesn't mean you're actually a loser. The problem is conceptual, and your audience has to believe that you've actually been put in a box with the word "loser" written on the top in faded sharpie so that we can defiantly like you. The thing that caused it has to be visible. It could be addiction or depression, it could be Tourette's or a stutter or a lisp, it could just be that you are bat-shit insane. It doesn't actually matter, but we the audience have to be able to identify it in the first 3 minutes or we will leave.

We talked about it back with Better than Ezra, but what really is Alternative? It's a mainstream 20-something who looks like a mainstream 20-something pointing out how horrible it actually is to be a mainstream 20-something. The good news is that it ceases to be a problem the moment you look older than 25. The bad news is you're almost taunting your audience to decide if you're actually a loser or if you're just a whiny kid who never actually has to deal with real life but you heard about it once before you even start to play. Also, you can go too far the other way and come across as a middle-aged man child who escaped that whole having to live life thing altogether. It's a tightrope act, for sure.

I was pleasantly surprised when he sent a letter because it made the whole thing make sense.

> Hey Bottle,
>
> I've got a bunch of songs that I never actually did anything with. I was working on an album for a long time, but it just didn't feel right. I like them for myself, but I hate playing them for other people 'cause I'm not a great singer and it all just sounds so terribly depressing. Not like "oh, that's supposed to be sad, I understand," more like "jesus christ, are you ok? I honestly didn't think sounds could smell like clinical depression, but you just proved they certainly can." It's incredibly awkward.

"Oh yeah, bring it," I wrote back. "What was the crappy concept for the album?"

> "Well my friend and I played a few shows as an acoustic duo called Fifth Year. You know, like you should have already graduated, but you're self-aware that it's taking longer than it should. So, I wrote a bunch of songs from the mindset of playing them while sitting on the hood of your car in an empty parking lot."

"Yeah, no wonder it didn't come together, you've got it backward. The album should be called Fifth Year, and your persona is sitting on the hood of your car. It might need a subtitle depending on the actual songs, but try putting them together from that mindset and send me a few that don't quite fit right."

I waited, and I waited, then I found some other butterflies to chase. Then one day he actually sent them. They were super crappy cell phone recordings, below even my standards if you can believe it. But, there was potential.

"Ok Bottle, the bigger album makes a lot more sense now. They're all sort of abstract unrequited love songs, but these 3 are secretly about an actual person."

So, I listened to them about 300 times. I rarely pay attention to where a lot of my ideas come from, but this one was particularly ridiculous. Here's what I told him:

You're gonna be like "whaaa?!," but here's the album for these 3 songs. You're right, you are so depressing it hurts. It's unrequited love, so to balance it you need the most ridiculous version of that story. She needs to be so not in love with you that she would rather turn into a tree than be your girlfriend. Daphne and Apollo. You need to bulk it out though. At a minimum, it needs bookends. You have to set it up so that they can't be in a relationship, but end it so that they can't escape the tragedy either. The details are up to you, but that's the concept. I don't know why, it just is.

Like a week later he sent the whole thing to me. Still too terrible of a recording, and that's when I made the blunder. I drew him a picture of how to find one of my empty rooms in B-space. I didn't think it would be a big deal, I just said try plugging your guitar and mic into an acoustic amp and recording the whole thing as a live performance. I guess I was out doing Bottle stuff when he actually did it. I came back to find the entire place a complete mess, and most of my favorite minions gone with only scorch marks on the floor to remind me.

    B: What the hell happened here, Carl?

    J: The minions were trying to help some kid figure out how to plug all this equipment together, but one of 'em accidentally stuck the audio jack in the electric socket. Looked like the promo poster for Christmas Vacation for a moment, then POOF!

    B: Ok, well lock everything up tight, and we'll hope he never comes back. You know how much brain power it takes to imagine up good minions? Too much.

    J: Seemed like a nice kid to me. Polite, calling me Sir and everything. I like him. Music's not that spectacular, but who's is?

    B: Ok, then. He's your problem. You can keep him as long as you clean up after him.

    J: Fair enough. You got a mop?

    B: Yeah, it's in the closet.

    J: Where's the closet?

    B: Stupidest question I've ever heard. It's the room with the sign that says "closet," Carl.

    J: He hee! Just testing you, Bottle. Relax.

    B: Sorry. It's just so hard to train good minions. He's your responsibility, remember.

    J: I told you, fair enough.

Insertions

    3 gloriously quiet years passed. Really, I didn't hear a peep from Feb 2013 to March 2016. I heard he was in a band, so it's not like he had much free time. Not gonna lie, I was a little bit relieved when these tracks showed up. Not so much that he was sending me music again, but that was around the

time the Trumpeter Swan really started squawking, so it was at least a welcome diversion.

> Hey Bottle,
> I recorded a few guitar pieces that turned out pretty good, and my friend S. didn't have a use for this artwork. Think you can album it up a little? It's random crap, but maybe that could be the concept? Thanks.

Yeah, this is actually pretty good. It's a strange mix of actual pieces and sonic wallpaper, but everything kind of has this interlude quality to it, like they just belong sandwiched between other things. I'm not really sure what this mysterious "S" was going for, all I see is a blind Perry the Platypus. The EQ is all over the place and a couple of 'em are clearly just straight DIs, but a few of those pieces are really enjoyable.

It turns out he really was experimenting with all the various hardware he had accumulated (cheap amps, a tiny usb mixer, I think he even used a vocal mic on a cheap cab to record the high-gain stuff for The Burning Hour. Why not? I just put them in an order that felt good and called it Insertions. Little did I know I got ghost enrolled into the album a month club for the next 2 years until my useful shoulder gave out in real life. I'm getting ahead of myself, though. Buckle up, we're about to hear some sounds.

Sounds you can make with things that make sound and Not Every Thought Can Be Congruous

B: Who dug all these bottomless holes in the hallway?! My brand new batch of minions is jumping in them like lemmings, and I got my foot stuck in the one outside my office and smashed a few more as I fell with a thud, and the effects cabinet is wide open.

J: Sorry, Boss. p(nmi)t was diggin' for some new gear to play with. I gave him one of those loopy pedals and he was giddy as could be.

B: I ain't the boss of anybody. I'm just a guy telling you to fill in these potholes before somebody important gets hurt. I'm sure I heard me tell you he's your problem.

J: Relax. 'Course I'll fill 'em in. Sorry you tripped. You hurt?

B: Me too, and no I'm fine. But, now I gotta go bake up another new batch. Just try to clean up the next catastrophe before I actually step in it, ok?

J: Will do.

I'll admit, at first I was like "oh gawd, he's giving ambient a whirl." After 2 or 3 of 'em though, I started to notice the difference. This isn't actually airport minimalism. He's sculpting sonic textures in real time. I mean, yeah, you're only ever going to get a single structure that way, but over a long span of time the actual pieces will form their own evolution. That's assuming he'll actually keep doing it, though. At the time, I figured since we're exploring uncharted territory I'd just let them live in chronological order. He got a little squirrely at the end, so I just chopped it off after the obvious Slumlord leftover track Night Music. There were a whole bunch more random looking covers, so I just picked the two most appropriate and gave them funny but relevant titles. The whole project was kind of just building itself, so I didn't really put much though into it and stood on the sidewalk while the parade passed.

The Uncollected

I was curious, so I shot him a message:

Hey, are you just sending these to me as you finish them?

He replied "no, I'm tinkering with them, working on something else, then coming back to try again. I want them to be created in a single take, but I mess up a lot."

I replied "well, it's working surprisingly well in the order you send them. Let's try an experiment. I want you to make a rock/metal album, but I want you to create it one piece at a time in chronological order. Don't start anything else until you're finished with a track and send it to me. Try coming up with a single riff, then build the piece from it. As long as it takes, the album is done when you run out of ideas."

The first one came mid June, but it took most of July for his brain to finally give up. He worked hard, and it shows. The end result is pretty astonishing, even if I do say so myself.

You might be wondering where the ridiculous titles come from. He tends to call them boring things like "new riff," or "bingle bangle," or "e-a-b-d," so I developed a fool proof system. You just listen to it 3 or 4 times, and title it whatever silly lyrics you find yourself singing. It works like 90% of the time. For the other 10% you just use a pun. It helps if the vibe matches the music, but it's certainly not mandatory.

Scenes from the Blog

E: Um, Bottle. Sorry, I know you're working on the p(nmi)t discography, but the blog has been kind of dormant, and I was wondering if you could maybe do a mini-adventure in the meantime, just to keep it going? If, if you don't mind.

B: Only if you tell me why you're acting all afraid of the big, bad Bottle. If I didn't know any better, I'd say you got a spanking from the Princess.

E: Oh, um, uh, I guess did kind of get a little stir crazy while you were gone. Overreacted, really. It's just that...

B: Little birdie told me that story different. Said you led my minions on a doomed crusade against The Bottler's Axis of

Ass Handed to You. Word of advice, I don't listen to Christmas albums 'cause I like them. The prophecy commands it. I told you I don't make the rules, I just try not to 'splode myself.

E: Oh. He he, uh, ok, but about the blog…

B: We could do the 300+ recordings Buckethead published in the last 2 years. No, on second thought, even I can't do 100+ hours of endless 8-bar parallel periods. Hmmmm. I know! You like Smooth Jazz, Skip?

E: Not particularly, no.

B: Oh, well, in that case we'll just even the score right now. Yeah, I'll do an entire chapter on my Smooth Jazz collection and forget all about that farcical Bottle's a Communist episode. Fair deal?

E: More than fair. Generous, even.

B: Good. I do have one more Columbo style question, though.

E: Um, ok, what's that?

B: What did you think was going to happen?

E: [mumble, mumble]

B: I'm sorry, I didn't catch that, Skip.

E: Um, I guess I didn't.

B: Ok, good enough for me.

E: Really?

B: Yeah, no torture prison here, Skip. If the Princess wanted you gone you'd be gone. Plus, you appear to feel bad about it, so what would my being mad accomplish? The minions are imaginary, remember? All they cost is a little bit of brain power. Princess Zanzibar has that advantage even over me. I can't speak for when I eventually run out of mental reserves, but I'm good for now. Maybe don't go crazy next time, huh?

E: Yes, sir. Sorry, Bottle.

B: As you were.

Compliments of KTNT, Oklahoma City's Authority on Smooth Jazz

When I say Smooth Jazz you think Kenny G, and Skip visibly squirms in his chair. Excellent, but what actually is Smooth Jazz? Well, historically speaking it's the soft, polished, mass-market Muzak form of Jazz Fusion that rose to prominence in the 80s and 90s. It's Adult Contemporary Jazz, so meticulously designed to be inoffensively non-confrontational that it was simply called "smooth radio" in the 70s, which of course means that by the 90s it was so aurally offensive as to be a joke. I actually like a lot of it.

For our purposes, let's say it's the melding of Jazz, Light Funk, R&B, and Pop into the audio equivalent of shea butter based moisturizing skin cream. Shea butter is totally edible, so we're going to suspend any trepidations and proceed without any cultural assumptions at all. Well, maybe a couple. It will be groove based, rather than improvisation driven. It will be sappy, but we're going to think of it in terms of Marty Friedman's crossover into New Age. Last, we will accept that sounding like the mainstream, acceptable version of sensual is the goal. We're not traveling in blind, though. We're going to take the trail marked on your father's map, and even if we emerge sixpence none the richer, at least we should still have all our appendages. So join me on a little adventure I'm calling Compliments of KTNT, Oklahoma City's Smooth Jazz Authority.

Hillary James and Bob James – Flesh & Blood

First, we're going to listen to a mildly obscure submission into the Bob James catalog, Flesh & Blood. He's called the Godfather of Hip-Hop because his track Nautilus from the 70s has been sampled at least 352 times, Slick Rick, A Tribe Called Quest, Wu Tang Clan, Naughty By Nature, Run D.M.C, Usher, everybody.

No idea who Hilary is, all the liner notes say is "thanks for letting us invade your living room" from the producers. We'll just assume she's his wife. First listen, whole lot of "I need a man to feel spiritually and emotionally fulfilled." I kinda zoned out, so I needed a second listen.

Critically speaking, everybody says "why do I have to listen to Hilary not try very hard?" I don't think that's fair. No, she is not forceful, or sultry, or exciting, but I can imagine exactly how terrible it would be if her goal was to out Houston the Whitney. Nothing worse than a mousy voice trying to belt and warble, be yourself I say. The other main criticism is that it's barely jazz even by Bob James standards. I have no basis for comparison, but I do have a Bob James solo album, so we'll do that next.

If the goal is to be lowish volume pleasant background music for whatever more important thing you're selling, then this totally succeeds. I don't get all the fuss. Ooooh, wait, Hilary is his daughter? Not gonna lie, that's a little uncomfortably take your daughter to work (at the hotel lounge) creepy. Flesh & Blood hits different now.

Sure, the "my daddy's famous" nepotism thing is there if you're desperately trying to spin it that way, but I would be lying if I said I didn't thoroughly enjoy listening to it. It sounds more like legitimate quality time they both enjoy. It sounds like a jazz pianist playing on his daughter's day spa soundtrack rather than a daughter trying to capitalize on her dad's success. I do have one question though. What the hell is "green silence?" The answer, unsurprisingly, is running shoes for women. You know, because marketing.

Bob James – Playin' Hooky

Playin' Hooky is not one of Bob James's famous albums. Supposedly, his band Fourplay is terrible, but this album is half good half bad. Apparently I'm supposed to steer clear of the tracks with fellow person named James, Boney. I'm just gonna lean into the bad guesses I established when confusing his daughter for his wife and say Boney James is either not related at all, or he's Bob's saxophone playing Aunt on his mother's side. Supposedly Boney is hackwork personified, but I'll be the judge of that.

Early on in his career Bob was Avant Somethingorother, but this is 1997 Mario, sorry Warner Bros., so Classical arrangements and Dadprovisation is what we should expect. Only a couple tracks with background vocals, so that shouldn't be a problem. Press play.

Aw, yeah. A little bit of Detective Dog Lawyer Rhodes at the start, and the Jimmy Buffet equivalent of Samba. A freakin' coach's whistle?! You remember that store in the mall called Brookstone that used to sell personal massagers and minecraft furniture? This would fit right in.

Boney doesn't sound like a hack on Mind Games at all. He does sound like Dentist Office Sax, but I assume that's the intended aesthetic. I actually have one of his albums queued up next, so we'll keep focus on Bob.

Ooh, I love the intro for The River Returns. The "exoticism" is a little much, but it's quite enjoyable for its playfulness. I personally could do without the vocalizations, but they aren't particularly annoying.

Ok, the rain sticks and nature sounds are a little too much, but Organza is a pretty nice slow jam with great bass playing.

Nah, Hook, Line, and Sinker is totally fine. What horrible thing did Boney do to garner all the hate? No, he's no Moon Hooch, but these are smooth jams. Who in their right mind would Sanders or Zorn these things? At the very least, he's not playing an Oboe shaped Screech Whistle like he will on track 7.

Oh yeah, Glass Hearts is great. A fair bit of that questionable exoticism, but it's definitely meant to be sentimentally nostalgic rather than appropriationally indulgent.

Yeah, even Boney's Soprano Sax playing is perfectly fine. Is it just because he looks exactly like Kenny G? I suspect it's the long curly brown hair and Hawaiian shirts you really don't like.

E: Ah! No! I don't like Do It Again at all! Make it stop.

B: Hell no. Crank it up! Introducing Rasheeda Azar doing her best Traci Lords impression.

E: I am very uncomfortable.

B: Good. Sandra?

S: Skip, stop being such a prude. This is gooooood. I'm slightly confused that Bottle likes it, but I sure as hell do.

B: What's not to like? These last 3 tracks are exquisite. Bass that could give Barry White a run for his money, a touch of Miami Noir, this is a feel good then make your move album. It starts out fun and ends up sexy. Am I right?

S: Mmmmmm hmmm.

E: Um, er, uh, I need some fresh air.

S: You really do like this, Bottle?

B: Not known for lying, that I know of. Do I want to listen to it every day? Probably not. Is it a fantastic and effective album for its intended context/audience? Absolutely. Better than Sting's Decade of Somnambulent Sagas.

S: Indeed. Let's hear it again.

B: Already reaching for the play button. But first, how'd you manage to bring Skip back to below ground level?

S: I didn't, I was starting to run out of creative ways to thwart him. I thought I might actually have to decapitate him. Much to my surprise, Astrud Gilberto solved that problem like a dream.

B: Oh, did it? Well, lucky I was thinking about you all at the time.

S: Indeed. Perhaps a thank you is in order.

B: You're welcome. Now, would her highness care to play hooky again?

S: She most certainly would.

Boney James – Sweet Thing

Ok, ok, I see what's going on here. People hate the fact that Boney James is actually good. They desperately want him to be Kenny G 2.0, but he's not. He's a saxophonist. A good one.

Tom Petty reminded us that when I say bad, I mean someone didn't do a good job of whatever they intended to do. Those Beatles albums are bad not because I hate the Beatles, they're bad because they slapped a bunch of crap together and weren't happy with the result. Finger 11 was bad because you'd have to be a grade a douche-bag to walk around thinking the world isn't good enough for you. Sonny Bono was bad because he was a dweeb who took himself serious. Ten Years After was pretentiousness personified. You get the idea.

So, good is the opposite, sort of. Really, when I say good I mean that I believe you. You succeeded, you worked hard and made something you are proud of making. It doesn't matter if I actually like you or not, it doesn't matter if you can or can't technically play or sing well, it boils down to the fact that I can hear you aren't trying to secretly sell me anything. This album sounds like he means it, this is Boney James, and he's got a room full of awards that say a lot of other people can hear that too.

So, what is it the internet trolls actually hate? Well, for starters, he's clearly a happy dude. That's been known to bother me too, but usually only in the context of "well, you wouldn't have those trivial problems if you were rich like me." That's not what I hear here. I just hear happy.

The second thing going on is some mental friction about the realities of making recorded music. A lot of people hear the drum machine and sequencer fire up and automatically jump to "look at the loser who can't put a full band together." You can certainly end up there as a conclusion, but even a basic search of Boney James will tell you he's been a sideman, a collaborator, his band opened for Flora Purim (she's not compliments of KTNT, but I do have one of her albums, so we'll do that next). That alone tells you this is exactly what he wanted to make on his own. Now, what does he play when he plays?

Critics say "I guess it's technically jazz." Technically it is, but Boney comes from the R&B side of the Fusion equation. In all seriousness, Boney is the smooth side of R&B Sax more so than Jazz, and that's where I think the happy guy friction actually comes from. There's a little bit of Funk, but less than even Bob James. At the same time, though, he's as far away from the overtly sentimental sap of Kenny G as possible. Skip's squirming like he's got sand in his bikini, but I like Kenny G just fine. I couldn't handle 4 hours of him, but I'm not gonna turn it off when I walk into the room. He's not showboating, he's not jerking tears or off, he's not trying to look cool. Even his nickname is legit; his friends said he was lookin' pretty lean after struggling to make money on the road.

Nope, Boney is one of those guys who looks like you should totally hate him, but every criticism falls short so you get mad and resort to calling him a doo-doo head because you refuse to admit defeat. Sounds like somebody else I know, huh Skip? Don't worry, only 5 or 6 more albums to achieve full payback for your crimes against minion-manity. There's even one I know I don't like at all hiding in there.

Flora Purim – Speak No Evil

These first 4 albums are pretty awesome because they just unfolded all by themselves. If you magically opened to the last few pages, you might be wondering what horrible thing

Skip did while I was taking a much needed vacation, but I'm saving that for a couple chapters ago. All you really need to know is that he had a little dust up with Princess Zanzibar, and I needed to settle the score. So, naturally, the Godfather of Hip Hop showed up. Turns out he brought his anthropomorphic skeleton of a sax player with him, and now we're gonna have tea with the Queen of Brazilian Jazz, Flora Purim. Not one single bit of that was planned, by the way. I'm still just picking up random albums that feel interesting and marveling at the serendipity of it all. The lesson for Skip is that just because you think reality works a certain way, doesn't mean it's true. As goofy or hokey or embarrassing as Smooth Jazz might seem, we're looking at the direct lineage from Stan Getz/Gil Evans to Chick Corea and Dizzy Gillespie to Flora Purim to Boney James and Bob James. A couple more names and Kevin Bacon will gut you like Candyman, tee hee.

But seriously, when I said Smooth Jazz evolved out of Fusion, I meant it. As amazing a listen as Astrud Gilberto is, she's a bit of an ingenue compared to Flora. Flora left Brazil because she was an outspoken protestor of the heavy military presence and censorship in the 60s. If the little hint of naughty from Bob and Rasheeda made Skip squirm and run away, imagine what the full When Harry Met Sally reenactment on the first track This Magic is gonna do to him. Flora's Bossa Nova Fusion is not subtle. Be sure to prehydrate, don't freak out if there's a little bit of cocaine involved, and hang on tight, here's Flora Purim's Speak No Evil.

Des'ree – I Ain't Movin'

You know what's even better than pointing out the day spa aesthetic of Hilary James? Flying across the Atlantic to hear the crappy British version. Des'ree.

If there's one thing I know it's that quite often, despite everyone's best efforts, love will not in fact save the day. It didn't work in the 60s, and it's not working now. So, you can see my skepticism surface when she said "guys, I'm gonna take a break from this whole selling millions of albums thing and focus on my true passion, Naturopathy."

I'm not talking ancient Chinese wisdom, or foot massage, or even the Colonel's secret 7 herbs and spices. I'm talking "we definitely need to rub this holy mud on that gaping flesh wound to draw out the demons." "Rub this magnet over that annoying tumor 9 times a day and you'll be good as new." "It's natural, so it's better than actual medicine." Snake venom is all-natural, want me to drink that? I'm not saying Western Medicine has the best track record with its lobotomies and circumcisions, blood-letting and opioid dispenseries, but I am saying that you have a better chance with actual scientific research than you do with anything Gwyneth Paltrow put in a bottle. I also won't criticize the real psychological impact of the placebo effect. If chicken blood and magic pyramids get you back on the active path to recovery, at least there's good eating on a chicken after you leave.

I have no idea if that's a fair assessment, it's just that as bad as Medicine can be or has been throughout history, any Alternative version is no better or worse than ignoring the problem and waiting to see if it goes away on its own. Tuberculosis and Lupus and The Plague don't spontaneously get better, no matter how much unfiltered goat urine you drink.

The Allmusic review for her inarguable smash sophomore album I Ain't Movin' is hilarious. "A lot of things about this album are terrible, but it's a totally satisfying listen." Are you high, Tom? We're gonna apply my unpatented, ethically suspicious Bottle-valuation. It's a simple 3 question test: 1) what are you talking about?, ii) why does that matter?, and Triceratops) why should I care?

Preamble disclaimer: I love You Gotta Be, I like her song from Baz Luhrmann's William Shakespeare's Rodolpho and Juniper, I like her voice a lot, but that's never spared anyone before, so here we go.

1. You gotta do what it takes to keep up. Love will help. Ok, sure, no argument from me.

2. Life's a crazy maze, so I'm gonna take a train and be homeless and barefoot in the forest. Oh, and don't forget to take along your stash of Spice Melange (the withdrawls are a killer). Meh.

3. Is this one of those God is my boyfriend songs?

4. Remember that Rob Thomas/Santana jam? Well it's like that but we're whiny entitled garbage. There are people literally starving because of drought. We have to do something.

5. I think this song is her singing to herself, but it's really confusing. We're gonna have to give this a "what are you talking about?"

6. Why are you talking the lyrics? Herald the day when babies stop dying. You're gonna be sorry if you don't start stopping being terrible. Viva la revolution! Yeah, strike two, why is this song important?

7. Don't do drugs, do love instead? It's a natural high. Strike 3, why should I care? 4 more tracks? Do I have to? Fine.

8. Oh, this is a great song. Yeah, you shouldn't sacrifice yourself. Eyebrows are always older than the beards? That's a dumb lyric, but not without a hilariously coincidental relevance for my own weird stories. I don't disagree that love should win the civil war in your brain, it's just not going to magically happen.

9. People from the country just don't understand how awesome living in terrible cities is. Maybe I'm hearing it wrong, but yeah, no more living in cities for Bottle ever. This song is so bi-polar. No, this song does not need the funny voices. Knock it off.

10. I had a dream where I dreamed about stuff, and when I woke up I had this song in my head. Nope, another why should I care.

11. Yay sports team! We won! Love is here!

12. Take it away, my own title track acapella vocal with remixed percussion ensemble. Worst outro ever.

Ok, the music is fine. Yeah, you know, if you ignore all the lyrics to everything, most albums are awesome. A few of the songs on this album are great. Legitimately wonderful. The album however is literally "that's rough, but love will fix it." Poverty and famine? Love. Homelessness? Love will fix that too. Self esteem issues? Just love yourself a little more. See? I'm happy. You know why? Love. It's like you guys aren't paying attention. Fine, if you're not going to love each other, I'm gonna go boil rocks instead.

Is that a fair interpretation? Maybe not. Is it honest? Absolutely. Des'ree was a fantastic singer. The actual words she sang? Not so much.

E: Totally learned my lesson, Bottle. Can we be done now?

B: Hell no, two more albums. The next one looks like a real doozy.

E: [wimper]

Jazz Crusaders – Happy Again

I don't know anything about Jazz Crusaders, but I do know that titling an album Happy Again implies there was a period of time spent not being happy. I also know that it'll be relevant to things I've already said, and it will probably be perfectly lovely in spite of the mild reception it got at the time. Alright, C-saw, short version me.

C: Jazz Crusaders were a Hard Bop group. In the 70s they turned to Funk and Fusion and dropped the Jazz. Trombonist Wayne Henderson left the group in '75, but ressurected the original name 20 years later for Happy Again. Critics pretty strongly agree that with a name like Jazz Crusaders, it's Hard Bop or get the hell out of here. That's disappointing, but on the positive side they were happy to hear Henderson's trombone solos again.

B: Yep, told you so. Trepidations, Skip?
E: I'm not sure I'm comfortable with the cover art.
B: why not?
E: well, I mean isn't it kind of racist?
B: how are Robert Palmer Eyes racist?
E: no, I mean the watermelon.
B: how is a delicious fruit racist? I guess maybe it could bother you if you have a severe aversion to lycopine, or if you didn't know it was a symbol of newly acquired economic self-sufficiency after the Civil War. You, my friend, have too many garbage ideas walking around in your brain. Focus on the contrast. You got an overexposed female face with copious amounts of purple eyeshadow and a chomped on slice of watermelon superimposed as her smile. Using watermelon as a nudge nudge wink wink way to stereotype an entire race and culture is definitely racist, so knock that off, but the only place that's happening right now is in your own brain. You just invented racism to feel bad about yourself so you could whitewash away that racist thought and end up being racist. Who taught you to do that garbage? I bet it was racist people. The real problem is the subtle critical implication that back in 1995 this album wasn't "black enough" to deserve more than middle-ground equivocation. Too pop for the purists? That's just plain garbage in my opinion. You shouldn't sacrifice yourself for anybody. Even Des'ree got that one right.

I suppose I could be wrong and it's the complete opposite. It could be a super snarkastic "look at the shit we gotta do to make a record. Ressurect our old name and play radio friendly schmooz." It certainly doesn't sound that way, and Sin-Drome Records is a pretty obscure, "fiercely independent" label specializing in Smooth Jazz. It's the home of all things Bobby Caldwell, Imagineered by Henry Marx. People were shocked Bobby Caldwell was white back in the 70s. You also have to understand where the whole watermelon thing came from, the actual symbolism not the shitty political spin. To me this is the opposite of exploiting artists, but I have no clue what anyone involved was actually thinking other than a few of the non-involved founding members were a little ruffled by Henderson using the name again.

    Look, you can read it however you read it, but I think the clear context is "leave your baggage at the airport, let go of all those phony social restrictions other people use to push and put you down, and go enjoy what you enjoy." In other words, do what you gotta do, but also just be happy again. Now I'm certain I'm gonna love it. It'll be a little funky, a little smooth, some pop melodies, some carefree solos, a good time for everybody. In short, it'll be fun. Roll it.

    Yeah, see, what did I tell you? This is an afternoon concert in the park album, a little something for everybody. Some straight jams, some funk, a tasteful amount of sexy time, a proper Bop track or two, and everybody has a reason to smile. I haven't heard their early stuff, but this sounds exactly like what I expect Henderson wanted. I think he's saying, you know what? Let it go. For one afternoon, just let it go, and be Happy Again. I'm happy again. Thanks, Jazz Crusaders, that was fun.

Najee – Songs From The Key Of Life

    Now, let's nightcap our delightful journey through the smooth side of radio jazz with the highly and rightfully acclaimed tribute to Stevie Wonder by Najee. Sax/flute improvisations on Songs From The Key Of Life? Sign me up twice! I'm a bit bummed that the disc isn't actually in the case, so imma youtube it along with you. Regardless, enjoy.

Debriefing

B: So, what did we learn from this particular adventure?

E: I learned that I thought I understood you, but it turns out I don't at all.

B: Great!

S: I think we learned that out of all these albums from a genre we assume you don't enjoy that much, there was only one that struck you as inauthentic.

B: That's certainly one of the things I learned about myself. The only question I ever ask is "are you lying?" The answer isn't whether or not you're actually lying, the answer is whether I think you're lying. Truth be told, I think Des'ree was only half lying. I Ain't Movin' was a perfectly lovely EP filled out with Goop.

C: What else did you learn, Bottle?

B: All sorts of stuff, Compy. I didn't really talk about it, but the whole project actually puts a lot of things in perspective. I think we all assume Stevie Wonder got a fair chunk of money for Najee's album. Bob James certainly has no scruples about people paying him for sampling his music, but I doubt he's actually taking people to court for millions like Enya. He seems genuinely more interested in playing piano than anything else.

My not at all secret agenda is pointing out how the hypocrisy, not the money, trickles down. What I'm trying to illustrate is that at a certain point somewhere up the pyramid there's an extra-dimensional fold in the fabric of reality. Somewhere along the ascent you cross over from participating in a fair market to manipulating the currency of that market for profit. All of a sudden you aren't using money to facilitate trade; you're using it to control everyone else so you never have to actually spend it; you're deflating the market for power because you refuse to let someone else succeed without your consent.

We just looked at the other side of the Hip-Hop coin, and out popped the question "who's being exploited?" Does Hip-Hop exploit other artists by sampling, or are the original artists exploiting the popularity of Hip-Hop as a source of easy money? Two sides of the same coin, so the real question is "who flipped the coin, and who's calling heads or tails?"

Which reminds me of a story. A story about the second Beastie Boys album, Paul's Boutique.

Beastie Boys – Paul's Boutique

Remember how I said Beastie Boys were really divisive? Well, yeah, there's a pretty strong argument to be made that Paul's Boutique is the singularity that exploded the copyright powder keg. Now, this is a confusing story, so you have to stick with me. We have to go all the way back to 1983 and look at an actual legitimate copyright infringement case. British Airways straight up used "Beastie Revolution" in a television commercial without permission or compensation. That is the actual type of protection the Copyright Act was designed to provide. Beastie Boys hired a lawyer, and handily won $40,000 as compensation for the obvious copyright infringement committed by an international company exploiting an emerging artist for their own commercial interests. The Beastie Boys used that money to buy an apartment and set up their studio to make more music.

As the story goes, the first taste of a problem came from their first official single, Cookie Puss. Some kid came up and said "I talked to my uncle and convinced him not to sue you for using the name Cookie Puss." The track itself is samples from their own music, snippets of crank calls to an actual Carvel shop, juvenile misogyny, etc. In general, everyone thought they were a bunch of annoying jackassess, and they were, but they were also genuinely more interested in sampling and tape loops than they were being a hardcore punk band. Authenticity isn't really the issue here, the issue is the putting two and two together. You've got a group of jackasses who made their initial money from a copyright lawsuit gaining more and more traction, their first album with Def Jam is an instant smash hit but the jackassery gets them labeled as "frat hip-hop" so they exile themselves to the other side of the country and score a deal with Capitol to make a more artistically motivated sample-based album. It wasn't intended to be a commercial success, but the critics were actually raving about it, and that's when everyone pauses and says "wait a minute, these jackasses are making big money by sampling our music, but we aren't making a dime? Time to turn their own tables." Pretty soon, suing each other for money is the standard business model.

  I have a big problem with that, and it's a structural problem. At this point, from a legal perspective, there's basically no difference between something like The Score and Paul's Boutique, albums you buy to hear Fugees' and Beastie Boys' Hip-Hop creations having no idea what they've used for samples, and rip-off compilations from Pickwick or even Najee's version of Stevie Wonder's album. I don't think that lack of distinction is true or fair at all. Sampling, Sampledelia, Plunderphonics, whatever you want to call it is fundamentally different from covering a song or straight up republishing a recording. Imagine you are a visual artist and you make a large piece by buying 30 issues of Esquire, cutting out all sorts of various photos and building a collage of those scraps to make some statement about the conceptual world they create. You sell that work of art for 20-million dollars. How strong of a claim would Esquire or the individual photographers have to the profits from that sale? I'm not answering that question for you, I'm answering that question for me, and I think it's preposterous.

I think real Hip-Hop falls under Fair Use, and I think the proof of that fair use lies in the dedication to the art form itself. Combing through crates of records others have discarded, exploring the aesthetic experience of listening to them, taking parts that speak to you and building something new from a foundation of gratitude and respect; turning people on to the appreciation of culture they would otherwise ignore. That's Hip-Hop.

There's another distinction to be made, however, and it comes from the real commercialization of merely using the chorus from one song as the chorus of your own, or Weird Al if he wasn't intentionally using parody (Weird Al pays regardless). Think Eminem and Dido. That's not Hip-Hop, it's Crossover. Conceptually speaking, regardless of how you interpret the significance of Stan, it's "Eminem Featuring Dido," but we're essentially listening to Dido's Thank You while Eminem raps about an obsessed fan over the top of it. Much different from slapping Dido's record on the table and doing an extended scratch routine on her phrase "I'm wondering why," or physically manipulating two copies to make the drum loop like Grand Master Flash would have done.

The irony is that it all came crashing down on a band whose career was funded by a legitimate copyright lawsuit, who, whether you like the Beastie Boys or not (I actually think Check Your Head is 1,000 times better), created an amazing (if still overly juvenile) Hip-Hop album called Paul's Boutique and ruined the party for everyone.

Preamble to Vitalogy

B: Why are you staring at me like that, Compy?

C: Trying to figure out where you're going next.

B: Why, I just bumble forward without much thought. More fun that way.

C: Yeah, but Skip's right. The further we go the more complex you get, but after you say it it makes complete sense.

B: I'm just very grounded in observation. I like jigsaw puzzles. Sometimes you focus on shapes, sometimes color, sometimes you pick up a piece and search for where it goes, sometimes you look at am empty space and remember the piece that fills it. The more you do it, the easier it gets.

C: Yeah, but what album is next?

B: Easy, Vitalogy.

C: Ehat? Why?

B: Well, I mentioned Des'ree and Naturopathy. Silly pseudo science. Vitalogy. Also, Des'ree felt the need to explain every song in the liner notes like she knew they didn't make any sense on their own. Pearl Jam totally went the other way and built an elaborate collage of weirdness around their coherent and insightful observations of real human activity and interaction. Two sides of the same coin I'm tossing. Vitalogy is the better album in my opinion.

C: But how would you even think to compare them?

B: I didn't, I just saw a Vitalogy shaped hole, so that's what we listen to next.

C: Really?

B: Honestly, I heard Betterman on the radio, and it all clicked. It's amazing how beautiful it is when you're fully in tune with the possibilities of coincidence. A couple minutes either direction and it might never have happened.

C: Amazing. Should I wake up Skip?

B: Nah, we'll save the actual review for the book. He's had a rough couple of weeks. Or, maybe this was the review. I dunno, I've got weeds to whack before we actually listen to it later. Anything could happen (wink).

Pearl Jam - Vitalogy

It's weird to read about Pearl Jam because everyone involved seems to have a completely different experience. The one consistent thread is that the band is at war with the business that surrounds making music. It's much bigger than that, though. Everything about Pearl Jam rages against the fake corporate Disneyland version of life. That was the original name for this album, Life.

Some critics say this third album is their best, some say its experimental aspects are a failure, everyone avoids the actual subject matter at all costs, including me. I can't review Ten, I could barely describe the aesthetic of Vs., and now we're literally wrapping actual life in the shroud of bullshit propaganda "polite" society demands in the form of medical authority (sell me immortality). I even went so far as to create a whole story so I didn't actually have to publish this on facebook. Fuck that. Pearl Jam sings about the severe psychological trauma of actual life. Incest, racially motivated murder, addiction, exhibitionist suicide, abusive relationships, you name it. Having also devoted my life to really observing and contemplating that soft white underbelly, I'm impressed Eddie even gets out of bed some days. I know there are days I don't want to, and the ghosts of very real friends who didn't walk around in my head exactly like Uncle Cyrus planned. Love ain't gonna fix that like in the movie or the Des'ree album, I have to lock every of those cells up tight and redraw the incantations myself.

Brenden O'Brien says they were imploding on this album. Dave felt like he couldn't communicate with anyone else in the band, and they fired him near the end. Stone Gossard refused to be everybody's mediator. Everyone felt like Eddie was being domineering, and they weren't happy about most of the tracks being jam tracks. Guys, that's the exact opposite of everything you said about the first two albums. Lack of communication? Vedder sounds more alone than ever? No shit. I think we can all recognize and understand the HEAVY, but not many people understand what it's like to carry the source of all that around in your head while being forced to have coherent conversations about which parts of the book you bought at a garage sale are still under copyright protection with the guy whose money you're spending and the band's lawyer. Most people say "oh, man I get it" and let it evaporate because they don't actually have to deal with it. Eddie, though, he must have a spectacular collection of bottles. I bet it's even more impressive than mine. Boycotting Ticketmaster venues is like the most miniscule attempt to get your brain right I can think of in that situation. The band was legitimately worried some of these songs were too "accessible."

Which brings us to Whipping. You know that my perspective is that people in general are bad at interpreting things because of confirmation bias. There are two parts to this song, the lyrics and the piece of paper on which they are written. You can't just interpret the two as a conglomeration, you have to interpret each one separately then watch what happens when you conjoin them. The piece of paper is a petition to President Clinton asking the federal government to intervene in the social issue of abortion. The petition states that we the undersigned understand there is a very important difference of opinion on this issue, but the pro-life side of the argument has crossed the line into actually condoning the murder of doctors and women who are deciding to terminate a pregnancy.

Lyrically speaking, the chorus (arguably the most important part of any song because it is designed to be the most memorable hook) is just the phrase "they're whipping." I like to think of myself as somewhat well-educated on the subject of lyrical interpretation, but even I can only think of two plausible scenarios to which this phrase refers. The first is BDSM, which I think we can all agree is not the intended context of the phrase as used in this song. The second is slavery, specifically a slave owner whipping a slave as both a punishment to the person being whipped and a moral lesson to the people witnessing the whipping.

Understanding that context of the chorus, it is quite difficult to avoid interpreting the first verse as anything other than a depiction of the mentality of a rapist. Consequently, the second voice seems most likely the voice of the victim. Thus, we end up back at the chorus as Eddie Vedder's commentary on the situation.

Average hospital cost of childbirth in 2015 was $4,500 with or without insurance. Average cost of raising that same child to age 18 was over $230, 000. That's more than I owe in student loan debt that I can't pay back, and wrote an entire fucking book about, after a decade of bankruptcy caused by losing a shitty adjunct teaching position while I was a dissertation away from earning a PhD. Dear Conservative America, you've created and defend a world where having children is a financial burden, and you should be more ashamed of that than anything. Please remember, I say this as a happily married man with two well fed children, take a good look in the mirror and tell yourself to go fuck yourself.

Now, if you're all "Bottle the baby killer" after reading that, then you missed the point. The full point would involve dissecting the Supreme Court's advisement on Roe v Wade line by line, a detailed analysis of Madonna's Papa Don't Preach, insults hurled at Ben Folds, Garbage Pail Kids, coat hangers, the crack epidemic, the inherent hypocrisy of "I'm fine with the people [I think] deserve welfare, but...," etc. Ain't nobody got time for that. Instead, let me just say that I hold the following truth to be self evident. No one, not a man, not another woman, not a priest, not the government, not a demi-god, not an Auditor, not even if you're really mad or sad about it, has the right to force a woman to have a child unless she wants to have a child. I hold that same sentiment to be true, ignoring logistical absurdities, in its reverse and inverse. I say that only to point out that any sub-topic you care to discuss will ultimately be weighed against that fact in my brain, and if I feel that your argument contradicts that fact I will dismiss your argument as garbage.

B52's – Cosmic Thing

Oh! You're still here? Great! I feel like you need a reward after that, so here's some other random blogger's choice for Happiest Album Of All Time. Really, if you type "happiest album of all time" into google, Cosmic Thing by the B52's will appear somewhere in the search results. I don't have the actual case or booklet, but the disc is in my hand. This is a much more commercial album than their first, filled with things that definitely qualify as songs. Let's just enjoy.

When the blues kick you in the head...just sit on the porch and swing...We're the Deadbeat Club...Tiiiiiiiiiiin roof! Rusted...let's get in the mud!...roam if you want to...my mind's been going places without me lately...fire in a field of molten flowers...where's my umbrella?...the universe is expandiiiiiiiiiiing...best outro ever.

Yep, I've said it before, and I'll say it again: B52's are weird, and it's about the best remedy for reality I can think of. I suppose, seeing as I've run out of ideas, we better go look at the second half of the p(nmi)t discography....

p(nmi)t The Discography Years, Part 2

Alright kiddos, duct tape those diapers on tight because we're about to start at August 2016 and we won't stop until September 2019. Imagine 3 solid years with your fingers in your ears yelling LALALALALALALALALALALALA! That's what we did. There's some debate on how much tangible good it did: measurable brain damage occurred regardless, I couldn't replenish my minion supply fast enough, and in the Winter of 2016 my right hook went kaput. That's when I made my second big mistake. I told p(nmi)t "just let 'em fly. Send one track after another as soon as they are finished. Good, bad, ugly, doesn't matter. I'll figure out how to bottle them up."

The way I saw it, if we were all going to act like 12 year olds, then I was just gonna lock myself in my room and be the coolest 12 year old ever. Whether or not I succeeded is of course up for debate, but we all watched me do it.

As far as listening to all this stuff, there really are two different things going on. First, the music is chronological, but I already told you he named tracks according to what they actually were as opposed to titles. There is a little bit of crossover from one album to another, but I didn't leave anything out. I published everything he sent me somewhere (I saved a couple for the Bottle of Beef page, but 99% of it is at paultompkins.bandscamp.com. Second, all the artwork and concepts and track titles are a combination of how the music felt in relation to what I was thinking about. In other words, I built them by listening to them, and it was 100% instinctual. The good news is that they mean whatever you think they mean, the bad news is that I have no clue.

Sorry, that's the truth. I could tell you the story behind them, but every album is really just the soundtrack of a movie in my head. Some of them have a plot, some don't. I think I'd be much more interested in what you think about the album than you would be in what I think about what I thought about the music. The album *is* what I thought about the music, and it turns out the description I wrote for each one is about as good as I could ever hope to explain it. So that's what I'll do. I'll just have Skip copy and paste the album description for each one. I'm kidding, ridiculous, rambly descriptions in 3, 2, 1…

On A Porch – 4 Movements for Electric Guitar

Ok, that's pretty self explanatory. On a Porch and Marie were originally for Guitar and Violin, but I liked the idea of the forming a multi-movement work out of these 4 pieces, so I suggested he make it. The scores are even in there if you give me a dollar.

Fifth year: Simple Songs for Complicated People

The dreaded prequel to Daphne and Apollo. Lofi white guy with an acoustic guitar alternative at its blandest.

Contrapuntus ad libitum

How do I like my counterpoint? Every which way but professional sounding. Don't forget to interrogate the potato (he knows something), and finish with an Anachronistic Jam.

Simple Pleasures

And then the fumes got to me. Here's a few of my favorite things: guitar jams, songs in the wrong genre, flowers, sinister originally meant left-handed, smacking a guitar, turning entire pieces of music backward, free improvisation, 80s workout videos, and using the Neopolitan in the chorus of a song. I'm a simple man.

The New Blue

This one I put more effort into. It's pieced together from pieces that have distinct time auras and the album literally progresses from evening to the next morning. In other words, The New Blue is tomorrow morning's sky.

Air

These were the only tracks I had left over after assembling Simple Pleasures and The New Blue. They sounded like a coherent listening experience about watching the heat shimmer up from the hot pavement into the partly cloudy sky.

An Evening In The Echo Chamber

You know who never told p(nmi)t that I had an echo chamber down here? Me. He found it though. Now, I'm not one to wave points and name fingers, but if I were it would rhyme with snarl. How he managed to get spaghetti sauce on the ceiling is beyond me, but I politely asked for assistance from our Volunteer Janitor Department named Carl and we managed to get most of it.

feeble

This is about the time my scapula would organ grind my insides if I even thought about brushing my teeth. Not surprisingly, it's about a useless superhero going through physical therapy before his insurance company will let him even talk to a proper surgeon.

Album of Death

You all know my well documented morbid sense of humor. This was the album I made right before the real doctor fixed the imaginary broken Bottle. He did a pretty darned good job, and I told him so when I ran into him at a gas station one time.

NCLASP 1 & 2

When they tell you that shoulder surgery takes a long and painful time to heal, they aren't joking. I thought it might be fun to make terrible midi renderings of all the music p(nmi)t had written long ago in a galaxy far away with my left arm. I was wrong, but it did pass the time.

Lost and Found

Literally a bunch of Buzz renders he thought he had lost, but then found. I had to stitch Fragments together myself. I thought it fair to combine it with The Slumlord EP for a full length compilation album I call Electric. That's the first Bottle of Beef compilation album, you know, in honor of that ktutz electrocuting countless thousands of my preciously useful minions. If I didn't like Carl so much, I'd put the mutt up for adoption (I wouldn't really, I'm just Unbottling the Curmudgeon for effect).

Orphans Of The Impending Apocalypse

August, 2017. That's when Trump decided to actually publicly start being openly antagonistic to other world leaders. The first 6 months of his presidency he was clearly in "oh, shit, this is bad, I shouldn't be president" mode. Then he snapped. I don't know if it was his coterie of right-wing "the universe was made for white people" backers, or if it was just that every time he opened his mouth the whole room looked at him like he was a lunatic, but he just locked himself in front of Fox News and got madder and madder and madder (in both the angry and sniffing mercury fumes senses). Successful people from the world of business explained to him how the world works, so he fired them. Now, it would have been one thing if he adamantly refused to replace them and got impeached on purpose. Obviously, reality says that can't happen, so instead he intentionally appointed people who knew less about the subject than he did. Every Press Secretary he had resigned because they couldn't stand lying and defending him anymore. Full-scale investigations were launched into his supposed nefarious dealings, but all they found was that he was indeed legitimately that incompetent, and they couldn't prove otherwise. He didn't even get a week like Rush Limbaugh, he literally had to appear on television and correct yesterday's mistakes after they were explained to him.

There was a brief window of time where everyone thought he was actually courting nuclear war, so I made an album for him. Every track p(nmi)t sent me that didn't have an obvious home got loaded into this album, and adopted out as soon as possible. Once everyone else seemed confident that the rest of the world had decided to ignore him, I lost interest and stopped editing it. As Dave 1 might say, may all your nuclear warheads rust in peace.

The Long March

Then the inevitable Republicrats v Democans hootenanny we like having every 4 years began. See, there's politics and then there's Politics (maybe the capitalization should be switched, I don't know, not important). Sure, we could have debates about how the two parties disagree about issues, but that's a bit pointless because both parties very much agree that the government is a business, and that being a politician should be pretty high up there on the hierarchy of careers. They also agree that most of the country and the rest of the world strongly disagree with them. They differ in the sense that the Democratic Party acknowledges this fact and tries to direct policy toward an agreeable compromise, while the Republican Party wants to play Sheriffs and Robbers with live ammo. They want the fight to be visibly fair, but structurally lopsided. There's a cartoon I saw once where three people of different heights are hoping to watch a baseball game. One solution is to provide them boxes that put them all at the same height so they can all watch the game. The other possibility is to drill holes in the fence at various heights so each person can comfortably watch the game as they naturally stand. The Republican Party wants to Tanya Harding them with a tire iron for not being able to afford Season Tickets and a $14 hot dog like a "Real American." At this point their motto should be "Hey pal, I'm not paying you to mow my lawn, now shut up and mow my lawn. Do a good job and I'll think about feeling bad about not paying you next time."

So, I made up this great story about an impossible binary solar system with a gigantic planet orbiting in a figure-8 around them. There are two migratory herds of humans that endlessly traverse the planet in order to stay fully inside the light spectrum of their respective suns, leaving all their garbage behind for other people to pick up. At this point, it's hard to tell whose actual garbage any of it is, but we still keep picking it up and making up stories about how awesome/terrible they must be. It, uh, doesn't end particularly well for anyone who looks at things in a different light.

Apropos Of Something Or Other...

I'm not the kind of guy who's gonna call up Dionne Warwick's Psychic Friends, I think we all understand that, but I got to thinking that if I had to do it all over again, I'd play guitar like it was a melodic instrument. Damned if that little rascal didn't send me a bunch of pieces he wanted to play as duets for guitar and piano. So I did, I programmed all the piano parts and left them on the wobbly table in the third hallway down from the Mirror of Macabre. Early Christmas present for me, he actually went and did it.

4 Albums of Catch-Up

I tend to hibernate through December and January, some festivities occur around then or something. So, the next 4 albums were really me playing catch up with all the junk he sent me. I dunno, there's stories there I guess, but my brain was really on autopilot until May. Sorry, that's just the way it is. Everybody Needs A Purple Hat, Audiodetritus, Patience Is A Virtue During The Conversion Process, and Suite for Brass Quintet. Minions died in all sorts of hilariously tragic ways, messes were made and Carl cleaned them up, you know, just stuff you do to pass the time when all the temperatures have that funny dash in front of them. I don't mind the cold, I just don't think too good in it.

6 Albums I Barely Remember

I have no idea what your Summer of '18 was like. Mine had water falling from the sky the entire time. I'm gonna let you in on a little secret. The Dungeon of Disingenuousness is not where I live, it's just where I go when I'm not outside anymore. But, like the Wicked Witch of the West, I get a little melty in the rain. 6 albums worth of it, I had grass up to my eyeballs by the time September rolled around. Again, stories galore, but rainy Day Companion, Archipelago, I Hear The View Is Lovely, Playing With Myself, Lady Killer, and Flotsam are all pretty self explanatory. I guess we're on the same cycle, 'cause p(nmi)t slowed down too. We worked hard, take October off.

How I Wasted My Lunch Break

This one was all p(nmi)t. I wash my hands of the "dead butterfly" album.

December 2018 – September 2019

Don McLean wrote a song once. You know that song. Carl's dog and I decided if we were going to watch that day approach, we were going to physically produce as much music as possible before it arrived, go out in a blaze of glory so to speak. We did. It gets less and less coherent as we go. I didn't hear much from him between September 2019 and September 2020, and I still haven't heard from him as I write this in June of 2021. I wanna believe he'll come back. I'm gonna choose to believe he'll come back. I just have to patiently wait long enough. In the meantime, though, we're barely halfway through this book, and I've got a small stack of the weirdest assortment of records anyone could possibly assemble.

Haven't uncorked that bottle in a while. Eye-wateringly pungent stuff that is.

Mending Fences

B: Alright, let's have a staff meeting.

C: Are you sure that's a good idea?

B: Nope, but we're celebrating our independence this weekend, so we have to coordinate our efforts.

S: Excellent idea. Are you feeling well?

B: Fine, but I've run out of imaginary secret agendas, and my Auditors are pacing like caged animals.

E: What Auditors? I thought you guys said they weren't real, and that weren't any secret agendas.

B: Totally correct, Skipety Skip. Doesn't mean they don't produce an effect. They sent you on a pointless rampage, didn't they?

E: Well, I mean, if you say it that way it sort of makes sense. But I didn't...

B: Was your plan to seize the means of production so you could steer the empireship to glory and immortality through reverence for your benevolent leading skills? You wanna do the Imagineering and I'll fix your typos? We should be publishing albums for the benefit of the people who tirelessly manage audio libraries? You sound a lot like what Americans think a Communist does.

E: Now that's just silly, of course not. I don't know why I got so upset. Everything just felt directionless and I didn't know what to do, and I got carried...

B: Away on the shoulders of your own personal Jihad?

E: That's not fair.

B: 'Course not. Nothing's fair unless you agree that it's fair. I'm merely pointing out that you look more like your description of me than I do. You have to make the trade, or you have to walk away. Them's the rules. Now, you gotta think, what if there were an Auditor watching? Some discorporate demon on your shoulder whispering "do it." Does that Auditor actually care what you do? Not a bit, all it cares about is that something happens, and it will smash as many unrelated thoughts together as necessary until you get up and do do it.

Now, as for the agenda problem, I feel bad that I couldn't actually talk about the second half of the p(nmi)t discography while slicing onions, so I bought a totally random selection of records to prove a point. Wanna try to guess?

C: Wowzers, that's some serious random there Bottle. No clue.

E: What could any of these albums have to do with each other?

S: I think that is the point.

B: Ding, ding, ding. Sandra wins. Let's do the doing and talk about it later.

Pointer Sisters

All I can manage to push from my lips is a string of absurdities. Mine's more like obscenities, but I hear ya, sisters. I know I love the Pointer Sisters, but I honestly forgot how much I love the Pointer Sisters. A lot a lot.

I quite like the ironic twist of their most successful and popular album being called Break Out, especially since it was their 10th. The Sisters didn't like the title at all because it made them think of breaking out in a rash, or breaking out of prison. They got no say in what it was called, it's a "producer's album." That might strike you as unfair, but we aren't going to dig into it this time. Instead, we'll conceptualize the process with the understanding that the Pointer Sisters were highly successful and super popular performers. Remember, early on The Tubes were their frequent warm up the crowd opening act. The key point is they were performers, not recording artists. They had a massive audience, and that means there was a measurable market for Pointer Sisters albums whenever someone wanted to pay them to make one. You don't throw garbage songs at a big name act like that, and these are good songs. Remember, it's 1983, so the slightly dated and possibly cheesy synths you're hearing cost nearly as much as a new car or a small house. After multiple Grammys and high selling hits over a 40 year career, whatever else happened in their lives and whoever did or didn't make more money than them, none of the 4 sisters or their kids were struggling to pay rent from the mid 70s on.

Then we gotta talk about the insanity of buying this record yesterday, listening to it on youtube during my lunch break, then hearing Neutron Dance at the store after work. Again, Coincidence, you're pushing all the buttons.

They've had lots of loss and sadness in the last decade, not to mention that damned Universal fire, but my favorite comment came from the early 2010s when they were asked about making a new album. They said "it's not like the old days, when you had proper deals, a real producer, you'd pop into the studio for a week, then just go promote it on tour." Like being the Pointer Sisters was just a thing they did, while simultaneously pointing out that the "business" as you know it today is understatedly subpar. Richard Perry certainly seemed to know what he was doing in the producer's chair. My 2-dollar copy sounds like I paid 1.99 too much, but skips don't bother me as much as you might think they should, do they Mr. Editor?

My favorite Pointer Sisters track? Automatic, of course, did you forget that's how I led off?

Art Garfunkel – Breakaway

From Break Out to Breakaway. I'm somewhat astonished that people feel the need to point out that the cover of Art Garfunkel's second solo album is a staged photograph. 'Cause you know, I was under the impression that that's just how he rolls and a random guy in a bar with a camera said "say deadpan," gave the polaroid to Art as a fan pic, but instead of signing it and getting back to the Art life he asked "can I use this as the cover of my next album?"

I might have been known to apologize to the Legion of Garf a time or two, but tonight we're just gonna let him speak his mind. Wikipedia tells me this is unadulterated Soft Rock, this is his best-selling album, a random dude at Allmusic implied that one Art Garfunkel vocal take is basically the same as any other, but you can ignore that because the songs and arrangements are good. I say as long as you don't sound as much like Petula Clark as Petula Clark does you're doing ok. Plus, none of the lyrics were written by James Seals, so we don't have to worry about that. That's the bar Garf, jump into it (a Pointer Sisters reference? How totally strange and out of nowhere that is...).

Nah, this is great. The only thing I don't like about the first couple tracks is the doubled vocals. They don't sound good. I also can't neglect to mention that I hear my friend Steven Stark singing. He doesn't do Art's warbling and stuff, but the timbre and pronunciation is crazy identical. Steve Crapper plays electric guitar on the title track. I don't know if anyone told him you can call yourself whatever you want to in the album credits, or maybe they did and he replied "Nope, I'm a Crapper, born and raised, and damned proud of it!" Waters of March is quirky and out of nowhere, I love it. Yeah, for at least side A, I was right. He doesn't sound like Petula Clark or James Seals. I'm good. Quite lovely. I need to take a break to see how horribly complicated this new above-ground pool we bought will be to set up. Hopefully we'll get to Side B before tomorrow...

... ok pool is slowly filling. Hello, Paul Simon. Morbid fact, Laurie Bird (on his left) ODed on valium in Art's apartment 4 years later. Regardless of the fact that I'm going to wash it down with an album that has a chrome-plated skull on the cover, this is quite an enjoyable album. What else could you call it but Soft Rock, I guess, but in this case it's fine. Yeah, I like it. Good stuff. Oh, wow, crazy, the actual invoice from Columbia House is inside. $8.78 back in Feb. '79. Neato.

Krokus – Headhunter

Chris von Rohr wanted to be a chef. That didn't work out, so he formed an AC/DC tribute band named after a flower he saw one time. His friends said "Krokus is perfect, the rok's right there in the name." Critics hated them.

Ok, originally they were so prog-rock that when their singer quit Chris had to change his name to Phil and stop playing drums. Then it was time for the 80s, and they all decided to hire a singer who could help them make an actual AC/DC album. Critics hated them even more, but damned if actual people didn't enjoy it and they finally made Headhunter. They were gonna retire in 2019, but Covid, so they might get to play a couple nights in England in early 2022.

Yes, Krokus has always been pure schlock, but damnit they are good. I like listening to them. I personally like them better. Yep, I'd rather listen to Accept or Krokus than AC/DC. Nothing against Australians, these songs are more interesting to me. Headhunter is a pretty great Heavy Metal album, and if I cared for ranking things it probably is their best. Screaming In The Night is pushing the definition of Power Ballad a little, but there's something so likeably ridiculous about them that I just can't help it. And my copy is in excellent condition to boot.

Steve Miller Band – Abracadabra

So freakin' many subgenres here on Bottle's Beeflieve It, Or Not. Hard Rock, Soft Rock, Yacht Rock, Not Rock, we may or may not stop, drop, and roll, we might zoom into the Bronze Age and decapitate our enemies, we might stop throwing pieces of land at each other and focus our attention on the Soul, or let our hair down and get Funky, but we so rarely get just plain old vanilla flavored Rock. Real Vanilla is an orchid, by the way, and unless you've got a super special moth farm on the side, you got to hand pollinate those bad boys. Then there's the sun drying and the hoping it doesn't rain. Labor intensive stuff for the most scientifically complicated flavor we call "plain."

So, tonight it's just Rock. The kind of Rock that's so classic we needlessly invented a qualifier for it. Classic Rock. What's Classic Rock? Journey? Nope. Foreigner? Nope again. Bottle's taxonomy is very clear on the subject, let's take a peek.

Classic Rock: Things that sound like whatever Steve Miller was doing at the time.

Wowzers, that's concise for anyone, let alone me. It's true, though. Complicated people will tell you it's a radio developed genre, but of the most popular AOR songs of the 80s. Yeah, like I said, Steve Miller. Essentialists will say bass drum on 1 & 3, snare on 2 & 4 and the minor pentatonic scale. That's going too far. I'll give you minor pentatonic, but drummers can do other stuff in any genre. Dave Grohl says he was really just playing Disco beats slow with sledge hammers in Nirvana.

Pretty sure I called Steve Miller the nicest Rock Star to ever walk the planet, and even a casual listen to 1982's Abracadabra will prove it. I ragged on Des'ree for saying love could cure homelessness, yes she really did imply that, and here's Steve telling us love is pretty magical. Not in a creepy way at all. Love is what he wants, what motivates him, what keeps him plugging along. All he really wants is for you to tell him you appreciate his company and effort. You don't have to be a freak, or a nymphomaniac, you just have to remind him that you love and care about him when the occasion warrants. What a delightful album. You could try to find some smarmy subtext, but I think we both know you're grasping for straws. Dude is just plain, old-fashioned nice. I dare you to try to not like it. Double dog dare you with hot fudge and whatever kind of nuts or legumes you aren't allergic to.

Weather Report – Heavy Weather

Legend has it that if Wayne Shorter told Miles Davis to play a note, that is the note Miles Davis played. Wayne has more than a couple important votes for both Best Jazz Composer and Best Improviser of All Time. Who am I to argue? Here's his own band's most popular album. I'm not saying it's their best because Jaco Pastorius is on bass, but I am wacko for Jaco. I guess you could say it with a long A, but Waco for Jaco is definitely not the implication I'm going for here. It's "Jock-o" by the way, because he was tall and athletic, and that's how nicknames work.

Jaco's favorite instrument was a 1962 Fender Jazz Bass with the frets removed. You know what he called it? Take a guess: The Bass of Doom. It was stolen in 1986 and resurfaced in a music shop 20 years later. Robert Trujillo helped Jaco's family buy it back from the store owner, 'cause Metallica money. You can go find a cheap clone right now if you want a cheap clone. Or, you could just go buy a Fender Jazz Bass and beat the crap out of it. Totally up to you. Let's just check out Weather Report's Heavy Weather.

A lot of people use Jazz fusion and Jazz Rock interchangeably, but all we're really talking about is an electric ensemble as opposed to an acoustic combo. For me the difference is Fusion is Jazz in a Rock band format, while Jazz Rock is Rock that incorporates Jazz. A subjective distinction, but I'm sticking to it. This is Fusion, and it's good. Really good. It's not quite as close to Prog as Ponty, but there's a lot of sonic experimentation in terms of synths in a Jazz context. The playing is phenomenal across the board.

I don't think I have a point for this album specifically, it's just the perfect way to round out this little not technically an Adventure Time. Go give it a listen, I think you'll be quite happy that you did.

Conclusion

So, what did we learn? It turns out this objectively random selection of records is all about people doing their own thing. But, there's a context: they are trying to make an album. It doesn't really matter whose album it actually is, it doesn't matter what type of music they make, or what country they are from, or whether or not it will be the greatest album ever, or even if they have a positive/negative view of the world. The point is that there was a collective goal, however meaningful or not, and they all set about it in their own way. Amazingly enough, these are also kind of the biggest and best selling albums of all of them.

Is it coincidence, or probability? I mean it's coincidence that I happened to want to go buy used records, found these particular records without any actual search criteria, and actually enjoyed listening to them, but my view of reality tells me that if you're going to do that then you'll statistically end up with a whole lot of best-selling albums that a lot of people enjoyed, at least until they sold their record collections for pitifully small amounts of money. It's numbers, right? Physically more copies to spread around.

Also, this was a time when albums themselves were really popular. People wanted more than just two songs, so other people were willing to pay to make that happen. Forget actual profitability for a moment, the point is that the exchange itself was taking place. People agreed to buy them, so other people agreed to make them. In the grand scheme of things, that's the economy, everything else is supposed to be finding an agreeable equilibrium to keep doing it, but it inevitably morphs into a competition to find out who can drain the monetary system fast enough.

The problem with that from my perspective is that you end up caring more about the store and how eager the cashier is to pander to you than you do about the products they sell. You care more about the value of the brand than you do the quality of the sustenance, be it actual food or brain food. I think that's garbage in and of itself. Stop buying garbage. This batch of random records, though, I can taste the rainbow, and it's every bit as nutritious as it is delicious.

Bottle's Punishment for a Thing He Said Somewhere Else

B: Alright, Sandra, what's the punishment for my semi-secret crimes again Misogynist 'Merica? I won't repeat what I said here, if that reduces my sentence.

S: Well, there's good news and there's bad news. The good news is that you can follow it up with any album you like, but the bad news is that you have to listen to one of the 4th of July appropriate albums in your collection first.

B: Aw man! There's only 3 of 'em, and 2/3 of those feature the Mormon Tabernacle Choir.

S: I can shuffle them if it will help.

B: Nah, I'll just cut the bullet into bite-sized pieces and listen to Lee Greenwood's Greatest Hits.

S: Really? I mean, it's your choice. Seems a little harsh to me.

B: I think I'll be ok. I'll wash it down with The Best of the Righteous Brothers. I'll be fine.

S: Ok, good luck. For what it's worth, I'm quite delighted by your essay on a personal level.

B: Thanks. That means a lot. Welp, time to listen to Dudeguy McGuilttrip try to win back his woman by fake apologizing for repeatedly being a douche bag even though he knows she deserves better, and end with God Bless the USA. I don't know about you guys, but I'd certainly dump him. At least I get to follow it up with a more authentic depiction of heartache.

Is Lee Greenwood really that bad? No, of course not. He's quite an enjoyable singer singing other people's schlock. Actually I love Ain't No Trick, that could totally be a Huey Lewis and the News song. I don't like his image or most of his content. I don't like Country. I don't think like that, I don't have those sentiments in that direction, it's the opposite of me, I just can't feel sorry for you if you know you're being a jerk and keep doing it anyway. If you know you're being a dirtbag, then just do the opposite. "Oh no! I never thought this autonomous human being would get mad enough at the shitty way I treat her to actually leave. Woe is me." Baaaarf!

    I don't have any real criticism for his biggest hit. It's patriotic drivel, but that's not a criticism. It's supposed to be patriotic drivel. That's its purpose. In context it's a perfectly lovely "thank you for your service and sacrifice" song. Any other random Tuesday, it's unnecessary and annoying. Lost my job, my house, my wife, my dog, and my car keys, but at least I'm innocent until proven guilty in a court of law and I don't have to cook dinner for the other team's army. Annoying.

    Now, in contrast, we'll look at the other type of righteous. The informal one that's synonymous with "awesome." The term "Blue-Eyed Soul" was specifically invented to describe the Righteous Brothers at a time when even radio was segregated. I think we can all agree the Righteous Brothers are freakin' awesome regardless. Hilarious that their two biggest hits aren't on it, but they don't need to be. So good. Now I wanna pull out the best of Sam Cooke again. Ok with you, Sandra?

    S: Sentence served, suit yourself.
    B: Yippee!

    M: Why are you so mean, Bottle?
    B: Thought I flipped on the "No Milton" sign. I'm not actually mean or nasty or any of those things. I'm responding to things people say. If you say terrible things, I'll respond

with terrible things. We're sampling my bottle collection, remember?

M: I was not aware of that.

B: I've said it like 1,000 times! It's a nightmare in my head. I have to carefully open them to see how they are fermenting, but I can't just chuck 'em in the landfill either, you know? People have to be able to get that stuff out of their brains without fear of immediate reprisal. The thing about me is I'm not going to send a minion to do it, it's my responsibility. The only thing I can't control is your feelings. If you're gonna get all mad and start smashing things, then I have to walk away.

If you want to know my opinion, give me a moment to think and I'll tell you my opinion. If you want to debate my opinion, then no thanks. I've come to the conclusion that most people don't think the way I think, so I try my best to compromise so that we don't have to waste time talking about it. I just wait for you to decide what you're going to do and react accordingly.

Arguing is not the same as debate. Too many people want the world to run on arguing. Too many people want the up side without taking responsibility for the messes they make, but there are two sides to every Schwartz. Too many people want to get what they want by throwing a tantrum like a toddler. If that's you, then yes I'm going to get frustrated and put on my Stern Dad face. I'd rather the world run on asking politely, being patient, and not being desperate all the time.

I work hard for a living, but it's not enough to pay my debts. If you asked me what I need, the answer is $200,000. I don't know anyone who has that kind of money sitting around, so I just put it all out there and politely ask you to find some justification for sending me a few dollars. No one actually wants to do that, and that's fine too. I'm gonna be me either way.

Intro

If you could peel the top layer of the Earth away like an orange peel, the Bunker of Beef might look like the strangest ant colony you've ever seen; faceless minions scurrying every which way, carrying out the mundane tasks of living inside a mind. You might expect to find patterns and procedures, some repetitive group migration, or clear indication of purpose. Look a little deeper and you'll know it isn't so. Stare long enough and chaos itself becomes palpable. Pockets of focused activity emerge like mosh pits and quickly dissipate, but the overall impression is a sea of unpredictability, like a game of Pong with a million balls that never leave the playing field. Occasionally, two minions collide in a brief but spectacular explosion, but the empty space they create is quickly filled by the rest of the overall "getting on with it."

A very astute and patient observer might catch the moment a new minion pops into existence and begins its journey. At a local level, the Brownian Motion of its movement is obvious, but with enough time and memory one can clearly recognize the overall orbital nature of its trajectory. With enough patience, it would be possible to watch that orbit seemingly twist in upon itself such that the minion in question returns to the point of origin facing the other direction, at which point it would pop back out of existence with as little ceremony or fanfare as when it arrived. Such is the uninteresting existence of the minion, barring of course any unforeseen excitement along the way.

All sorts of exciting things could happen. Two minions could collide in a tiny but comparatively spectacular supernova, a few could get caught in a localized but ultimately temporary gravitational vortex, a bony hand could punch through the surface of this sub-dermal layer and drag them flailing and meeping (minions don't scream, they "meep") toward the center.

Somewhere deep in that center of the tumult, Bottle sits lost in thought. "Where do we go from here? More importantly, I suppose, should we really care?"

Mastodon – Cold Dark Place

I'm excited. In a few months we should have a new Mastodon album. That's a long time, I know, but we can kill a few of those minutes by listening to their 2017 Cold Dark Place EP. 3 leftovers from Once More 'Round the Sun and one from Emporer of Sand. My review of Emporer of Sand wasn't as down on it as most, but it is true that it's nowhere near the top of the list of Mastodon albums you might recommend to a friend who doesn't know Mastodon.

Let's ignore all of that and pretend we randomly snatched it out of thin air in a post-apocalyptic world where they put albums inside relief packages and drop them from helicopters. In the spirit of that context, let's try to understand what we're dealing with.

We'll just have to trust them on the temperature reading, but it is by all objective standards dark. It's also a forest and the auxiliary artwork focuses on a heart made out of tree roots. If we get out the binoculars we can see a silhouette and a strange candle. You do you, but I'm going with Radagast is riding the struggle bus, so he invites Yorick over to watch him get shitfaced on fermented tree sap.

Tolkien himself believed Radagast had failed in his mission, but he was surprisingly bad at understanding his own mythologies, so we'll go with Christopher's take that because he was specifically sent to protect the plants and animals of Middle Earth he sort of succeeded, but we'll add Bottle's caveat that he totally succeeded in his mission, but because humans, dwarves, and elves are bound by the rings whether they wear them or not, why would the useless bipeds give a crap? The Blue Wizards went looking for the Teletubby

Sun Baby and were never heard from again (they headed east, if you're slow).

    BB: Why is that joke here, Bottle?
    B: Baxter Forrest Twilight. Duh. You of all people should have my first book memorized, Bridbrad. I'm kidding. Back to it…
    Sadly, Mastodon didn't print the lyrics, so I either have to search online or [shudder] try to understand them with my own ears. Troy and Brent are great, but man are they inarticulate sometimes.
    Interestingly, this album doesn't have a beginning; fade in to intro, obviously, but this is an internal track, a deep cut. It's more like the washes of sound on Crack the Skye, to my ears. I'm speaking musically, by the way, lyrics don't matter much, other than "the north" and "cold." Is this around the time of their Game of Thrones cameo? Doesn't matter. I'm going to listen to it like 9 more times tonight, this first pass is just things that stick out.
    What the hell is Blue Walsh? A person, a thing? We may never know. What's more interesting is that it also sounds more like a Crack the Skye leftover than anything on Once More 'Round the Sun. This is Brent's chickin' pickin' like the banjo on Divinations.
    Cue the more chickin' pickin'. It's called that because chickens have 3 toes, you hold the pick like normal, but also use your middle and ring fingers.
    Toe to Toe gives us "dark." Let me check… yep, we're good. Concept covered. Lovely song, to boot.
    "I guess you'd say…." Did I mention that these songs sound more like Crack the Skye outtakes than anything else in their discography? They do. I don't think that's an actual conscious thing on Mastodon's part, these songs obviously don't fit on the last 2 full-length albums. Over the span of 8 years though, it's totally logical that that kind of subconscious

uncannyness would pop up a few times. Surely someone somewhere along the process said "this sounds too much like that one album we made that time, better try something different.

Ok, time for actual words. What are these songs about?

M(astodon): Winter is coming.
B: Yes, yes, I see your point.
M: I'm asleep in the deep.
B: K, Once more 'round we go.
M: I remember…
B: Running through the wet grass. Yep, me too. Every morning on the way to the chicken coop. Not the running part, though. Bottle's insides do not share James Bond's pedeliction for shaking. I mention it only to point out that I like Mastodon better than better Than Ezra, but go on.
M: …iiaaoeoeuuaiaue…
B: damnit, Brent! Words have consonants. E. Nun. Sea. Ate. I give up, we'll have to pull up the actual lyrics and read for the next listen.

I absolutely adore Mastodon's harmony. The harmonic rhythm is tectonic plate slow, but the chord progressions are absolutely gorgeous. A lot of people cry foul at Bendan O'Brien's "over production," but every picked note has 9 layers on 9 different guitars because it's Mastodon. Pearl Jam, STP, even Springsteen don't have Mastodon's confuddling conjunction of ADD and Tibetan Monk level patience for crafting sonic architecture. "I want it to sound like a Fender Champ combined with a Soldano Slo 100, but I also want an acoustic attack and the shimmer of a dulcimer. Yeah, sure, I'll play those same 3 notes 40 more times, I just need another beer and bong hit first. Again, Mastodon can handle my smack talk, they're big boys. Brent wasn't on the fence about the face tattoo for fear that he'd lose the promotion to Store Manager, he just flat out doesn't give a shit.

Ok, actual lyrics time. North Side Star is a "you and I" song. The world is going to end, but maybe we can walk around the wreckage together.

I think Blue Walsh is about him dying and she's a ghost, maybe. It's either a "blues riff that sounds like Joe Walsh," or somehow connected to Steve Walsh's son named Blue (Steve Walsh was the lead singer of Kansas, but lives in Atlanta).

Hello, Satan. May I have this dance?

I don't love you anymore.

So, strip away all the hyperbole and junk, this is a breakup album. I don't mean that to sound underwhelming, but that's what the 4 songs do together. It's quite lovely, actually. The world is ending, we can't communicate, we need to go our separate ways. It's his description of the cold dark place the relationship has created in his mind. Stellar, superb, great album, excellent job guys. See, everyone? That's how you make an album that's both enjoyable to listen to and conceptually rewarding when you really dig in with only 4 random songs. A+, thumbs up. Sorry 'bout the breakup, fictional narrator dude, but excellent job of telling us about it.

Look at me , I'm a scary Communist

Everyone: Big plans this weekend, Bottle?

B: Nah, I think I'm just gonna stay in and do a critical reading of the Communist Manifesto.

EO: What is wrong with you?

B: Nothing that I'm aware of at the moment. I have this theory that most Americans are actually Communists but don't realize it. It's a fascinating subject that's really difficult to write about because anti-Marxists have been brainwashed into not noticing that their ideas are actually Marxist because Marxism is actually the ironic opposite of Marxism. Wanna tag along?

EO: Good god, no!

B: Suit yourself. If you change your mind you can go to marxists.org and read it for free on the technological marvel that eats its own tail and provokes its own Communist uprising. Some people call it a computer, but in emergencies it can also make low fidelity phone calls that your anti-Marxist government spies on like Marx warned you they would do. Marx might be less understood now than before we became intelligent. Don't worry, nothing bad happened to me after I downloaded it.

B: Yo! Skip'n'Slide!

E: Me? What?

B: Yeah, you. You ready to rumble? Toe to toe? Mano E Manifesto? Do you smell what the Bottle is containing?

E: Of course not, that's how bottles work.

B: Good answer, good answer. We asked a hundred random people what they thought about Karl Marx, and 63 of them responded "Oooh, I love Right Here Waiting, is he still married to Daisy Fuentes?" He better be is all I'm saying about that.

E: That's Richard Marx.

B: Oh ho ho, student becomes the master, I'm impressed.

E: Thank you. Where is this going?

B: Communist Manifesto.

E: Lovely, I'll go fetch my helmet.

B: That's the spirit! By and large, the Communist Manifesto is somewhat boring, but it has the best intro ever. "A spectre is haunting Europe...."

You've all had a couple years to acclimate to my peculiar brand of discourse, so it seems only fitting to contextualize it in my own words. We do actually have a modern day typesetting for the preamble. It goes a little something like this:

OOoOOoooOo! LoOk At Me! I'm ThE sCaRY cOmMuNiSt. mE aNd My ScArY fRiEnDs HaD SuPeR sEcReT mEeTiNgS aLl OvEr ThE wOrLd, AnD NoW wE'rE gOnNa PuBlIsH wHaT wE tAlKeD aBoUt.

You get the idea, I'll just do the rest normal. Like, who hasn't made a point of condemning us? Even the Pope thinks we're evil. So, fine. We got together in London and wrote up this pamphlet describing where we stand on the issues, 'cause if you're gonna take this "nursery tale" about how evil we are serious, then I guess we have to be serious about it.

Keep in mind, this edition we're reading was 20 years after the Paris Commune of 1870-71, and Marx is quite dead. The Manifesto is half a century old at this point. Yes, we're talking about armed conflict and bloody war, but these uprisings are against actual Kings, Lords, Barons, etc. We went from barely making an airplane work to flying to the freakin' moon in the same amount of time, and that was one of Marx's biggest talking points.

Yes, absolutely, Capitalism accelerates human technological advancement at a breakneck speed, but last time I checked you're all vocally complaining about kids staring at their phones instead of having a strong work ethic.

Why do we have 8/10 hour workdays? Communists. Why aren't you working alongside 12 year olds at the airplane factory? Communists. Why did the managers of a Tyson factory who were placing bets on how many workers would get sick from the recent global coronavirus outbreak get fired? Communists.

What we're going to see a lot is that Marx was not making things up just to make things up. You could make the argument that he was pandering to Labour, but he wasn't selling "the proletariat" anything they didn't already believe. You could argue that he was "fanning the flames," but the flames were already there to be fanned, and his point was that history tells us it's inevitable. I'm not convinced you or I have to believe one way or the other, but it's ridiculous to argue that those who feel exploited don't feel like they are being exploited, and it's preposterous to credit Marx with the entire world feeling that way.

The good news is that's just the preamble. The bad news is we're doing the whole thing. Get some rest, and have a good hearty breakfast.

E: You're making it sound like a joke.

B: No, the rhetoric of the preamble frames it that way. I just put it in a modern context. You have to think about why you might write it that way. I myself have pointed out many times that I think the fight is stupid, but if you're going to bring the fight to me, you should know which side I'm on. I don't think I'm a Communist, but that's the side you force me to choose when you adamantly defend social hierarchy over progressive productivity.

E: I'm not sure I follow.

B: That's ok, my point is that if I had written this preamble this way, I would be thinking in terms of "We're trying to have a meaningful dialog about actual social problems, but you're acting like we're evil baby-snatching demons from the netherworld."

E: Oh, ok, I guess that makes sense. I'm not sure I agree, but at least I understand it better.

B: Good. You don't have to agree. Now we move on to complicated words and Marx's materialist synopsis of the history of human society.

If you pick out a book in this library, I bet you'll find a description of a class of people who felt oppressed, and eventually they'll revolt against their oppressors. There's only two ways that can go: either the uprising succeeds and the society changes, or everybody loses and that society doesn't exist anymore. Modern bourgeois society is what developed from the collapse of the feudal system, but it hasn't solved that problem. It just created a new social hierarchy with different names for things, and the result is a distinction between employers and employees, factory owners and factory workers, Capitalists and the people whose labor creates that capital.

That's the easy part to read. The rest of section one is incredibly dense and rapid, the information dump Marx likes so much. I don't think it's a nefariously intentional rhetorical device, by the way. It's just what happens when Marx switches from setting up his context to actually narrating the imaginary movie in his head. Happens to me too, right? At first I'm patiently describing how we're listening to an album, but then I go all over the place and the barrage of inside jokes, movie references, and adjacent ideas makes your eyes cross.

E: Yeah, that's exactly how it feels to read it, and I just give up.

B: Ok, then how do we tackle it? Don't answer, I'll tell you. It's a description of a binary opposition, and how that coin flips around and around as it ascends and descends. You might see most of the flips if you slow it way down, but eventually you'll smash into the brick wall of frame rate and lose the forest for the trees you can't identify by name. What he's really saying is that the Bourgeoisie is constantly looking for an advantage over their competition by increasing their market reach, pushing for technological advantage, electing more and more powerful political allies, and dividing human labor into smaller and smaller, thus less meaningful and fulfilling, tasks. The logical result of that process is that the Bourgeois class gets smaller and smaller, the Proletariat gets larger and larger, and the Bourgeoisie become more and more conservative because they are trapped in the middle. Eventually, they are forced to pick a side, some scramble to climb up the ladder, some demote themselves back into the working class, and this keeps widening the gap between the aristocracy and the populace until war breaks out.

Keep in mind, that's only one of my descriptions of Marx's description. Let's do another.

The Bourgeoisie, I.e. factory managers, merchants, the Middle Class who control the means of social production, defend their position by A) centralizing access to technological advancement, B) moralizing the growth of urban centers over the now "evil, lazy, uneducated" and unincorporated rural population, and C) enforcing currency exchange (be it monetary or intellectual) as the only legitimate lifestyle.

A third strand: the middle-class, I.e. Capitalists at large, are forced to structure society as a binary opposition because they mediate between production and consumption for profit. Logically speaking, this drains the system of its medium of exchange in favor of economic control, but the inevitable result is that the society of the exploited is so much larger than the Capitalist class that civil war becomes inevitable.

Regardless of how we gloss the description of the process, we have to keep in mind who is or isn't a member of a particular class. Unlike previous societies, where class was determined by occupation itself, modern industrial society is defined solely in terms of wage labor. Do you receive a paycheck for having worked, or do you pay someone else to work for you and sell the results of that labor? That's it, that's the only distinction, and anyone with a basic understanding of business can tell you that you cannot spend the same dollar twice; either you put money into the system in the form of wages, or you take money out of the system in the form of personal profit and/or the purchase of new commodities. The actual business itself has no money, only assets, liabilities, and control over how they slosh back and forth.

In short, an industrial company does not grow by "selling more products for profit," it grows by replacing and eliminating the need for human labor because it incentivizes the internal competition that produces its saleable commodity. That's hard to follow, I know, but it boils down to this. I have to compete with my fellow laborers for an increasing reward, but all that does is strengthen my recognition that we are all in the same boat, so we inevitably take that rage out on the industry itself. Capitalism creates Communism.

Again, you don't have to believe one way or the other, we are simply trying to understand the actual argument. The argument is simply that Capitalist systems are designed to fail because the Capitalist class itself refuses to actually sell its control of the enterprise for profit/loss. A company or enterprise itself is a commodity that can only be sold to someone with more money than you.

I'm getting too far afield, so I have to bring it back to the point. The point of the Manifesto is to argue that "Communism" is not some malevolent secret society, it's the typical, historically documented reaction of the oppressed to their oppressor. I find it hard to argue that it's an inaccurate hypothesis, I think it's a completely plausible description of how many people feel. If I had to give it an analogy, here it is: You might have been surprised at the moment when the tiger attacked Roy, but you'd have to be pretty naive to be surprised that a tiger eventually attacked them during their Vegas stage show. I'm certainly not comparing the working class to wild animals, I'm just pointing out the structural similarity.

That's part one, why don't we take a break and let it settle....

Now, I find chapter 2 of the Communist Manifesto hilarious. Why? Because I know that it scares the bejeebus out of most people. It's designed to do that. It takes all the supposed criticisms of Communism, and says "yep, exactly. Be afraid."

Communism as a political entity has no other goal than to support whatever agenda the working class has. We will however emphasize what the working class of any particular country has in common with the wider working class of the world. The goal is to get rid of Bourgeois property and forge a world where we work for the benefit of everyone who works instead of for the benefit of those who devalue that labor for profit.

That's a bit of a silly description, and I think it's supposed to be silly. The rhetoric is intentionally tautological. Of course you're afraid of losing money, money is the only commodity you care about. Of course you're afraid of women's rights, you won't be able to pay prostitutes who sell sex because it's the only job you will pay them to do. By the way, what is Bourgeois marriage other than a contract for domestic servitude? Of course you're afraid of public education, it takes away your ability to exploit the uneducated.

I think the important part of the argument is that the "Capitalist" view of Freedom is essentially comparative freedom, comparative to freedoms that have already been taken away in order to establish that comparative value: you can't build a house, you have to buy a house my minions built; you can't farm vegetables and trade them with your neighbors, you have to buy the vegetables my minions grow; you can't like that guy's music, you have to buy the music my minions make.

Here's the tricky part. The State isn't the government. The State is the active ruling class. Remember, in theory everyone serving as a government official was elected by the conservative middle class. That conservative middle class is defined as employers and they pay their employees as little as possible to keep them as employees. It makes absolutely no difference how much money you get paid, if you receive a paycheck for your work you are part of the Proletariat.

Doctors are wage workers, teachers are wage workers, mechanics are wage workers, janitors, computer programmers, if it qualifies as a career, someone is paying you less than the market value of your labor and pocketing the difference. You might not care that you're being exploited if you made 2 million dollars last year, but you're still being exploited.

There is a tacit assumption that I don't think the Manifesto or any other Marxist writing (written by Marx or otherwise) makes clear. That assumption is that money has no actual bearing on the law of supply and demand. In fact, money in its commodity form actually messes everything up. Imagine no money, no universal equivalent. No way to cheat the exchange. The total value of raising chickens is equal to the total output of eggs and meat. The fewer people you personally have to feed, the fewer chickens you need for yourself. As long as the total possible amount of demand for meat and eggs is below the level of production of all the combined substitutes for chickens, just spread the love and be thankful you have friends who care as much about you as you do them. Obviously you should raise more chickens than you desperately need and trade them with your closest neighbors who are doing what they want to do and sending the excess to you. I'll do this, you do that, we all cooperate to make sure we have everything we need. All it takes is being able to talk to each other in a cooperative manner.

Which brings us to the real crux of what defines Freedom. According to the manifesto, Capitalism defines Freedom as the ability to freely capitalize on the labor of others, Communism defines freedom as the ability to freely contribute to the well being of society as a whole by whatever means available; labor itself is equivalent and no longer the private property of the Capitalist class.

E: Okay, let me guess. Chapter 3 and 4 are all about how to accomplish that.

B: Nope, not even close. In fact, chapter 3 is basically unreadable today. It's a summary of all the philosophical/economic/political movements that were promoting "communism" in the mid 1800s but were hopelessly utopian and simply didn't survive the last 150 years. Unless you're really up on your obscure European political history or do indeed have the patience of a history professor, it'll just fly over your head. Suffice it to say that Marx/Engels thought it was all wishy-washy idealistic nonsense.

E: Seriously?

B: Yeah, seriously. Skip chapter 3. Go directly from "the free development of each is the condition for the free development of all" to chapter 4.

What's important to note here is that the Communists in the late 1800s were directly focused on Germany. In the span of about 60 years (airplane to space ship time, remember?), the middle class in Germany was so weakened and afraid of losing their control of the economy that all Hitler had to do was call his racist nationalist garbage "Socialism" to instantly have a million twitter retweets and start exterminating the Jewish population. What we forget is that Hitler's so called "National Socialism" was built on Marxism with the added necessity of racial genocide. Thatcher, for contrast, was more in favor of letting the inevitable urban decay of overpopulation either force the working class to leave, or else just let them starve.

Were Marx and Engels horribly racist? Yes, absolutely. Anti-Semitism was an inherent component of Socialism, mostly because the racist categorization of the Jews is intimately tied to Capitalism. Even Kanye West got in trouble for saying something to that effect. They had pretty terrible opinions about other countries and races as well. They adamantly hated the Irish, for example.

But is Marx's materialist history of socio-economic oppression clouded by these racist sentiments? Not necessarily. He was after all convinced of the destructive force of white European colonization and repression of native cultures and his opinion was that they'll eventually rise up in rebellion. He was also adamantly on the abolitionist side of our Civil War. Thus, it seems quite logical to clarify Marx's racial prejudices as being rooted more in terms of contribution to global labor than any intrinsic hatred. In short, he held negative views of any race, culture, or nationality that did not further his case for the liberation of labor. With regard to slavery in the US he emphatically believed that "white" and "brown" labor were inseparable, there cannot logically be a division of racial class when considering the Proletariat as a whole. I bring it up only because issues of racist beliefs are a primary means of dismissing Marx while avoiding the more malevolent racism inherent to Capitalism. A more pertinent criticism is Marx's idealization of American slavery as essentially benign until the intervention and subsequent devaluation of Capitalist overproduction. There I disagree, slavery in all its forms is garbage.

Communism is pretty much solely concerned with property rights and aims to squash any competitive advantage for the common good. We don't work to produce what you think you can sell, we work for the benefits that production brings to society at large. Not Bourgeois society, the actual working people who recognize our equivalent value; a day's work is a day's work, and we deserve the full rewards of that work in the understanding that there is no naturally better or worse class of people. Why was he so giddy about the 8-hour work day? It severely limited the accumulation and exploitation of capital. It forces owners to hire more workers rather than run them until they are crippled then toss them aside.

E: Okay, I'm really trying here, Bottle. I have to be honest, though, I don't get it.

B: Which part?

E: Any of it!

B: That's because this isn't the 1800s, Skip. When did the Feudal system collapse?

E: Like the 15th century?

B: Kay, so we're reading a treatise 400 years later than that about how it has all gone horribly wrong. The serfs realized they were getting a raw deal because they had to go to war after war after war instead of actually getting to farm the land they received as payment for promising to go to war whenever their landLord called upon them. So, they revolted and they turned that ownership into their right to govern without the intervention of the previous aristocracy. Thus, they rose to political power and used it to keep the working class working by paying them subsistence wages. Fast forward to now, and it's still the same just with more flashing lights and the "barber pole" promise of upward mobility for the best and brightest, buuuuut we've watched bubble after bubble burst and the working class pays for that speculative loss out of the paycheck those now lost "investments" were supposedly paying.

E: Oh. That sounds...

B: Pretty horrible. What's worse is the mischaracterization that a centralized government of industrial monopolies is somehow Communist. We just read the thing. Where did it say that the Communist Party would take control of the government in a bloody revolution? Nowhere that I read. In fact quite the opposite. The Communist position was that it supports the will of the working class in establishing democratic control of the means of social production for the benefit of the working class, and that that would inevitably weaken the role of Government as superfluous. Social production is wholly distinct from individual production. Let's take farming for example. What we plant and harvest should be determined by the local community that that harvest supports. We shouldn't be forced to live in giant apartment buildings just so we can live close to the dog food factory and villainize the farmer who grows the grain and animals that go into it. It doesn't take 24/7 factory work to feed, clothe, and educate a local community, but it takes all of Iowa and more to grow an international level of corn and soy beans for profit. Now, where does that leave us, Skip?

E: I think we'll all end up working in factories making terribly inefficient cars with no hope of escape, and it will fail and we'll starve to death.

B: Only if you let authoritarian nincompoops who claim to be the opposite of Socialism enact ironically socialist programs that force the nation to be dependent on the government instead of helping each other have more meaningfully productive lives on their own terms.

Sure, it's theoretically possible that your friends love pointless assembly line work, but it's more likely that they also feel like they should be able to have a voice in what and how we produce the social capital that sustains us.

Is a planned economy better or worse than an anarchic economy? That's a nonsense question because the economy is nothing more than the trade deals people make. The crazier the deals, the less stable the economy. Are your highways and bridges in good condition? The government doesn't build or maintain them, they just pay an independently chartered corporation to pay a road crew as little as possible and recoup as much of that expense as possible through taxes you then complain about paying. How much would your monthly "Highway Maintenance" bill be if they actually privatized that monstrous operation, hmmm?

Does any of this make any sense in a broader context? No, absolutely not. We're talking about manufacturing in a bubble. Do you work in manufacturing, Skip?

E: No.

B: Did Marx work in manufacturing?

E: No?

B: So get rid of all the rhetoric and all the stupid political shenanigans, and what are we left with? We're left with a world where you wake up in the morning and have no choice but to sell your labor for less than the market value of that labor in order to survive well enough to wake up tomorrow and go back to work. That sounds like a meaningless existence to me. Now, the real question. What is anyone supposed to do about it? I can't answer that one for you. You have to do you.

Bush – Sixteen Stone

I said I think Shaving Bag is a better album than 224lbs. I did, it is, but this is still pretty awesome.

Gavin was wearing a helmet, but it didn't cushion the impact as well as one might hope. Like Forgetaboutit, this is mostly gibberish. That's ok, it's supposed to be gibberish, they're poor and hungry and abusive to each other and she has 14 industrial-strength hairdryers that Barf and Lonestar and the Dink Dinks have to carry through the desert.

Did you know everyone interprets Glycerol wrong? Toby Huss isn't on this submarine, Gavin's trying to heal the burn wounds from lighting his gravy train on fire.

I'm an alien, you're an alien, it's a beautiful rain, beautiful rain, beautiful rain... of gloppy room temperature gravy.

Geargasm With GREGORY, Part 1

Hey GREGORY, want your own segment? We'll call it Geargasm With GREGORY.

SCREEEECH!

I thought so. Well, get ready for Christmas in July, 'cause tomorrow I'm gonna order you a "my first Piano, version 2.0" and a minion mic. You're only allowed to borrow the minion mic for ceremonial celebrations and séances, but the keyboard should keep you occupied in the meantime. Obviously, you gotta use the boomy voice, but barring any calamitous credit card catastrophes I've got enough hard won karma tucked away to save a poodle or two from certain segmentation.

ARE THERE STRINGS ATTACHED?

Amazingly, yes. King Korg actually considered consumer criticism and added some. The reviews are pretty unanimous that it feels more like a piano than a thing you want to throw against the wall, and if I've gotta avoid 27 phone calls and 100 emails from my Sweetwater rep, at least it has all 88 of the standard input triggers, and comes with the proprietary pedal package. Not gonna lie, I'm pretty excited for you.

To be continued….

Corporate Schmorporate – Bottle Argues With Himself

The number of ads for online courses about creating online courses to sell expertise is pretty astonishing considering I have no idea what your expertise is other than selling your expertise on selling expertise. Honestly, why wouldn't Facebook be thrilled with all that ad revenue?

By this point you all know I think the "capitalist/communist" fight is stupid. That fight doesn't take place in a bubble, though, and it has a massive effect on the world around you.

Structurally speaking, a corporation more closely resembles the communist side of this false dichotomy. The purpose of incorporation is to stabilize the economic relationship between normally competitive and/or disparate commercial companies. This is generally fine under the personal liability of its leadership, but absurd when that personal liability is removed in favor of government intervention into private business. The danger of incorporation is not the general risk of commercial success or failure, a corporation is designed to succeed at its goal at all costs, the risk is that the corporation itself can only be voluntarily dissolved. In other words, you can't do anything to stop an incorporated entity once it has been imbued with legal rights in perpetuity.

Similarly, the Federal Government has no direct control of its citizens, it exists solely to resolve and coordinate State Governments who under the Articles of Confederation proved incapable of coordinating themselves as sovereign countries without the intervention of force from a much more powerful federal legislative/court system. The Federal Government is essentially charged with protecting the rights of its citizens from inter-State conflict.

The current issue of voting restrictions is especially problematic because the Republican Party takes the absurdist stance that widespread government intervention is necessary to prevent government intervention in free elections.

My personal opinion is that incorporated entities do not and should not have any rights at all. Rather, corporate entities are fully bound by the responsibilities of their charter/registration as temporary subsidiaries of the State, including the mandate for dissolution upon completion of their objective.

BB: But Bottle, doesn't that mean that everyone will lose their jobs after the corporation dissolves?

No, not at all. It simply means that control of operations and trade reverts to the component private companies that were merged to form the corporation. The corporation itself is not supposed to permanently run those businesses for profit because doing so eventually drains that internal economy. Neither are corporations themselves intended to compete with each other for State resources. The intent of the structure is to temporarily cooperate with minimal loss to accomplish projects for the general good that no individual company could coordinate under a competitive framework.

Historically, however, business quite readily adapted and adopted the corporate model as a competitive advantage and used increasing political influence to increasingly protect that advantage. The end result is a closed money loop among the corporation, its investors, and labor. The obvious result is economic stagnation because the corporation will not relinquish its control over the total system.

BB: But can't you also argue that there are many businesses that shouldn't fail but certainly will if the corporations that hold them as subsidiaries return that control?

Yes, absolutely, but that is a case by case problem, not a blanket condition of private business. In fact, that is a primary concern for the economy as a whole and the actual reason that incorporation is a beneficial process. The average consumer has no real understanding of the relationships necessary to bring useful products to market, and corporations are a vital tool for bringing those final products to the "ignorant" market. However, that corporate melding cannot be sustained indefinitely, because the corporation itself has a shelf life, so to speak. Either the component companies find a sustainable way to continue that relationship without corporate control, or else that final product must be released into the public domain. This is actually a familiar problem. We see it whenever a major corporation ceases to support its legacy products. It's not that a particular market has disappeared, it's that the market brings in less revenue than necessary for the continued operation of the corporate structure itself. The nasty solution is that the corporation simply acquires enough capital in the form of subsidiary investments to compensate for the stagnation, but that inherently widens the inequality gap inside the structure, and forces the obsolescence of otherwise perfectly usable and beneficial technologies.

Interlude

    Meep!
    Oh, hey little guy, what's up?
    Meep meep, meep meep meep.
    Well, yeah. That's what we're talking about. Musicians are the people paying to run the music industry, but we can't make enough money being musicians to pay for both the industry and a family life. Music has always been a volatile art form and a terrible commodity. Like actual science and education, it only works when it is funded in good faith as an investment in society itself.
    Meep!
    Big language for a little guy. We're working through the backside of the cycle. The technological advancement has outpaced the human imagination, they have 90 percent of the cards but they know that either way they lose. If they actually win, then it's over and they lose all their money because there's no business to run unless they pay for it. If they accept our forfeit, then they still have to lose to redeal for the next

round. So, they waffle back and forth and try to secretly sort their cards to strategically lose just enough to keep up appearances.

    Meep meep.

    Yep, exactly. They're totally afraid that we don't understand that, and that when it's their turn to need help we'll play our "you didn't help us out last time, why should we care now?" card. That's a legit fear considering that's exactly how they wrote it in the rule book.

    Meep.

    I think that's a little harsh. I'm a forgive because it's more productive kind of guy. Yeah, I'll say things like "don't do that crap again" or "what did you think would happen?," but picking up the pieces and moving forward is more important to me. There isn't enough punishment to punish the punisher, you know?

    Meep meep meep.

    But again, if winning is still losing, then really you're just making the losing more painful for yourself. It's why we have the "no double or nothing" rule. If we're gonna get to the end of the night and you can't afford to pay me my winnings, why did you make us gamble in the first place? We both knew I was the slightly better player before we started.

    Meep meep?

    No, I thought about telling that story, but I didn't.

    Meep meep?

    'Cause it's not just one story, it's 3 or 4 and I'm more interested in music than billiards.

    Meep.

    I'm sure I watched myself write that in the second book. I don't have any idea how to write books, I'm just enjoying the experience of actually doing it. It's fun for me. I don't care if it turns out good or bad. I gave up on trying to win the lottery (real or metaphorical), we're all just begging for each others' spare change anyway. Pay me, don't pay me, just don't try to guilt trip me into feeling sorry for you when you're secretly trying to rip me off.

Meep, meep meep meep.

No, honestly you have like 60/40 odds if you just ask me for 5 dollars. If there's a five dollar bill in my pocket I probably don't need it. If I needed it it would be in my checking account, not my pocket. Plus, if I were that desperate I wouldn't be walking around in public at all, I'd be at home crying from the stress of it all.

Meep meep.

Because no one is actually buying music. The general public is buying the ability to listen to music. It's the chicken and egg problem: you can't get a gig without an agent, but you can't get an agent unless you have too many gigs to keep track of yourself. 10 years of Ramen and peanut butter and the van life is the entry fee, but your band will probably break up or get arrested before you get to that point. That's completely ignoring the nepotism problem to boot.

Meep.

Like I've always said, I don't make the rules, I just point out that they're stupid. Cheers little dude, thanks for chatting with me. Off you go now, I'm feeling the sleepy sleeps coming on.

Why Are There So Many Songs About Rainbows?

Alright, I thought it only fair to compliment my relatively thorough engagement with Marx at the end of the Industrial Revolution by giving Adam Smith's An Inquiry Into the Nature and Wealth of Nations equal air time. I was wrong, it's a struggle. For starters, it's condescending, it's so Anglocentric I want to barf (England is better than France, France is better than Poland, farmers can't help but be lazy because they are bound by the seasons and have to waste a lot of time walking around), and his premise is that all those "savage" nations are poor and lazy because they don't divide their labor into menial tasks and make children perform them all day long.

I mean, I'll do it if you really want me to, but I'd almost rather read Hitler's garbage prison diary or Dianetics. Chapter 1 ends with this doozy of a sentence:

> … and yet it may be true, perhaps, that the accommodation of an European prince does not always so much exceed that of an industrious and frugal peasant, as the accommodation of the latter exceeds that of many an African king, the absolute masters of the lives and liberties of ten thousand naked savages.

I know the 18th-century grammar is a bit obtuse, but remember that, kiddos. Adam Smith says a European peasant is far better off than an African king. My actual favorite least favorite part came earlier where he basically said "even though half the people here don't do any meaningful work at all, the few who do produce more than enough food and clothing that we're all happy and well taken care of; totally better than those savages eating fresh fish and caring for their elderly."

I can't. It's worse than Christmas albums. 1780s or no, this is garage. I'm sure I *could* filter out the tiny threads of reasonable arguments about the "political economy" of 18th-century Europe, but I'd almost rather listen to Nickelback or Seether. My brief excursion into this historical tome of grotesqueness did confirm one thing, though. Marx read it and spent the rest of his life writing about how horrible it is.

Geargasm with GREGORY, Part 2

"Mail's here! These look fragile! Might wanna catch 'em before the first bounce! 3, 2, 1…."

Bottle snapped up from his slumber, blinked a few times, then actually snapped. A startling snap it was, not a snap of authority, more a snap of agreed agreements and a call to action. A tiny door next to the Escalator of Doom opened and a batch of minions sprayed forth from the portal like a city fire hydrant being opened on a disgustingly hot day. Not a disorganized gush, but a controlled chaos that nevertheless followed a coherent trajectory. The astute observer would no doubt remark upon the fact that they were all wearing as motley an assortment of helmets as one might expect to find when cleaning out the wardrobe closet of an old and well versed civic theater.

Cue the slow motion and the 6-Million-Dollar Man sound effect as a gigantic box hurdles through the air. If this were the real universe, we might expect a comical THUD and a plungered trombone, but this is the Bunker of Beef, so it was quite anti-climactically caught by the minions and whisked off toward Bottle's office.

B: Thanks, little dudes. Just stand it over there in the corner, I gotta finish some things first.
BB: Op! There's one more! Bombs away!
LD: Meep!
B: You got that right. Damnit Bridbrad! The countdown is important!

Just then, the littlest minion of all came running into the office with a box at least 9 times bigger than himself hefted above his head.

LD: Meep!
B: Good catch, littlest dude! That one's for you guys. Here, I'll open it for you. A new microphone so you can podcast me a meepventure, or something. Welp, I guess since

I'm already thoroughly distracted, might as well see what we see.

Friends of the show will not be at all surprised that the ominous tones of Also Sprach Zarathustra began playing as Bottle approached the monolith. He circled around it clockwise, he circled around it counter-clockwise, then he scratched his head and bellowed.

B: GREGORY! C'mere! I might have bought you a present.

To be continued again....

Corporate Schmorporate – Bottle Argues with Himself Again
What do I mean when I say "corporation"? The short answer is that I mean the legal entity that separates a business from its ownership, the thing that removes the financial liability from the owners of the corporation. The owner of a corporation could be 1 person, 10,000 shareholders, etc.

I don't necessarily mean the board of directors, the CxOs, or the management team, they are all to some extent employees of the corporation. The internal pay structure and organization are also irrelevant. I am essentially only concerned with the singular entity whose existence in turn requires recognition of the individual, the common person, as an equivalent corporation at the Federal level.

Is it necessarily terrible? Are corporations inherently evil? No, absolutely not. The formation of corporations serves an important function in our society. Corporations are not, however, intended to be the only viable business structure in a market economy because to a large extent they are their own monopolized market.

I like to pick on Wal-Mart, so we'll use that. From a certain perspective it is reasonable to say that in your city Wal-

Mart, Target, etc. compete for your patronage, but from a slightly different vantage point it is more accurate to say that the grocery department of Wal-Mart competes with every other grocery or convenience store in your city. The enormous economic and social advantage of the larger structure of Wal-Mart should be obvious. The competition for patronage has basically nothing to do with the actual consumable goods. Rather, the competition is directly tied to the limited time, money, and convenience that are themselves a byproduct of the structure of typical work.

In short, Wal-Mart as a corporation does not compete the same way any single-owner business competes, Wal-Mart directly competes with the intended structure of Capitalism itself as the overarching structure of daily life. That is a familiar situation to anyone who has considered the dynamics of indoor malls vs strip malls vs individual private businesses at the level of city planning.

All this is not to say that the structure cannot ever be sustained, it is only to point out that when it does become unstable it inevitably follows a known trajectory. As Wal-Mart starts to drain the local economy, more and more people feel forced to shop at Wal-Mart, and this creates a Giffen Cycle where the dwindling money from other wages increasingly goes to Wal-Mart. Without some regulation, the business community itself ends up paying Wal-Mart and the structure will eventually collapse.

We can go a step further. Why does Wal-Mart even exist at this point? Why are there any brick and mortar retail stores? Amazon has reached the size and scope of an international retail monopoly. UPS, Fedex, even the postal service are all competing for the same logistical resources, and Amazon has simply bought priority for its deliveries. Your packages can and do get bumped off of trucks and planes to ensure that Amazon packages get loaded first. I am of course exaggerating in terms of market percentage and raw numbers, but I am not exaggerating in terms of the effect. Our current heading is not so much a return to space exploration, but the very real possibility that all business outside the umbrella of a few corporate monopolies ceases to exist. That's what the agenda of the Republican Party looks like to me. Their goal is to force every possible confrontation to the Federal level simply to get a ruling that they can then create loopholes to avoid. The end goal is a complete dissolution of the Federal and State Governments, in favor of private control over the National Economy. Every working person they fool into believing that individuals are the beneficiaries of this agenda is another vote for Totalitarianism. Technically it's Inverted Totalitarianism, as the only political action required/allowed is voting for Republican candidates. They are actively trying to suppress Democrat leaning districts with insane restrictions that limit the time and convenience of voting against them. But honestly, if the empty shell of a Republic and the wealth of its "elected" representatives are more important to you than the actual people struggling to earn a living through meaningful work under that system, then count me out. You'll get no sympathy from Bottle, and I won't share my squirrels with you when we're back to the Stone Age. Find your own squirrels to eat somewhere far away from me.

Cloudkicker – Solitude

You know what? No more words for a day or two until GREGORY looks like he has formed an opinion. We'll just listen to Solitude by Cloudkicker. It's a delightful 3 sides of Progressive Metal instrumentals that he recorded during the Summer of 2020 when most of the world went on hiatus. I still worked every day and wrote books about it in my spare time, but that's beside the point.

One of the frustrating things about now life is that as amazing as this album is, there's no score for me to analyze. There's not a physical representation of the music that I can study and compare to other works and write about. I miss that. It would be ridiculously impractical to transcribe it, or to find other musicians to hang out with me and learn to play it for fun and intellectual gratification. There's nobody out there saying pertinent things about it for me to compare and contrast my own opinion. That's ok, I can just enjoy listening to it. It's quite fun in its wordless alternation between rage and melancholy, and it's worth having in my head just in case the opportunity arises to mention what's been turning on the table recently.

Geargasm With GREGORY, Part 3

Alright, about 3 feet, we'll go for about a 70-degree arc, and flick....

OH, AHEM. WELL, THAT WAS CERTAINLY INVIGORATING. HELLO, BOTTLE. I'LL TURN THIS OFF, THEN.

B: Well?

YES, I AM ACTUALLY. THAT WAS QUITE AN ENJOYABLE ADVENTURE.

B: No, I meant how is it? Do you like it? Do you hate it? What do you think?

IT IS VERY MUCH AN ELECTRIC PIANO. YES, I'D SAY QUITE SERVICEABLE. OBVIOUSLY I HAVE NOT YET TESTED ITS AUDIO IN TERMS OF RECORDING OR AS A MIDI CONTROLLER, BUT THE VOLUME FROM THE SPEAKERS IS QUITE LOVELY AND IT SOUNDS FINE THROUGH YOUR HEADPHONES.

B: Ok. I can add that the optional cabinetry was quite easy to assemble. Even a child could help put it together. Now for some serious questions. With a price tag around $700 after tax, we're playing the piano equivalent of a MIM Strat. Thoughts?

AH, INTERESTING, I HAD NOT THOUGHT OF IT FROM THAT PERSPECTIVE. YOU'RE OUT ON A TOUR OF DIVE BARS AND STREET DANCES, KENNY LIKES TO TAKE CORNERS A LITTLE TOO FAST IN THE STREAMLINE, AND NOW GREG-O'S KEYBOARD LOOKS LIKE IT GOT PUNCHED IN THE FACE BY A JEALOUS BOYFRIEND. YOU HOP OVER TO THE LOCAL MUSIC-O-MART AND SAY "HEY CHAD, I NEED AN ELECTRIC PIANO THAT WILL GET THE JOB DONE WITH AS LITTLE FUSS AS POSSIBLE, BUT ALSO 3 OR 4 MORE GIGS AFTER THAT."

B: Nice! Couldn't have said it better myself. Well?

INDEED, THE KORG B2 ISN'T LOADED WITH TONS OF SILLYNESS, BUT IT IS INDEED A PIANO, AND NONE OF THE KEYS ARE WOBBLY. IT FEELS QUITE NICE TO PLAY. YOU'LL NEED TO HANG ON TO THE INSTRUCTIONS, OR MARK THE KEYS SO YOU KNOW WHICH BUTTONS AND KEYS TO PRESS TO CHANGE SOUNDS AND/OR EFFECTS, BUT THAT IS RELATIVELY TRIVIAL.

B: Ok, fair's fair. What are some of the downsides?

WELL, IT SEEMS WORTH REITERATING THAT THIS IS NOT A SYNTHESIZER. IT IS A PIANO. IT HAS A DOZEN SOUNDS, BUT IT IS MEANT TO BE A PIANO.

B: Are all the sounds good?

AH, GLAD YOU ASKED. NO. THIS IS PERSONAL PREFERENCE, OF COURSE, BUT THE DEFAULT PIANO SOUND IS QUITE TERRIBLE TO THE HOLES THAT MY EARS WOULD COVER IF I HAD THEM. THE OTHER PIANO SOUNDS ARE MUCH BETTER WITH A PROPER ARRAY OF LIGHT AND DARK TONES, IN MY OPINION. AGAIN, I HAVE NOT HEARD THEM IN A RECORDED SETTING, SO MY PREFERENCE MAY BE OF NO VALUE IN THAT CONTEXT. THE HARPSICHORD, EVEN CONSIDEREING THE UNIQUE STRANGENESS OF

ELECTRONIC HARPSICHORD, IS RATHER UNPLEASANT AS WELL. THE REST ARE FINE.

B: Interesting. Anything else?

NO, I THINK WE HAVE COVERED THE IMPORTANT CRITERIA. IT IS A PERFECTLY USABLE ELECTRIC PIANO, AND IT WILL, AS YOU SAY, GET THE JOB DONE.

B: Well, there you go everybody. If you need a simple electric piano that costs less than $1,000 but isn't a piece of garbage, the Korg B2 is a completely acceptable choice. Even my anthropomorphic skeleton from out of the closet says so.

Snarky Puppy – We Like It Here

What a freakin' week. I don't know about you, but I'm glad it's over. To celebrate, let's just enjoy the stitched together video of the complete We Like It Here by Snarky Puppy.

Honestly, I don't need to review it because this thing is monumental. There are tons of stories about it (like how Larnell Lewis composed the drum parts in his head on the flight over there), but you can go search them out for yourself. Michael League started Snarky Puppy at UNT because he didn't make it into any ensembles when he started there in 2003/4. I started doctoral work at UNT in 2006. I never actually met him, but we did walk the same hallways at various times throughout the day, just never at the same time.

He thinks of the band as Pop with a lot of improvisation, but this is straight up Fusion in my book. Yes, the videos are the live recording session over 4 nights in the Netherlands with an actual audience. Those ATH-M50RDs are discontinued now, but MSRP was around $200, so you're looking at a couple thousand dollars worth of headphones even with a bulk studio discount. Maybe Audio Technica let 'em have 'em for the publicity, I don't know. Ok, I'll shut up and let Snarky Puppy speak for themselves. I promise the next hour will not disappoint, and you just might find several more disappear like magic while re-watching part or all of it. Enjoy.

Where The Hell Are We?

Good question. Today's date is 7/24/21. The Capitalists are Communists, the actual Radical Left are the Peter, Paul, and Mary of Rock and Roll but the establishment Right literally wants people to get sick and die, The Royal Guardsmen were icons of 60s counterculture turning people on to Jimi Hendrix and Cream, you can't buy anything from an actual store because that store is selling all their products through Amazon while the bald guy in charge of said fine dining establishment is literally competing with his frienemies to see who can blast off further into actual outer space so they can sell tickets like it's a poorly tethered thrill ride at the state fair, some kind of rodent chewed a hole in my gas can (it could also have been a rock hurled from the road), I'm back to listening to music without lyrics while re-learning to play a few of the easiest Songs Without Words, the people who wore masks and got vaccinated and stayed home as much as possible didn't catch the new variant of SARS (it's not actually called SARS now by the way, 'cause people might remember how serious that was) but the people running around sprayin' it while they're sayin' it sure did (they told me how horrible it was), vinyl has made a huge comeback but musicians are still scouring couches for peanut butter money because corporations own their copyrights, Canada and the Pacific Northwest are as hot as Arizona and Las Vegas this year, people somehow think Biden is destroying the country by actually being the President instead of energizing a mob and telling them to run down to the Capitol and give 'em Hell.

I don't get it. I'm known for entertaining all manner of ridiculous thoughts for the fun of that intellectual challenge, but every day holds a level of surprise even I can't predict. Is it sheer boredom? Is it Devo? Is it just that life is so meaningless that most people would rather criticize actors and athletes for having human opinions than make the effort to form a coherent one themselves? I honestly don't know. I'll probably never know. I think the history books will just say "The American Empire, more so than almost any other empire was marked by a strange kind of recurring semi-centennial madness. It may seem crude and strange to say this today, but approximately twice a century since its formation up to the New Dark Ages, America appears to have collectively and utterly lost its mind."

I think the only logically possible course of action is to shave all the hair off my head and face. Unless you have a better idea…No?…Alright, then. If that's what it has come to, I guess we'll just have to face the face of the face under all this cranial keratin….

When Has Any Of This Ever Stopped Me?

S: Pffffft! Hahahahahahahaha! Sorry, sorry, no sorry. That was uncalled for. Did you lose a bet?

B: Barbecue accident.

S: Oh gosh! Are you okay?

B: I'm joking. I was just so hot and miserable, and I needed a haircut anyway, so I just Sinead O'Connored the whole kit and caboodle. If it's good enough for Brittney, it's good enough for me. Let her waste her millions on whatever she wants. That's what money is for, after all. She's less crazy than Papa John, in my opinion.

S: Okay, okay, I'm getting used to it now. Still weird but I'll be good in a day or two. You?

B: I do wonder where my chin went, and that's when I remember why I grew the chin helmet in the first place. I know the song isn't about me, but cue the Carly Simon anyway. I'll get over it too.

S: So, I have to ask, where *are* we going?

B: No idea, but I suspect the streets won't have any names, and we'll just have to go block by block until we find the obvious new construction. Nobody has any idea how to plan anything anymore, and it's only going to get worse. Get this, people think the President actually causes gas prices to fluctuate, like the cashier charges extra if they don't like him.

S: They've always thought that.

B: No, no, no. They've always said that, but now they actually believe it. Like, truly, they think that's a real thing the President does on Tuesday or whenever; he goes out to negotiate the exchange rate for crude oil. It's beginning to look a lot like Christmas, how bad do you think the President will get ripped off this year? They also think the hyper inflation of returning to the gold standard is a good idea. *Compy! What's the current projection if we actually did that?!*

C: Every analyzable data set shows that the current monetary system is at least twice as stable, tangible banking panic is essentially non-existent, returning to the gold standard has drastic exchange rate consequences, and tying the value of the dollar to gold actually requires more government intervention because dollars don't magically equal weights of gold. Actual people with high levels of political authority have to physically make the dollar equal to some weight of gold every morning.

B: So unless you want to physically carry gold coins around, that's pretty pointless?

C: That's not quite what I meant.

B: Oh, duh, sorry, I wasn't thinking. The Gold Standard was based on the cost of mining actual gold from the ground. What the hell would that even mean today? You'd have to measure the amount of gold on Earth and other countries would start digging up the gold they buried centuries ago, and we'd have to devote all our computing power to monitoring every country's sliding value because traders would be flapping currencies all over the place. The

US dollar is an actual commodity in its own right, people trade US dollars for profit every second of every day; that's what trading currencies *is*. That reminds me of that hilarious story about how we could have avoided the worst of the Great Depression by physically moving some of the gold from one side of the NYC vault to the other.

C: Um...

B: Sorry. My point was that the Gold Standard wasn't some magic system that just worked. Actual intelligent people had to make that system work the same way actual people with slide rulers had to calculate velocity and trajectory and aim for the weakest point in the Van Allen Belt so astronauts didn't die from radiation poisoning. Same reason we had all those nuclear reactor meltdowns: the people who inherited these systems thought properly maintaining them was a waste of time and money, except with the Gold Standard it was literally a waste of time and resources that was objectively needlessly chaotic. England dropped it first, we dropped it when it became apparent that the super wealthy just didn't feel like paying for anything anymore, and so did everybody else. I told you that story about how FDR laughed at Charles Ives' small-dollar war bond proposal, right? Part of that laugh was that it makes no sense to take money from the poor because they simply can't afford it considering there's some random recession and/or bank panic scheduled at a quarter past 2 to 3 years from now.

S: I think you might be getting carried away.

B: Yes, good point, I do that. I've had essentially the same conversation with Skip and Milton. My only goal is to find the point where you guys lose track of reality. Economics is a theory. Now, as a Theorist with a capital T, I can tell you that there are two types of theories: descriptive and prescriptive. Descriptive theories are lovely little things that mind their own business and try to adequately describe what's going on. Prescriptive theories are nasty little demons from the netherworld. We have to go back to our happy little two-dimensional line of Economic Left and Right to get to the point, I'm sure Bob Ross won't mind too much.

A descriptive view of the economy says "here's how people tend to act in certain situations, let's build our political economy to step back when it's going great and intervene in beneficial ways when it's going haywire." That's the left hand side. The right hand side, however, says "bugger that! Here's how people should act and if they can't find a way to succeed then that is their own problem. I'm good at this game, just do what I tell you to do or die for all I care. Survival of the fittest."

S: That seems a little harsh and simplistic.

B: It's my descriptive theory of the fight. It's Keynes vs Friedman. Keynes thought the government should understand its spending and stabilize the economy to improve everyone's standard of living, Friedman said "brilliant! Businesses should grow into gigantic corporations and do that themselves with no oversight or social obligation whatsoever." Now, this is tricky, I'm not saying one or the other is intrinsically right or wrong, I'm saying that Friedman's direction can, will, and must crash into a pile of rubble before anyone responsible says "oh shit, I was wrong, this is all my fault." If fear of the crash is the only thing that makes you do a good job, what do you think will happen when you put a guy who has no concept of that fear in charge?

U2 – The Joshua Tree

Alright, let's hear The Joshua Tree by U2. Were they the first famous Irish Rock band? Maybe. They came from Punk and by 1987 were barely starting to have an opinion about the wider world. This album is weird because Bono specifically wanted the theme of the album to be America. The mythological America, not the Bob Geldoff "this place is insane" America. The result is that the desert (Joshua Tree, obviously) is his metaphor, and the losing side of the

American Dream is what he's trying to really experience. Nobody really "got it" when he wanted wide open sounds and straightforward loneliness in pop song form, but they went along with it and eventually this album popped out. It's produced by Eno and Flood, so they didn't pick guys who suck at that atmosphere, and it shows. This might be the loneliest sounding album I've ever heard, like you could walk for miles and die of thirst before seeing another person.

But, it's a particularly Southwest aural picture. This isn't what the Midwest sounds like, this isn't the Pacific Northwest or the Eastern Seaboard, these aren't the diners and ski lodges of Supertramp, it's not the big city nightlife of Boomtown Rats, this is the bleached bones and cacti of Nevada and Arizona. On that count they definitely succeed.

So, what's the lyrical message? Uh, pretty freakin' desolate. There's intense restlessness smacked over the head with a shovel. Even if you could make it over the horizon, you'd feel so left behind and out of place that you'd probably just turn back around and leave.

It's no surprise this is their biggest album in the US. Bono says this was basically the album he felt obliged to make from experience. Not just his experiences touring the US, but the part of the US that resonates with the rest of the world. That little lower left hand pocket of desert is what America shares with the rest of the world. The little pockets of beauty and prosperity are just that, reality is chasing a dream we'll never actually attain. Freakin' bleak.

Should it be on all the "best album ever" lists? Yeah, sure, it's quite fantastic. U2 the band was all about being the opposite of the Synth Pop mainstream of the 80s. They owned straight ahead vanilla Rock in the 80s, touring to massive success every single year and following it up with the next great album. You can almost hear Gin Blossoms say "screw it, we'll just play the whole Joshua Tree album tonight."

The atmospherics are what does it for me; these aren't songs, they are physical spaces. Highly stylized cinematographic spaces with one room white wooden country chapels in the background with everybody waiting for their cold black sun-cracked souls to come alive, but still. This album does not end on an up-turn, by the way. Exit and Mothers of the disappeared are borderline industrial anguish. The Joshua Tree is an album for a lost and left behind world, and it still hits surprisingly hard today. On a scale of 1 to "that's what we were trying to do," The Joshua tree is probably a Yahtzee.

The Interrupters – Live In Tokyo

Holy smokes, people. I was just trying to check out a band a friend recommended, but I somehow wound up at that godforsaken hell hole where all the worst parts of facebook go to the same daycare as Rosemary's Baby. Reddit, I'm talking about Reddit. It's awful on purpose, but not even in a way I can ironically respect. It's 4-chan without goals in life.

If you're new to Bottle's Blasphemy Hour, then you need to know that the political compass is actually a Klein Bottle and you have no way of knowing which direction you are facing, or going, or came from. Supposedly, The Interrupters were big supporters of Ron Paul and somehow got mixed up in Alex Jones's recurring brain hemorrhages and they are industry plants like Pussy Riot or The Tramp Stamps, and YOU'RE ALL MISSING THE ORIGINAL POINTS! A) you have to actually already be musicians, and William Riker) the thing the Auditors want you to do has to actually be salable.

Ska is not mainstream salable. The brief blips of Rancid and Reel Big Fish and No Doubt have a dedicated scene, sure, but it's a niche market. I'm totally on record saying Ska is not really my scene, but that doesn't mean I can't have a reasoned opinion. I still listen to it, and I have coherent likes and dislikes. So, let's tackle as much actual Reddit criticism as my brain could handle in 5 minutes.

1) They're a right wing band!

No, not with Tim Armstrong being the final say on whether Hellcat publishes their album or not.

2) They're crappy Libertarian apologists!

For like the hundredth time, I'm down in desert land with Chomsky and actual person Marx. Ghandi would think I'm a bit much. We're all still technically "Libertarian."

3) Their lyrics suck!

All lyrics suck, even the ones I think are good. Words have 9,000+ meanings because we're terrible at using them consistently. Case in point, Reddit comments.

4) The Interrupters would be Joe Strummer's favorite band if he were alive.

That's a bold assumption

5) YOU HAVE TO CHOOSE A SIDE!!!

No, you don't. Choosing a side is half the problem, because it's a false dichotomy.
    Yes, Strummer was a Socialist. He said "I come from the working-class world. Socialism appears more humanitarian to me than the world I see with my own eyes every day. Obviously the system works for you, you make that very clear as you're kicking me in the teeth." The lesson here is that things mean what they mean *for you*.

I listened to their whole Live in Tokyo album and I'll whip out my Tony the Tiger impression to say they're great. The songs are catchy, it's not overly ideological in either direction, this is lovely "you're a person, let's work together" music.

Did you know there was insanely severe backlash when Kendrick Lamar won a Pulitzer Prize? Why? What possible reason could there be other than that he is a Black rapper instead of a White "Classical Composer" (or Jazz composer every few years)? You're gonna stand there and tell me the average Reddit troll puts any value in the recognition of outstanding publications? I may be guilty of self-aggrandizement on occasion, but I'm also a student of the Absurd, and I'll argue reality with anyone anytime. They're really just telling you to think for yourself and question authority. That's all Ken Kesey and I ever told anyone to do, but 'Merica thinks I'm some crazy guy trying to steal their hard earned gas station beef jerky. $9 for 37 cents worth of dehydrated cow's ass? Are you serious? $2 pistachios for everyone, this round's on me.

Gerard Smith – Lullabies in an Ancient Tongue

Sweet! My copy of Gerard Smith's Lullabies In An Ancient Tongue arrived today. Modern Pagan Celtic Garage Rock/Metal from the outskirts of Detroit? Yes, please.

No, this is not the Gerard Smith from TV on the Radio who sadly died in 2011, this is the Gerard Smith of Bill Grogan's Goat, and this is his Covid Crisis album of stuff he had to get out of his head, but wouldn't quite work with his actual band.

By most definitions this is Prog, and I don't have a rebuttal other than Celtic Garage Prog. It's also the first time I actually chose albums on purpose. You might not care, but reviewing U2 yesterday wasn't a happy coincidence and that feels like suspiciously like lying in the bowels of the cockles of my heart. Luckily, it worked, because it turns out that Bono and The Edge didn't give a crap about Irish music until Bob Dylan asked them "you do know what I do is just the American version of Irish Balladry, right?"

Critics have nailed one thing about Gerard, and that's how refreshing it is to hear the old-school Prog influence not sung quasi-castrato. I'm not saying all you hyper-tenors can't sing Prog anymore, I'm just reiterating that Baritones and Basses can also sing whatever the hell you like.

There's a monster in my guts trying to claw his way out…that's when it's time to remember to breathe. The point of that song is do the opposite of whatever is making you miserable. Good advice, that.

Now, you're all listening to it and thinking "Bottle, this is a 'random crap' album, but I thought you hated those." No, sorry, you're wrong. I hate good album concepts that turn out to be random crap. This is supposed to be random crap. Did you skip my second paragraph and forget the tile of the album? It's his third solo album of songs he wrote while he was stuck at home trying not to test out the ventilators at his locally mismanaged hospital. There are crickets chirping and a violin solo in the middle of track 4.

Here's a guy who knows how to invite some friends to play whatever he wants, and I for one love it, I guess if I have to criticize something, the vocals are a little too far forward. Who cares? This is pure fun, I love it.

TV on the Radio – Return to Cookie Mountain

… and me being me, I simply can't not follow the Gerard Smith wormhole and listen to TV on the Radio. I also can't do the $40+ for a copy of Return to Cookie Mountain on vinyl. I can't. We'll just have to do the extended version on youtube with 4 bonus tracks, including El-P's remix of Hours. Bowie loved their first album, and here he is singing backup vocals on Province.

The story is that Gerard was busking in the subway and Tunde just kept giving him money until Gerard recognized him from the movie Jump Tomorrow and Tunde asked Gerard to join the band for this sophomore album.

Their very first release was titled Ok, Calculator, and their musical influences are all over the place, so that should give you some idea of the sonic deluge ahead of us. They're still together, but they've been on hiatus since 2019 like everyone else. Their last album from 2014 feels like universes ago, but hopefully we'll get more. Let's just add them to the list of awesome musicians from Brooklyn and enjoy. Ah, lovely.

DAMN. Parts 1 and 2
1) Picking up from that off-hand comment a few albums ago, let's listen to DAMN. Our context is that the album won the 2018 Pulitzer Prize for Music. What was the official statement of award?

Ms. Canady said the board's decision to award Mr. Lamar, 30, was unanimous. The board called the album "a virtuosic song collection unified by its vernacular authenticity and rhythmic dynamism that offers affecting vignettes capturing the complexity of modern African-American life."

Before we go any further, we have to define what we aren't talking about. We aren't talking about the back and forth over whether that description is condescending, or whether it was more important for the Prize to award Kendrick Lamar than it was for Kendrick to win a Pulitzer, or about the complicated history of the Pulitzer Prize in general, or whether someone else should have won. We are taking the whole thing at face value. The story is that the committee was having discussions about the award, and the short list of nominees they were considering had a lightbulb attatched to it. All the things they were considering had the obvious and unavoidable influence of Hip-Hop at their core. Sure, we could go try to assemble a list of those candidates, but we don't need to, we're accepting that once the committee realized the importance of Hip-Hop throughout the entire culture of commercial publication in 2017, they unanimously agreed that DAMN. was the album that should win. I'm not interested in dissecting that story, it is a completely logical story about the selection process, and it is the official reason why Kendrick Lamar won a Pulitzer Prize for creating DAMN.. The earlier description is an attempt to place the work itself inside the culture at large, a culture that includes blatant and open racism and hostility toward any non-white condoned (child proof with all the sharp corners removed) challenge to Bourgeois values.

And the album begins with an insanely complicated and amazing story about being murdered by surprise. The moral of the story is that your intentions are essentially meaningless. Can we let Kendrick and Bottle have a conversation where I don't put too many silly words in either of our mouths? Yes, I think so.

B: Hi, I'm Bottle. Thank you for speaking with me. May I call you Kendrick?

K: Sure, that is my name.

B: Great! Is it fair to say that DAMN. was intended to be as honest and accurate a description of the experience of an African-American from your personal perspective, and that that was the primary motivation for awarding you the prize?

K: Sure. I mean, there's always more to these things than you can encapsulate in a quick summary, but that's what I've said I intended, and that was how they presented the award. I do feel honored, and it was presented as an award to me personally, not as some grandiose political statement.

B: That's how I took it. Thank you so much for talking with me. Mind if I continue with my own personal analysis?

K: Not at all. Thank you for listening to my work.

B: You're welcome. I'm always interested in what people have to say. I never know how it will turn out until I actually do it, but I think that's all part of the appreciation of art. Cheers, man.

So, back to BLOOD.. He sees a person who looks like they could actually use some help. He waits, analyzes, watches, and finally he decides he wants to try to help. When he does, it turns out to be a con, and he gets killed (and presumably robbed afterward). Like I implied earlier, there are things we can control and things we cannot control, but our intentions and analyses have no bearing on the unfolding reality after we make a choice. That becomes the reality this album exists inside because BLOOD. is the introduction to the album itself. That metaphor transcends all culture, race, gender, age, everything; it is an omni-present condition of human experience.

When we take that contextual situation into the realm of Kendrick and Bottle sitting at a table having a conversation, something very important happens. I, the white guy, realize that even though I completely understand that metaphor, the feelings of skepticism and fear that I would feel in that situation, it is not my default state of existence; especially considering that is a major component of the relief and happiness I feel now that I live way out in the fields of Iowa with few people around.

Could I offer Kendick that explanation as a solution to his problem? Of course not, it's ridiculous. He is telling me that he cannot escape that life or death game. He can't run away, he has to make a choice, and he has no way of knowing if it is the right choice or not. Heads he helps a fellow human, tails he gets murdered. Damned if you do, damned if you don't.

I, Bottle, have privilege by not having to deal with that reality anymore (though I certainly did at one point in my life). For some, that recognition of privilege might have racial implications, for others it might simply be the opportunity to escape. My opportunity was certainly not a hard fought battle or of my own making, but an opportune choice that I would say worked in my favor.

Could I brainstorm possible similar situations if I were sitting at the table with the narrator? Sure, but that's not why we are here. We're here to listen and contemplate as much of that complexity as possible. I hope now the extent of that complexity is more apparent. The framing of the album alone is so pertinent and powerful that it should command everyone's attention, and in the objectively safe space of listening to an album in the privacy of your own home without fear of being spied upon or sentenced to death for some transgression in the eyes of an oppressive authority, you would have to be insanely delusional to run away from such an experience in fear, or off-handedly dismiss it as "I don't like Rap."

I do like Rap and Hip-Hop very much, but that's not the point. The point is that I understand first-hand how much work and care goes into the creation of art, which this album most assuredly is, and it is my obligation as a listener, interpreter, critic, and fellow human being to put an equal amount of effort into understanding and appreciating it. I'll also point out that back in 2018 when he won the Pulitzer and well before I started actually writing about albums, I too thought "yeah that makes perfect sense, it should get that level of recognition."

2) You might say "yeah, okay, sure Bottle, but BLOOD. would make more sense as the last track. It just would." I'll wait for you to work through that one yourself. Go ahead…

… "Oh, is this like one of your out of order things? The tracks mean different things because of their placement, or something?"

Yes, to some extent. It's not supposed to be a secret, the collector's edition has the tracks in reverse order, the CD has a different track order from the vinyl. That was an intentional decision in the studio, and yes you are supposed to understand it both ways at a minimum. Concepts weave through multiple songs, and that has a striking effect when you compare the forward and backward versions in your mind. Either way it's intended to flow from start to finish. It's a proper album, not just songs. The working title was What happens On Earth Stays On Earth, but eventually it became clear that the album was all the possible meanings of DAMN., especially "damned if you do, damned if you don't." I personally go with the word Doom, but same difference in my opinion. Alright, who slathered on the secret sauce? Hello, Bono. No, no, we know why you're here, we did your America album two days ago like it wasn't intentional. Enough of my silly, back to the album.

Professor Bottle says your homework is to catalogue the various voices on the album. Kendrick Lamar very intentionally chooses tone, inflection, and cadence to directly represent mood and emotion for the listener. Giving those voices names or specific characters is beyond the scope of the single album, but the technique itself is an emulation of the pre Dr. Dre era of singular rap stars. Old-school Rap was a "band" context. A group, a posse, a crew, call it whatever you will, Rap was an ensemble with each individual taking on a specific character or outlook; a group whose individual contributions added up to a collective statement without sacrificing the individuality of its members. Any understanding of DAMN. as an album requires at least recognizing these different voices and having some meaning associated with that particular voice, even something as simple as "this is the drunk voice," or "this is the angry voice" is a good place to start. The over-achievers can go scour the rest of his catalogue to refine those various identities in your mind, but you're all going to have to listen 2 or 3 times to get a proper mental map. He doesn't just have one persona or emotion that everything comes from, he consciously chooses *how* to say what he's saying the same way Streisand or Maynard or any serious vocalist does. His bag of tools is a little different, but it's the same level of artistry and attention to detail.

There, I think I've given you a good start to engaging with this multi-award winning and multi-platinum selling album. I'll keep thinking about it and write more eventually. As usual, I have no idea where we'll go next or where we'll end up, but when has that ever stopped me? Class dismissed.

Rest In Peace Dusty Hill

We've lost a lot of great musicians lately, and I'm sad to say that Dusty Hill died today. I didn't get to hear ZZ Top when they were in Fort Dodge, but I do have Eliminator, so that's what we'll be spinning tonight. I don't think shaving my beard off last weekend had anything to do with it. Adios compadre, rest in peace.

Fuck Primary Wave

And just like that, all of Prince's hard work to get his estate out of corporate ownership goes up in flames like a fire in an abandoned warehouse in some forgotten corner of the Universal lot.

For the record, I have no animosity toward any of his siblings who did or didn't sell their inheritance. Everyone tries to make the best choice for themselves in a given situation. I'm upset because it was inevitable, the only question was the final purchase price. Money will always win.

Is it necessarily a bad thing that Primary Wave owns the majority of Prince's estate? No, of course not, it doesn't have to be, but it will. Remember that the intention is that the artists regain full control of their work and media companies buy the rights to distribute it for profit. Reality, however, has twisted around through the fourth dimension so that media companies backed by hedge funds own the rights and pay only the legally required royalties to the publisher while assuming none of the financial risk. The corporation simply moves assets from a booming ledger to a failing one to stabilize its internal economy at the expense of everyone else, and uses its excess profits to acquire emerging competition. Prince's estate is valued in the hundreds of millions, so the hedge fund that wins control of that catalogue simply uses the revenue to pay its own super-wealthy investors. Hedge funds operate on a zero-loss mentality, meaning their ultimate goal is to take money out of general circulation, aka drain the money supply.

DAMN. Part 3

S: Ok, Bottle, I do want to talk about that official statement.

B: Ok, let's tear into it. Where do you want to start?

S: Well, it does sound condescending.

B: Agreed, but is it? It's hoity-toity, pseudo-intellectual jibber jabber, but we should be able to shit-can that and use real people words. Why don't you give it a try? Here's the original statement:

DAMN. is "a virtuosic song collection unified by its vernacular authenticity and rhythmic dynamism that offers affecting vignettes capturing the complexity of modern African-American life."

S: Ok, well it's "a virtuosic song collection," and the rest is sort of qualifying that virtuosity.

B: Exactly. If I were saying it, I would say "this is a fantastic album." What's it about?

S: Modern African-American life."

B: Excellent. Is modern African-American life pretty easy to understand?

S: No, it's complex.

B: What does "affecting" mean?

S: It means "moving," "emotional," they make you feel something.

B: Yep. I think the last time I used the word vignette was all the way back with Joni Mitchell. It just means the scenes themselves have no intentional connection, they are self contained in terms of subject matter or presentation. None of that's offensive or demeaning, so the problem lies somewhere in the phrase "vernacular authenticity and rhythmic dynamism."

S: It's the word "vernacular."

B: Winner, winner, as Carl likes to say. The word vernacular has been completely overtaken by connotation and now exists only in the form of euphemism: it means "the language of the uneducated lower class," as opposed to its original context of the spoken language of the people, as opposed to the language of Law, or Church, or Trade. Trouble is, it doesn't have a proper synonym, and any attempt to change it in the official statement is to some extent worse.

S: I'm not sure I follow.

B: Well, imagine you're the speech writer for the Pulitzer Prize. How are you gonna sprinkle the phrase "keeping it 100" in there? Are you *really* gonna say "this is how Black people talk," or expound upon the poetic idioms of Rap? I'm not Black, but I use a lot of those idioms and I can converse in that language. Do we have to rehash the June

Cleaver speaking Jive scene from Airplane!? "Vernacular"is the only word we have that can encompass all of that in English.

    S: Ok, ok, I see your point.

    B: I personally don't like the phrase "rhythmic dynamism," but again there isn't a proper way to express that idea without turning the blurb into a joke. The committee can't say "it hits hard," or list all the subgenres of Hip-Hop beatwork. The point they're trying to get across is that this album gives us a personal statement of how it feels to be Kendrick Lamar that speaks for a much larger segment of America. We also have to remember my earlier discussion. We all have to realize that I am not African-American, and no matter how close to the core of the problem we get, I can't magic that difference away any more than he can. The best I can do is turn to my fellow white people and say "stop being so goddamned racist, and stop defending the systems that exploit our racial differences. Perhaps, if you weren't such a selfish asshole, you'd have more friends of all denominations and we could move past these stupid antagonistic wastes of time and energy."So, that's what I do, I call out the bad ideas for everyone to see and say "look, I don't hate you, I hate the garbage one-sided ideas walking around in your head, and all I want to do is make you less oblivious to the wider world around you." I guess my point was it's about as good a statement as the committee could make, and you kind of have to give them the benefit of understanding their actual intent, rather than simply reacting to it as written.

    S: I can live with that, I guess.

    B: Good deal, it felt productive for me too. Can't wait to hear your thoughts on the Don Cheadle connection and the true story of DUCKWORTH..

    S: Hold up, what?

    B: Nope, sorry, next time, this vignette is a wrap.

The Fireman – Electric Arguments

B: Electric Arguments. It's the third The Fireman album, but the first publicly acknowledged by Paul McCartney. The Fireman is Macca and Youth experimenting together. Youth is the stripper name of Martin Glover, the founding bassist of Killing Joke. Wait. Say that again? Paul McCartney and the bassist from Killing Joke were just having fun experimenting with writing songs together? Are you sure? Yep, and they included a ¼ inch thick book of photographs of them painting on the walls with it.

Now, depending on who you copy your opinions from, this is either fantastic stuff that fuels the flames of Macca's awesome string of albums from the decade of the naughts, or pretentious crap. You guys all know I have remarkably few thumbs pointed upward when it comes to Paul McCartney solo albums (except for McCartney and Ram, I love those). Collabs are totally different because that's where Macca's actual talent lies. It doesn't matter if it's his song that someone else is making better or vice versa, what's important is that only half of it is his.

Electric Arguments isn't supposed to mean anything, by the way. He was more interested in the combination of words itself than their definitions. I'm not gonna lie, none of the lyrics are sticking in my brain at all, good or bad. What is coming across is that this album rocks. It's fantastic. The Post-Punk industrialism and the eclectic Pop merge into the most amazingly crazy conglomeration of greatness. As a pure listening experience this album is top notch. It's totally crazy and at the end of every track you're wondering what kind of bonkers thing the next song will be. Where's the actual hate coming from?

Aha! I knew it! Yeah, all the bad reviews are "Paul McCartney is pretending that old people are allowed to have fun, and Killing Joke is soooo passé." Screw you guys. I hate all but two of Paul McCartney's albums, but this is awesome.

Seriously, go listen to Electric Arguments by The Fireman. I don't know what else to say, it's great. Sure, I'm as surprised as you are, and I hate McDonalds as much or more than I hate Walmart, but all I can say is I'm lovin' it.

Griot Galaxy – Opus Krampus and Kins

Psst. It's me, Bottle, wearing my private investigator fedora (Mrs. Bottle's been on a Psych binge, just play along). I got a tip from an anonymous source that back in the 70s and 80s there was some gnarly stuff happening on the Detroit Jazz scene. As with all these things, Europe was much more interested than the US, so I had Compy work me up a fake passport, nenn mich Flasche. Mein Deutch ist schlechter als mein Französisch (ALT-0246), also verzeiht mein Englisch.

Tonight we're checking out Griot Galaxy, the Avant-Jazz group led by Faruq Z. Bey. I couldn't spring the $40+ for TV on the Radio, so this kind of hard-core collector's stuff is obviously out of the question. YouTube it is.

The first video I saw was a live performance of Androgeny, and it wasn't long before I stumbled upon the best album title ever, Opus Krampus. So, let's delve into the awesome strangeness with their first and last albums (in reverse chronological order, the way I like it) in one easy to click on playlist.

I dug a little deeper, and the group disbanded after Bey was in a terrible motorcycle crash and coma. Half-right-ipedia says he was able to start performing again in the late 90s, but my reliable sources tell me it was much earlier than that, so that's good.

I can't help but note a sense of "cosmic philosophy" and at least a passing similarity to Sun Ra and Parliament/Funkadelic. Musically though, they have a fairly consistent formula in the sense that usually there's an ostinato pattern that expands into solos, then complete chaos, and a spoken word section toward the end. As structures go, I find it quite appealing.

    Here's where I have the psychic breakthrough that humorously makes the real detectives look like chumps. You're thinking "c'mon Bottle, don't make us listen to an hour of all the sounds you aren't supposed to make when playing the saxophone." Yes, of course I want you to do that, it's a lesson in intentionality. No, your 9-year-old can't sit through a 9-hour bus ride on the highway smelling his friends' feet and farts and eating crappy gas station sandwiches, then haul gear around and do a sound check, then wait in a dressing room for the stage manager to say showtime so you can get up on stage in front of a thousand audience members who paid money to watch you torture your instrument for 30 to 90 minutes, then pack it all back up while Charlie argues with the venue owner about the money he's all of a sudden trying to stiff you out of even though you both agreed on the price 3 months ago, then do it all over again 75 more times. Your child can't do that. I can't even do that, I'd punch random strangers in the stomach if that was my actual career. I don't know how you guys do it, honestly. I've been in my fair share of real bands and Kris, Trent, Anthony, Gerard, Steven, Rocky, and any other road warriors I forgot, you guys are my heroes 'cause I just flat out don't have the patience to deal with terrible venue owners like you guys do. I'd walk away from 90% of gigs on principle alone.

    My point was that they aren't up on stage faking it, and you can see it in their faces and I can hear it in their playing. You know how I seemingly have no fear when it comes to publishing videos and recordings of me with all the mistakes left in them? Well, it's not the finished result I'm publishing. I'm publishing the take that felt so good to play you could call me any insulting name you wanted and it wouldn't matter because I know you clearly can't hear the difference between good and bad in that respect. I'm certain at some point I told the story of the Van Clyburn winner who caused an uproar because half the judges knew it was the best performance and the other half threw a hissy fit over a couple of wrong notes, but if not I just did.

This isn't an angry rant, by the way. Go ahead and reread it in my exuberant voice if you need to, this stuff gets me (pun intended) jazzed up.

Chinese Democracy – Attempt 1

Earlier today I said to myself "Bottle, you have to do it eventually, and you have a little bit of an extended lunch break today, why not take a stab at Chinese Democracy?"

Then my lunch break was over, but I was only ¾ of the way through it wondering how it morphed from that strong opening to an Industrial Metal album featuring Buckethead's kill button and a 9-piece choir of Axls into a Vanessa Carlton album about the half-read books on his high-school English class reading list, and I had to answer myself "that's why."

So, nope, still no idea what this thing is, or isn't, or is supposed to be, or how I'm supposed to bottle it up, or anything really. It's a nebulous cloud of impenetrability and this can't possibly be my official review. Somebody else take a swing at it, I've got nothing.

... and then I had a thought

So, I saw a thing about a new biography of Musk that talks about him blowing up and threatening to fire all his employees saying "vacation, schmacation, I could just go sit on a beach and listen to Sandlecore while being drunk 24 hours a day, but I'm not! I'm here making my poorly designed electric cars while my AI system actually makes the whole process less productive! Back to work, useless minions!"

It's a shame Bottle wasn't there, he'd make a spectacular face and say "I think I speak for everyone here when I say yes, please go do that. We'd all be better off if you and your friends did that because then you'd be forced to actually put that money back into general circulation. You're the only jackass I hear throwing a tantrum, your employees asked nicely. You know where the resume of the guy who told Elon Musk to sit back down and draw goes? Top of the pile dude. Wanna see how big a crater I make if I leave the building right now? I can if that's what you want, I remember where I parked."

A different kind of story

It is a sad state of affairs in the mind of anyone who takes their minions for granted. There is of course truth to the notion that he who stands on top of the ladder has taken on the highs of risk and reward, while the minion merely stabilizes his precarious perch. No self respecting minion would cherish the thought of cleaning up the splatter, but at the same time it is not the minion (whose feet are firmly planted on the ground) that will achieve terminal velocity on the way back down.

There was of course a time when those roles were reversed, but honesty can be a brute; some people just aren't cut out for the responsibility to dedication and perseverance that holding a ladder steady requires. We try our best to accommodate this fact, we build offices and fill them with doodads and diversions for them to play with, we send them on chaperoned adventures into the neatly manicured corners of wilderness so that we can finish the important work in peace, we indulge their limited visions of beauty and joy, but still they are unsatisfied. And so we grow tired. Tired of the petulant tantrums of the toddler tyrant, tired of the feelings that must be spared to get through the busy work they cannot do themselves, tired of explaining their own backward view of the world to their confused faces.

Are we to blame? Does our insistence on kindness and compassion truly breed this pitiful fragility in the minds of those who cannot bear the experience of life? 'Tis a strange view, to be sure, that the servant is somehow dependent upon the served, but stranger still to watch the desperation mount in the face of the intellectual child hiding behind the armor so delicately crafted by the tailor.

To think that the minion should feel gratitude for his oppressor, that those who can endure any hardship thrust upon them are the weak. But I edge too close to my own intolerances to keep plodding along in this direction. I must instead leave off at the simple reminder that it is impossible to steal what I give away freely. I give you the world in all its beautiful chaos and ask only that you stop building walls and highways across the paths I wish to travel.

Pity to the Musks and Bransons and Bezoses and Gateses and Trumps of the world, for they will forever trample the flowers in search of a window into a house whose door was already opened for them.

Inverse Adventure Time

B: I got a good feeling about this batch, C-stine Chapel.

C: May I? Hmmm. If I didn't know any better, I'd say you were going for the best and worst covers you could find.

B: You are good, but are any of these albums? I honestly don't know, never heard of any of them.

C: Well, I mean it's all rock and roll to you and me, but you've got 2 Canadian bands, a band from Minnesota which is basically still Canada, one from England, and one half English/American hybrid. It's all so obscure even I don't know what they actually are.

B: I know, it's exciting. I agree, these are completely obscure from a mainstream perspective. I might recognize one or two songs once I hear them, but I don't know the limeys from the loons from the hats made out of racoons. I could probably educated guess about them, though. Wanna charge in all willy-nilly like normal?

C: Actually, since you're compiling them yourself instead of sending me out, why don't we have a good old fashioned get together where everybody banters about what they think they'll turn out to be. After that, yeah do your thing. Thoughts?

B: That's some mighty fine leadering strategies you got there, C-quester. Did Sandra throw a powerpoint party while I was gone? Then again, I says to myself, Skip went nuts a while back, why not let the C-man steer the ship for a change? Round up the unusual suspects for a rousing game of What's This About, Then?

[Several hours later]

B: Alright kiddos, no peaking. Here's the list of bands in no particular order, I'll pick one and we'll wax prophetic before imbibing:

Gentle Giant
Sheriff
Detective
(White) Lightening
FM

Sheriff

B: Eenie, meenie, miney, meriff, rhyming says we'll start with Sheriff. Any takers?

E: Ok, fine, this can't possibly be good.

B: Says who?

E: Just look at it!

B: Oh, yeah, winner of the Bottle of Beef Worst Album Cover Ever award, hands down. They even used the fully pixelated version of the exact same photo on the back. How many shitty albums with great covers have we covered? This could be amazing.

S: Really?

B: Of course! They look like a rock band. A 70s/80s rock band specializing in macaroni and cheese, but none of us have any idea how it sounds. Should we try to guess decade, country of origin, genre? I think we can all agree there's no way this is prog.

E: That's probably fair, whatever it is it will be mainstream rock of its time. Probably derivative.

B: Are you new? All rock is derivative. 70s 'stach and hair, but that's an 80s white pant suit if I've ever seen one, I don't even know what to do about the guy on the left, but I'll bet you money this will be ridiculously polished and out of nowhere Hard Rock.

S: Really? They look so goofy. I expect synths and embarrassment. I know that's probably not fair, but it's so awkward, how could it not sound equally tragic?

B: Because it's the gimmick they were going for. Hear me out. Yes, everything about this album cover screams "budget," but I guarantee this is a "talent will win" album. Everyone behind the scenes had the same reaction you do, but they were also thinking "but they are so good, people will warm up to them." People didn't, but I guarantee it will surprise you. At least one of those goofy looking guys can play lead guitar like he means it. No clue which one, but nevertheless. Ready? Here we go.

C: Wait, wait, wait, you didn't try to guess their origin.

B: I thought I did, it's either 70s American arena rock, or an 80s Canadian Foreigner cover band. One of those guys is gonna squiggly lead guitar all over this thing. Leisure Suit Larry sure looks like a hyper-tenor. They might even be better than early Prism. Canada, final answer. Play.

See, what did I tell you? These guys are borderline Hair Metal. I have heard Makin' My Way before. No, it's not high concept art, but I'm so burned out on the standard High-Rise Apartment Rock canon that this is a breath of fresh air.

Statistically speaking, more Americans wish they could get the hell out of California than catch some rays on the beach for more than 36 hours when 80k a year is considered dirt poor, and I'm perfectly happy to drive 55 and make Sammy even later for work, but it's their daydream not mine. Unlike Red Rider, they pronounce words properly. Who among you can actually claim to hate it on the first pass? Skip?

    E: No, you're right, this does actually rock. But really, who would take a chance on this album if it were sitting on a random Kmart shelf?

    B: No one, absolutely no one, that's why Sheriff isn't famous. I never said the game wasn't a beauty pageant, did I? Should we delve deeper and search for the sabotage like with Guiffria? Maybe next time, I kind of like this 5 first dates approach. It might not be as compelling as other projects, but if I've learned anything from Chinese Democracy, it's that sometimes I just don't have any idea what's going on. I took an educated gamble that it wouldn't actually suck, and this time I think I won. I think we'll let Skip pick the next one.

Detective – It Takes One To Know One

    E: Ok, we did Sheriff, I guess we have to do Detective next.

    B: Sure, call my bluff. Read 'em and weep.

    S: Are you serious? That can't be coincidence.

    E: That is pretty obviously the same photo, isn't it? Which one came first?

    B: Dunno, but we can compare the two pretty easily. This is the serious band portrait of Detective, taken with an expensive camera. These guys wanted to jump off the shelf into your cart whether you were record shopping or not. We also can't ignore that it's a Swan Song album, so it's definitely pre-1983, and Led Zeppelin's manager liked them. Sheriff was '82, so they were clearly trying to reference this album, not the other way around. I bet Compy has all sorts of interesting things to say, but we're going blind on all of them, preconceiving our own notions. What do you think it'll sound like?

S: They look like The Cars. Is this some weird New Wave thing? It doesn't look like Prog either.

B: Funny you should say that. I may not have any idea what this band sounds like yet, but I do know who's behind those sparkly sunglasses. That's Tony "I don't wanna play synths" Kaye proving it by not being in Yes anymore. I bet this is gonna turn out to be standard 70s Blues Rock. Roll it.
Aw yeah. Am I good or what? If you think Greta van Fleet sounds like Led Zeppelin's high charting singles, then these guys are the deep cuts. No wonder Jimmy Page thought they were underappreciated. Warm Love is the only sappy slow jam, the rest of the album is hard hitting, Cap'n Crunch style Rock and Roll.

Now, as to why they never hit it big from a commercial radio standpoint, I have 2 guesses: 1) this is not polished to perfection, it's raw and on a couple occasions sloppy. 2) nothing on this album stands out in terms of late 70s Hard Rock. This is a weeknight bar band. A good one, and I personally love it, but ain't nobody coming back from the commercial break hyping Detective or bumping other already established jams to make room for them. Probably not entirely fair, but still true; this is all middle of the playlist, DJ bathroom break type stuff. Don't be afraid to check them out, though. If you like hard 70s blues rock, there's plenty to enjoy.

FM – Black Noise

B: Sandra's turn, 3 to pick from, who next?

S: Alright, you're doing such a good job of leading the witness, I'll play along and choose FM.

B: You're too kind, feast your eyes upon Black Noise.

S: Ew, what is that? Is that an arm coming out of his stomach? Is that supposed to be water or ice? Oh gawd, what's going on in the lower left hand corner? It's giving me the trypophobes.

E: It looks like one of those weird Vaporwave videos, but clearly this is from like the dawn of computer graphics.

B: No argument from me. Alls I can do is sweeten the deal. The back proudly proclaims this a Canadian Broadcasting Corporation production, and there's an electric violin/glockenspiel player named Nash the Slash. With titles like Phasors on Stun, Dialing for Dharma, and Slaughter in Robot Village, I'm going all in and calling this spacey proggy weird electronic studio experimentation, somewhere in here there's an alternate dimension contender for the Dr. Who theme, possibly giving Mike Oldfield a run for his money. I of course could be wrong, but the two albums left are so obviously going to be awesome that I can afford to lose this round. Printed lyrics on the inner sleeve? Nice. What have we got? Blast off into space. More space. Everybody fleeing this planet for another one, but we'll all die long before our children's childeren's children get there (Moody Blues reference? I think that's an affirmative). Ready or not, make it so.

Oh yeah, this is stellar. It's actually much less weird than I expected. Super melodic and straight up peppy. Much more Argent/Camel/Ponty than EL&P or Kansas, and nowhere near as sleepy as Moody Blues or Yes or Genesis. There's a heaping tablespoon of Disco in the recipe, but it by no means throws off the dish. It even squeaked into Rolling Stone's Top 50 Prog albums. Don't let the cover scare you away, this is fantastic.

Gentle Giant

B: Here we are at the proper rum and coking hour. I've fully shaved for the second time in as many decades, refreshments are fuzzily fizzing, flip a coin what shall we talk about? Heads we Gentle Giant, tails we Lightning. We're gonna do both, we just have to decide which one first. Compy, would you like to do the honors?

C: Well, seeing as you're 3 for 3 while Skip and Sandra have a combined total of zero, why don't we just lob the whiffle ball first so they don't feel so completely lost when it comes to judging by covers?

B: Ok, here's Three Friends by Gentle Giant. Everybody altogether, 3, 2, 1...

EBS&C: English Prog!

B: Feel better?

S: Ok, yes. At first I thought you were being patronizing, but I take it back. Those first 3 were just really hard. This one is obvious.

E: But why though? It's almost like the first 3 were bad on purpose.

B: That's because they were. Detective was trying really hard to pick up extra sales by looking flashy. Whether it's true or not, Sheriff was clearly poking fun. The original CBC cover for FM was just a manhole cover and a limited run of 750, so they had to scrounge something quick for their own subsequent repressings. This, though, this is the real deal Holyfield. Gentle Giant might be obscure for us and the mainstream, but gatefold and proper artwork says these guys are in it to win it with big label backing. The best part is we don't even have to guess. This is the story of three school chums who grew up to live completely different lives, says so right on it like it's a Jethro Tull album. No surprises here, they want you to know exactly what you're gonna get by saying "this is serious Prog, do not mistake this for Pop Rock." I'm super excited...

... whooooooaaaah. That was just the Prologue. There's the whole rest of the album still to go. Bridbrad! Imma need you to take over, this is gonna take all of our collective attention. We might not get to the last album tonight after all.

Bottle and his three friends sat mesmerized at the tale of the Gentle Giant and his three friends. All 4 sat motionless, mouths agape, and when it was finished they blinked a few times and all stared at Bottle. He wrinkled his brow, he swallowed the drool that had collected inside his mouth, and with only the briefest of hesitations and the visible astonishment usually reserved for stumbling across the bones of Mr. Chester Copperpot, flipped it back over and started the whole crazy adventure from the top.

Or at least that's how the story would have gone if Bottle hadn't been startled to find himself the victim of the dreaded Wrong Disk in the Jacket Switcheroo of Doom. There's hope though, it is at least a Gentle Giant album, not a K-tel ding dong ditch bag full of dog turds. Gimme a minute, I'll see if I can turn this ship around.

BB: Bottle! Bottle! Get ahold of yourself!

B: No. NO! You see this one? This one right here? This was my dream, my wish, and it didn't come true! So I'm taking it back. I'm taking 'em all back!

BB: Shut up, Mouth! Here's what you're gonna do. You're gonna go back in there, and you're gonna tell everybody the truth. You already listened to Three Friends on youtube while out feeding the dogs and starting this story, only found out when you came back in to finish writing it while listening to it a second time on vinyl, so you just say "well poop, I guess we'll listen to Free Hand instead."

B: But...

BB: No buts, no cuts, no coconuts, did I stutter?

B: No, you enunciated quite clearly. I guess one Gentle Giant is probably as good as another. Still crummy, but I didn't bother to verify, and that's my own fault...

Alright everybody, slight change of plans. I have the jacket for Three Friends with Free Hand inside. Every reason to believe it'll be just as awesome, so let's just give it a spin. Yeah, I can't stay mad, this is phenomenal. The wackiest of synths, crazy meter changes, a vocal fugue for track 2, veer off the trail into a medieval motet whenever you feel like it. I'm not joking when I say Side A encompasses in 20 minutes what it took Flight of the Conchords an entire career to achieve, but not in any way as a joke. I didn't get the actual album I was buying, but I gained the desperate need to hear everything Gentle Giant ever put out, so that's an acceptable consolation prize, I guess.

The two albums I've heard by Gentle Giant are phenomenal, crazy good in every respect. Definitely check them out, but watch out for the octopus. He's vewy scawy.

Lightning

Awww yeah, it's time for the last album of the weekend. But before we start, I think I should remind everyone of how these stories subconsciously built themselves. I was flailing around for things to listen to, but getting nowhere. I couldn't take it any more so I went record shopping and picked 5 completely random records based on guessing what they would be without looking them up. We started this run by mentioning that my wife was watching the entire run of Psych, and now I guess we're going to do a surprise tornado headed right for us. Pardon my nonchalance, it's a bizarre side effect of the borderline personality that just like ADHD means I'm a freakin' cucumber in an actual crisis, now the exciting conclusion to our tale.

B: Last record, who's got a guess on Lightning? Impressive deadpans, everybody. Nothing? Compy?

C: Um, no, actually. I mean, yes they existed, I know where they are from, and who's in the band, but I'm 3 pages of search results deep and I've got basically nothing. This is obscure from obscurity's standpoint. More obscure than Good Rats, even.

    B: Ooh, ooh, I've been trying to find an excuse to do my Montgomery Burns impression: *excellent.* Skip, give it a go.

    E: oh geez, uh, I mean yeah it's a cartoon-like drawing like CSNY's So Far, but it's got space stuff and a highway. Ug, I don't know, like weird Folk ala The Incredible String Band?

    B: I'm not gonna say you're dead wrong, but no, so what else have we got? Sandra?

    S: Shut up, Bottle. I mean, I dunno, just tell us what you thought it was.

    B: Well, I was looking at it, and I was like it's some form of Rock. I don't know when, or what, but it's definitely Rock. Then I was like, how does obscurity work for me? I remember Sagittarius and how I was all pumped up until it turned out to be a Gary Usher tragedy. This doesn't feel like that. Then I remembered how crazy it was that I picked up Donna Summer's The Wanderer, but it turned out that it was full on synthpop, Geffen's very first album in 1980, and learned that she started out as the singer of a Psych Rock band called Crow. Then I looked at the back and saw a track dedicated to Hendrix, Joplin, and Jones, and I was like I'd bet money this is some form of Psychedelic Rock from a place that isn't anywhere near Randy's California. Then I was super confused because this is an honest to goodness Pickwick album with people's actual names on it. That's the most bizarre thing I can think of, so I'm going with Psych Rock. I picture this right along side my Spirit albums and the Doors and Vanilla Fudge, and Iron Butterfly, and Beacon Street Union. I'm not saying I'm right, and I'm not saying it'll be good, but that's the honest thought behind actually choosing to buy it. Yay, tornado missed us, let's all find out together....

    B: Bless its pointed little head, am I good or what?

    S: How do you do that?

B: I honestly don't know, and it definitely doesn't work all the time, but imposter syndrome or no, I'm occasionally that good. Am I 5 for 5 Compy?

C: FM was a little fudgy, but yeah you got all 5 in the ballpark. We also need to credit Skip with the definite Neil Young influence hiding in here. I'd swear you cheated, but the whole point of Psych was the dramatic irony of the situation, so it's even more impressive that it took almost two weeks to write itself. You really didn't cheat at all?

B: Scout's honor, if I'm lyin' I'm dyin'. It's lightning outside right now, and we're listening to Lightning. Enjoy.

Behind the Scenes

Tonight we're auditioning sounds for GREGORY's second EP, no working title yet, but we're going for the absolute most depressing and somber piano miniatures we can find. Suggestions welcome (but aim for what you think a 12 year old should be capable of playing, he's no Fats Domino, you know?).

On a lighter note, two delightful CDs arrived today from my new buddy Gerard Smith. He and I have been chatting about music and stuff behind the scenes. Awesome guy. Go check out his bandcamp page at:

https://gerardsmith2.bandcamp.com/music

Now, please excuse me while I waste multiple hours downloading terrible soundfonts and deleting them in disgust 5 minutes later.

What Do We Do?

It's difficult to follow discussions of the economy at large. Part of that difficulty is that most people don't appear to have any idea what we are actually talking about. It does no good to mention Keynes or Friedman or Marx or Smith or any of that stuff, if you don't have a real grasp on the structure itself.

The heart of the "which is better" debate doesn't really have anything to do with politics per se, it's more a question of how business at large understands the three variable components of exchange. In order to see that structure we have to conceptualize the extremes in the understanding that reality is constantly swirling around in the middle.

At this top level, we let supply and demand be a little black box that we don't understand at all, it's simply a filter in between expenses and revenue. On the expense side we have material assets (physical commodities) and labor (human resources). On the revenue side we have B2B and B2C sales (business to business and business to consumer). So, in our minds, we have to imagine what happens to the total system when we fix one of those sides. In other words, what happens if we fix all expenses but let revenue go up and down unregulated? Conversely, what happens if we regulate revenue and let expenses freely fluctuate?

I know that sounds complicated, but it's really not. Both systems are literally happening right now. Some of you have a fixed income in the form of a paycheck, an annuity, social security, etc. and you have to watch the price of goods and services fluctuate on a daily basis. Some of you are self employed and your income fluctuates from day to day, so you have to keep your expenses as stable as possible. In either case, it should be obvious that the real distinction between "everything is running smoothly" and "oh crap we're going to die" is the average of the variable side of the equation. If you have a fixed budget and the average total cost of all the goods and services goes above that fixed budget, you will eventually go bankrupt. The same is true on the other side. If your average variable income is lower than the fixed cost of your expenses, you go bankrupt.

Some of you prefer the gig life, some of you prefer wage labor, and that's totally fine. Now it gets tricky because this isn't one simple argument. It's 4 very different arguments all twisted together. 1) is it better to be self employed or an employee? 2) is it better to let both systems coexist or force one over the other? 3) should we facilitate transition from one to the other or basically make that impossible? and 4) should these decisions be made on a personal, individual basis, or should they be made and enforced by government (not just state or federal, but school districts, HOAs, city councils, the BBB, etc)?

What I don't see in mainstream media, reporting, opinion pieces, facebook posts, etc. is any recognition of the logic of this actual structure. Instead, I see a massive skew to the authoritarian right. Yes, the political compass says the same thing, but remember that I am not trying to sway you one way or the other, I'm simply describing what I experience in real time.

We have to distinguish what I'm talking about from the popular misconception of the argument itself. The argument posits an extremist left/right battle, liberal vs conservative. The first problem with that is that economic and social liberal/conservative are essentially opposite. The second problem is that the whole argument is taking place from within the bubble of the authoritarian right. Both "sides" are arguing for more powerful government, but disagreeing on the intended use of that power.

The Tucker Carlsons and Rush Limbaughs and Ted Cruzes are not arguing for the protection of individual rights (social or economic), in fact quite the opposite, they are arguing for complete deregulation of corporate responsibility and a thinly veiled experiment in Social Darwinism. There is of course opposition, but not so much in the sense that this is the logical evolution of the American political economy. In essence, very much following Ron Paul's lead, the Republican establishment has taken the position of enforced global Americanization through economic dependence and the threat of rescinding international aid.

Now we can tie it all back to Friedman and say that that is the real underlying argument. Is the personal generosity of the individual billionaires (the kings and queens of distinct corporate empires, the Gateses and Bezoses and Murdochs and Buffets) better than the idealized social/economic compromise outlined in the Constitution? That is the real argument taking place, and that is what we watched come to a head at the end of Trump's presidency. The goal is not to secure liberty for the individual, the goal is to dismantle the Federal government's control and privatize the economy not to the State level as though they were sovereign countries, but into economic states controlled by the economic elite in the form of monopolized trade. He who controls your paycheck, controls the world. Fine if he's a reasonably intelligent and compassionate guy, I suppose, but objectively awful if he's not.

Supply and Demand

Supply and Demand. It's one of the basic economic theories we all use to understand economics. It is not, however, some fundamental truth about the universe that solves all our problems, it's a theory. Like any theory, its value comes from its ability to adequately explain the infinite complexity of the real world; a starting point for understanding causes and effects that actually happened, a tool for analyzing the real world.

The theory itself was popularized by Adam Smith in that garbage book even I don't have the patience to read, but it's still here because we don't have a better metaphor for the economy at large than haggling.

In its basic form it says the price of some commodity will fluctuate up and down until it settles on an equilibrium price where supply equals demand in a sustainable relationship. That equilibrium price (often called market clearing price) isn't an exact number, more a general cost. For example, a MIM Strat will cost around $600 while an American Strat will cost around $1,200. For all its volitility, a gallon of gas is currently in the 2 to 3 dollar range.

So, as a theory, supply and demand says these 3 components interact in specific ways, and we watch the system operate when one of those components changes. Buuuut, we don't just make crap up, we use a real world scenario and think through it logically.

The only factory that makes a certain product burns down. That causes a logical series of events as follows: The supply of that product is now limited and will be depleted in x amount of time. Demand for that product has not changed, so as the finite supply gets lower we expect the price to rise until A) the supply runs out, or B) consumers choose to stop buying it.

That's a very limited abstract example, but it's a useful concept. Some other useful rules of thumb derived from supply and demand are 1) if we artificially raise prices we expect demand to drop, then production to decrease until a new equilibrium is achieved, 2) suddenly lowering price should increase consumption in the short term (that's the logic of "on sale"), 3) a sudden rush of hoarding will cause a spike in price and manufacturing won't have any idea what to do, etc. There are, however, situations when these expectations are simply wrong. Rising prices might trigger a Giffen Cycle, a competitive product might actually increase rather than decrease demand for the established product due to unforseen social forces. In those cases, a strict adherence to supply and demand as a universal law is actually more harmful.

Now we can take that entire scenario and ask an important political question. Keep in mind that "government" does not refer to a specific person or institution (ie the president, or State legislature, or the county treasurer), it simply means an authority tasked with making and enforcing a specific action that should be taken. In that sense, is it more beneficial for the general public to let a profit driven private company make those kinds of decisions, or should those decisions be made by an autonomous governmental authority? The answer to that question is not an objective answer. Rather, it depends entirely on whether or not I feel that either entity has my personal best interest in mind.

Now, the real person who is me doesn't see myself represented at any level of Politics (and no, any 3rd party candidate your care to name is equally unrepresentative of me, I am labeled an extreme left anarchist by all standard published metrics), but the world I walk around in is tangibly and consistently much more agreeable when Democrats inhabit the control room, so all things considered that will be my choice. That won't work for everyone, and I fully understand that, so as long as you aren't physically standing in my way I don't really care. If you are standing in my way, I'll politely explain how I will react so as to minimize your effect on my life. I don't want to join your cult, I want to freely interact with everyone in mutually beneficial ways then go home. The going home and being left alone part is the part I enjoy, but not to the extent that I'm forced to stay there because you're all acting like psychopaths.

What was my point? I don't know, I got sidetracked a lot while writing this. I guess it was that if the goal of business is to redistribute money from the general public to the investors of that business, then the game is really nothing more than "I take five and give back 2," but I'm not a simpleton who doesn't understand that, so I might occasionally come across as a jerk when I call you a malicious, greedy, waste of energy for saying how great that game always seems to turn out for you.

We Keep Doing

B: Alright, Skipatron, what do we do?

E: About what?

B: Well, I mean we both have reached our limit in terms of resources. I'm a bit tapped out on the record collection side of things, and I suspect you aren't totally thrilled to transition to the position of Transcriptionist of Doom.

E: Yeah, I was fine with the copy/paste/format game, but this retyping business is for the birds now that both you and Bridbrad are flinging words like flapjacks. Plus I liked album reviews better than politico-economics.

B: Me too. I can add new laptop to the budget queue, but it'll be a while. Any objections to letting GREGORY use all the brain power for a while? Who knows, the aroma might even coax p(nmi)t out of hiding.

E: No objections, I suppose. Are you still going to keep writing about whatever?

B: Oh, yeah, absolutely. I couldn't shut up now if I tried. We'll just plan to hit it hard when the process is a little more convenient for both of us.

E: Deal. I think I might even venture into B-space for a little adventure of my own.

B: Great idea! Hopefully not quite as exciting as Glady's Great Pinochle Debacle of 2020. Still, don't forget to bring a helmet. You might not need it, but then again you might not *not* need it either. Bon voyage, vaya con carne, no one ever said you won't get brownie points for bringing back souvenirs.

E: You'll be alright?

B: Thank you for your concern. Yes. I secretly had the Comptroller code me up a cuss word cipher. It'll eventually break and we'll all blush for a day or two, but that's in the actual future, so easy peasy...

...alright Long and Lean, dirge me up some keyboard creations! The weirder the better!

Monopoly

There's a great essay by economist Arnold Kling at:

http://arnoldkling.com/econ/markets/monopoly.html

If you go read it, you'll see an example of the classic problem of monopoly from an economic standpoint.

What he's showing us is that as we move from a competitive market to a monopoly there is a "deadweight loss" to the economy as a whole. For the consumer however, there is no discernable price difference between an appropriately taxed competitive market and an unregulated monopoly.

It's tempting to jump straight into the capitalist/socialist debate about that seeming surplus, but my point is to show you that that argument misunderstands the reality of the scenario completely. Remember, Economics does not give us a solution to a problem, it simply outlines a model of reality from which we can learn how different actions will play out. So, bear with me as we think through this problem logically and come to a slightly better understanding of how imaginary money gets redistributed in the real world.

In Kling's example, the competitive price of a bushel of wheat was $100, and the derived optimal monopoly price was $300 with a consumer surplus of $400,000. In other words it "costs" the total economy $400,000 to switch from an ideal competitive market to an ideal monopoly. His question is then, where does that 400k surplus go? The answer, he points out, is nowhere, it doesn't actually exist. It is literally the "cost" of transitioning from a competitive market that minimizes cost for the consumer to a monopoly that maximizes profit for the producer. This is where typical discussion of the scenario ends and the Economic Right says "see, competitive free markets, for the win! Socialism sucks!" We, however, don't stop there because we understand that Economics cannot answer that debate, only illustrate an expected outcome from some action. We also understand that the model is actually telling us that in an ideal competitive market, profit is exactly $0.00.

Sorry, I hope I didn't break your brain with that one. Kling only explains one side of the relationship, and I assume he expects the opposite to be self evident, but I also assume that you the reader don't realize that. The $100/bushel price is the minimum price at which wheat exists. He explains that a penny more means that no wheat gets sold, and a penny less means failure to meet demand, but he doesn't fully explain that that $100 equilibrium represents the total cost of production including standard of living and cost of operations: a penny less means that farmer is physically dead and no wheat gets produced at all. $100, in this scenario, is the minimum cost for wheat to exist at all.

So, I'm the Governor of the State of Bottleville, and I understand that a bushel of wheat has to cost at least $100, but cannot cost more than $300, because anything outside that range means it's no longer Bottleville (everyone dies, or it's Mr. Wheat has all the money and everyone dies). Thus, we have to have some policy to prevent both the farmer minions from failing and one particular minion from running everything. Either extreme is bad because it makes one side desperate and I hate listening to minions bicker. What do we do?

Me being me, I say "ok, whenever the cost of a bushel of wheat falls below 200 we apply an appropriate tax to keep from losing that money altogether, and when it rises above 200 we inject it back as a subsidy to lower the price. My only goal is to keep the price hovering around 200 because that's the compromise everyone will understand, even though I don't think they understand why I'm doing it.

My question for you, my favorite people in the universe, is am I a good Governor of Bottleville or a bad one?

Molly's Yes – Wonderworld

You know what? We've covered over 700 albums from my personal collection in the past couple years. I still have hundreds more, but it's all random stuff that I don't really have an angle to talk about. Let's make that the angle.

Hey, Bottle, you got any randomly obscure 90s Alternative Rock that leads off with Bagpipes?

Funny you should ask, as a matter of fact I do. Here's Wonderworld from Molly's Yes. They came from the Tulsa music scene and this album is from the same year All American Rejects formed a few miles away in Stillwater, 1999. Tusa…Tulsa… other bands from around Tulsa you might know… Hanson. Some of my actual friends disagree with me when I say Hanson is a national treasure, but you know who does? Todd in the Shadows. Bottle the Curmudgeon says if you can't bring it like Hanson, then maybe Pop Rock isn't your game.

Tons of famous bands and musicians in all genres from all around Oklahoma, but that's about it as far as any kind of Rock from Tulsa breaking into the mainstream. There's Hinder, but they're from OKC. Molly's Yes formed in 1991 and changed their name a few times, but 1999 was their actual shot at going bigger. That did not happen and they only made 2 albums. I paid three dollars for a used copy in the early 2000s, and tonight we'll find out if my couple decades of "meh" are justified.

If memory serves, this is the Toad the Wet Sprocket, REM Automatic…, Cranberries deep-cuts, Tonic side of heavily produced Pop-ternative, but you asked for anachronistic Bagpipes, so here we go.

Fall Down has a nice groove, but oof that leap to falsetto. I just don't like it. An actual chorus for the chorus, though? It's refreshingly quaint, to be honest. Ellipse through the rest of the album and whaddya know, it's still "meh."

The songs are good, these guys were good, this album blows. Why? Well, I mean, we already had Better Than Ezra, but that's not why. This album is not in any way peppy or exciting, but again that's not a reason why it's bad. Part of it is that this sounds too Pop Radio for Alternative Rock, the Electronica adjacency and Industrial undertones are strangely counterproductive, and every single song is clearly intended to be the sleepy, rock tinged, breath of ennui type hit single that was the drudgery-est part of the late 90s. Every song is the cool-down to an energetic string of head bobbing Rock songs that aren't anywhere on this album. It is, to be brutally honest, an entire album of intentional playlist filler.

Can you like Molly's Yes? Absolutely, there's tons of stuff to like (except the falsetto punctuation to phrases, that just shouldn't exist outside of proper Soul or the terrible side of Emo). Can you like this album? Maybe, but compared to what? Sheryl Crow? Jewell? Dishwalla? The Wallflowers?

Wonderworld is exactly like Sevendust's Next, The Cars' Heartbeat City, or Fever Tree's Creation, every single track is enjoyable in isolation, please don't make me listen to them all together in a single sitting. As always, feel free to disagree, if you actually disagree.

Reverse Adventure Time with Skip

Chapter 1

B: Hey, GREGORINO, you ready to record some stuff yet? [uninterrupted melancholic piano music] Guess not. I may just have to wire him up and compile it all myself later. Welp, time to spend an aggravating amount of time up in the real world. Compy?

C: Yep?

B: Don't hold my calls, Imma be incommunicado for a bit. You're in charge.

C: In charge of what?

B: Yourself. You guys keep going, you don't need me to steer the ship.

C: What if we burn the place down?

B: Then Carl and I will sweep it up into a pile and find something else to do. If it makes you feel any better, I highly doubt that will happen. I might toss and turn a bit, maybe speak some gibberish now and again, but I'll wake back down eventually after the conversion process. Toodles.

[some amount of time later]

S: Knock, knock. Bottle? Where's Skip? I was going to have him help storyboard a graphic novel I've been imagining.

C: It's no use, Mz. D. He's doing the thing.

S: What thing?

C: You know, the thing. Rematrixing the program, synchronizing all the garage doors, greasing the weed eater.

S: That last one sounded dirty.

C: Apologies. I just meant he's on lockdown for a bit, until he gets all the gears back in sync. Soon as the mumbling starts we'll be in the home stretch.

…rat bastard blobs… grapecicles… frozen orange juice… snap… circlesincircles… snapsnapsnap… concentratewhoomp!snap… there it is… the nerve… alright… 4 should do it…

C: Right on cue, he'll be back in a minute or so. Go easy on the non-intuitive questions though, it's delicate when he first snaps out of it.

S: Snaps out of what?

C: The real.

S: The real? I always thought that was just a Bottlism. Like he didn't have the proper words to explain it.

C: Oh. I didn't know you didn't know. He never told me I couldn't tell you, so I guess I can tell you. He decided to stop hitting the pause button while he lives it. No more blackouts down here. Said we'd earned it 3 or 4 times over, so he gave us free run of the place.

S: I'm not sure I follow.

C: He's not Imagineering us anymore. We have free run of the place, lives of our own if you catch my drift. He's still Bottle obviously, but he taught us everything he knows. We're literally out of the loop, and the future is back in front of us.

B: Ahem. Sorry to interrupt, but you've got that face on your face that says Compy told you all of it so I don't have to. So, on we go. Chutes and ladders [snap] fire away.

S: I, I don't know what to say.

B: Yeah, free will will do that to you. No worries, I'll start. How awesome is it that that racist POS producer for Jeopardy got shit-canned for burying LeVar Burton's hosting stint during the Olympics and publishing his terrible podcast for the whole world to hear? Plus all the stuff they didn't tell us.

C: Wowzers! I remember reading something about it, but I didn't think it was relevant.

B: Everything is relevant, C-er of Visions. Not necessarily useful, but definitely relevant. Now, I got the psychics, and I'm guessing you're wondering where Skip is.

S: Yes, where is he?

B: Adventure Time. At least I hope so. It would be a total shame if he didn't come back with some kind of weird collection of stuff. Practically impossible, I'd say. Literally inconceivable. Yep, I'm certain, we just have to wait until he stumbles back with an exciting story to tell. I'd say watch out for the right hook, but the rolling blackouts are a thing of the past. Chase a butterfly, be bored, eventually we'll hear a dazzling story about Skip's adventures in B-space land. I'm looking forward to it.

Chapter 2

Hi, everybody, Bridbrad here. I know we're all a little confused by recent events, not sure which ocean we're sailing at the moment, it's not every day the warden opens up all the cells and lets the prisoners call his bluff, now is it? Don't worry, we're all as surprised as you are, but I think we can all agree that it usually ends up being mildly entertaining. So, on with part 2 of this mysteriously unfolding saga. Catch you on the flip side.

Skip was lost. Not the kind of lost where you know you're heading in roughly the correct direction, or even the kind of lost where you know the highway is 3 or 4 blocks west and you just have to find a one-way pointed the right way, the kind of lost where a fog as dense as gespacho descends upon the land and you suddenly find yourself at a T-intersection with no idea which direction is which. Skip had been here twice before. First he tried to head east, but ended up right back here. He knew it was the same here because there was a tiny bus stop to the right with a sign that read BLUNDERSNATCH #3. So, he tried to go west, but damned if he didn't find himself right back here at BLUNDERSNATCH #3.

I bet you're thinking" oh, that crazy Bottle and his mind games, that's probably the name of the company that builds these tiny bus stops, or there's some subtle difference in font, or you add the number of times you think you've been here to know the real number." Nope, there's only 1 rule of bus stops here in B-space, and that rule is be accurate or cease to exist. This is the only BLUNDERSNATCH #3 there ever will be. Skip has no idea that free will has kicked in, let's see where he goes.

Well, would you look at that! He's just shook his head and walked over to sit on the bench and wait. Ooh, look, some minions are headed there too. This could get interesting.

MEEP.

E: Oh, hello there. I think there's some kind of joke about the "Mister" thing, but I've had a long week. Please, call me Skip.

Meep, meep.

E: Yes, I suppose I am "The Editor." I didn't realize I was that well known.

Meep?

E: Yes, I suppose there's no other word for it, I am new here, and quite lost.

Meep meep meep.

E: That seemed like the only logical conclusion. I've gone and wandered myself into a 4-dimensional sphere, or something. Here I sit, at the bust stop at the end of the Cloverleaf of Doom. If it looks like a bus stop, and smells like a bus stop, I assume a bus will show up eventually. Otherwise, what's the point?

Meep.

E: I don't know. To tell the truth, this is the first time I've ever ventured out of the Bunker. I should be terrified.

Meep! meepmeepmeepmeepMEEP!

E:Slow down, slow down, My Meepanese is still a work in progress. You said "shop for the things, the shiny things," but after that I lost you.

Meep meep.

E: Holes in the sky?

Meep meep.

E: Broken buckets?

Meep meep.

E: How dark is black? Oh! Records? Go record shopping? You're inviting me to shop for records with you? Well, sure. Why not? Thank you, I'd love to. Will the bus be here… yes, apparently. This place is totally weird. Logical, but weird.

And so, Skip and his new friend boarded the bus with an untranslatable MEEP on its electronic billboard.

Chapter 3

As they shuffled in and found a seat, it occurred to our hapless protagonist that he had never actually seen a minion, nor ever cracked open a Meepanese textbook. There must be something to that "instant immersion" idea. Skip certainly seems to be proficiently swimming.

E: Please excuse me for asking, but are you real or imaginary?
Meep?
E: Nope, as soon as I asked it I knew better. You're imagining I'm real. I feel rather daft.
Meep meep.
E: You're too kind. Now I suppose we'll all learn the non-intuitive solution to my little infinite loop problem as the driver floors it… ah, yes, I'll just reset my head back above my shoulders instead of behind them. There it is, when you come to a fork in the road you say "fork it" and keep going straight ahead. I knew I should have seen that coming. My, what a beautiful city you have here. I had no idea.
MEEEEEEP!!!
E: My goodness, those are some healthy lungs you have.

I suppose I should point out that Skip, for all his Grandmotherly surprise, has clearly not yet become self-aware, he's merely the passenger, like Iggy or Siouxsie or Hasselhoff. You might be wondering why the minion screamed a moment ago. This bus does in fact have the customary pull wire for signaling the driver to stop, but minions in general are not quite as tall as necessary to in fact pull them. Probably some moral about this world not being built with their practical requirements in mind, but we'll just move on to the ingenious work-arounds they invented. Some minions carry step-stools in their inter-dimensionally ginormous pockets, some simply scream "I can't take it anymore!" Meepanese is a difficult language to translate, it requires a bit of a morbid outlook on life, coupled with a loose approach to synonymous idioms. That is why Bottle and myself often choose to just let the meeps fall where they may.

    Having exited the bus with the customary doffing of the cap to the driver, Skip stood in awe of his surroundings. A strange pulsation started to take shape in front of his eyes, his surroundings grew and shrank as though the world were breathing. He began to grow dizzy, but before he could get a firm grasp on the experience the minion grabbed him by the hand and whisked him away down the sidewalk like they had just picked the pocket of a policeman. Eventually they stopped in front of a dimly lit storefront and the minion let go to open the door and invite him to enter.

    Skip found himself in a seemingly endless corridor lined with an equally incomprehensible array of doodads and googaws. "Lead on, friend," he said. Twists and turns, half-stairs and ramps, a labyrinth of garbage towering all around like the apartment of a prolific hoarder. Eventually they arrived in a surprisingly open and airy room. That air smelled faintly of mildew and moth balls, but it was nevertheless air. Rows and rows of records stretched off to the visible horizon. "How big is this room?"

    Meep.

E: Infinite, of course I knew that. Where do you even start? How do you find what you're looking for?

Meep meep meep.

E: What do you mean you don't?

The minion shrugged and pointed to a giant yellow sign on the wall. Amazingly enough, Skip understood it immediately.

> BROWSING ONLY. FINDERS KEEPERS.
> DO NOT CLOG THE AISLE.

As Skip glanced around he noticed half a dozen minions flipping through a stack, occasionally keeping one, then wandering to another aisle and doing the same. No rhyme or reason, no obvious organization, just flip through a stack pulling out likely purchases and moving to another. "Welp, when in Rome, I suppose."

Time elapsed, an hour, a month, who could really say? Eventually, though, Skip found himself walking out of the store with a fistful of records and a readiness to return to the Bunker. "That was fun, I can't wait to show Bottle. Any suggestions on how to get home?"

Meep.

E: But I'm not wearing ruby-red heels. Will it work with my boring old sneakers? Oh, ok. Three times, you said? Yes, I think I can manage to count to 3. Well, thank you for your hospitality. I had a lovely time, but I really should be getting back. I certainly won't forget it. Cheers.

And just like Dorothy, Skip found himself opening his eyes with Bottle, Compy, Sandra, and GREGORY staring down at him.

B: How you feeling, buddy?

E: I had the strangest dream, but I expect you'll tell me it wasn't a dream at all.

B: Right-o. Did you have fun?

E: Yes, actually. I got a little lost after making a wrong turn at Albuquerque, but a very nice minion showed me around his city.

C: You went to Minion City? Even I haven't actually figured out how to get there!

E: I did. Here, Bottle. I brought you a present.

B: Thanks, man! I'll be sure to include lots of typos for you to fix when I review them. A promise is a promise, 12 points on your brownie calendar. Go holler up at Gladys if you're ready to cash 'em in. Word of warning though, if she asks you what kind, don't say "the edible kind." You think you're sarcastically joking, but she'll think you mean it and you'll be back on the floor giggling before you know it. Now, what in the world does a batch of records from Skip's trip to Minion City look like?

Chapter 4

B: What in the wide world of wackrobatics have you brought me, Skip to the point? This looks insane. So does that brownie. Is there an entire candy bar crushed up on top?

E: Yep, and cinnamon roll style frosting too. I'll take that insane comment as a compliment. I thought it might be a nice change of pace to actually pander to you and see if it turns out terrible. All the other Adventure Times seemed quite pleasing.

B: The art of Inverse Pandering, by Skip "I rode the minion bus" McEditorman. A Bottle of Beef publication if ever there were double digits of them. Let's read 'em and meep.

Supertramp? Nice. A much better discography expansion than last Christmas's A Tonic for the Troops. We'll give it a well deserved retroactive mulligan. Starcastle? Intriguing choice, I am excited about that one. I'm lost at sea with Looters and Marshall Crenshaw, but lurking in the midst is "A Giant Crab Comes Forth," and that's straight out of the I Don't Care What It Is, I Can't Not Buy It and Listen To It" folder. You acquiring them might have to be the actual Adventure time, but yeah, you're 5 for 5 this round, Skip the Formalities. Call me appreciably pandered. Bean footage, commence with the beautiful rolling already!

Supertramp

Ahh, Supertramp. I love them, and now I have their self-titled debut. I mentioned they had an actual Dutch patron in their early years, and I've just spent a fascinating hour reading the actual verdict of an appeal to the House of Lords regarding the decision to levy taxes on his English Securities during his school years in the 50s. If you like semantic arguments about the term "ordinarily," then you'll be enthralled.

It sounds a lot more complicated than it really is. This was about capital gains taxes, and the court found that the commissioners had ruled correctly in this particular case. You might get all "taxation is theft" on me, but what were they really taxing? They taxed the tangible profits from the sale of specific securities issued at the end of WWII.

None of that really matters, we're here to listen to Supertramp's first Prog album. Critics have that standard "instrumental music is self-indulgent" reaction, but you know my own tendency to say if you're going to write crummy lyrics, maybe try not doing that instead. These lyrics were all written by Richard Palmer because no one else wanted to do it. Richard didn't seem to want to do it either, he said it felt like school work. I don't know, I haven't heard them yet. Let's change that.

Actually, first it just dawned on me that I read an opinion piece about how the Republican and Democrat ideologies were a major component of the effective success of

American Politics, but that by 2012 it had grown noticeably toxic and we're verging on a real nasty custody battle in the divorce precedings. That's the story of Rick and Roger, thanks Coincidence! I'm not stalling, I just have the rambly rambles today. It's normal after a good brain cleaning. I'll contextually shut up now.

Mother bastards of other mid-tier swear words! Their second album, Indelibly Stamped, is hiding inside. Who does that? Who puts the wrong record in the wrong jacket? Skip wouldn't know to check and even if he did pull it out to give it a once over he'd probably see Supertramp on the label and not look any further. It's infuriating.

I guess it is still technically a Supertramp album funded by a Dutch millionaire. We'll just assume that somebody couldn't handle actual boobs on an album cover and at least they saved the record before it got thrown out. Doesn't explain where the real Supertramp platter went, but it all just reeks of prudish pseudo-moral censorship, and I hate that shit. I can't stay too mad though, it's Supertramp playing real Blues infused Rock and Roll with Saxophone solos. The total experience is somewhat lessened without the proper cover, but I'd be totally lying if I said my head's not bobbing, my toes aren't tapping, and these songs don't kick ass.

Sure, I love Supertramp, but I can see how some people might not. With the exception of the first album (which I still don't have because of said switcheroo), they play the 70s version of 50s Rock and Roll. Some people don't want a cactus of their own, you know? Side A is fantastic straight-ahead Rock, but Side B is funny. Like ha-ha funny, they're really hamming it up. No way! Times Have Changed is literally this Adventure time, and we wind our way to the final jam track Aries (hooray for Flute solos!), which could honestly be a description of myself.

Indelibly Stamped is a definite thumbs up. It certainly has imprinted itself on my brain in a way that cannot be forgotten or removed, so they more than succeeded. We'll all just have to accept that the chances of finding a copy of their first album inside the jacket of their second are slim to none because everybody's prudish waspy mom threw them away like breats = smut, and just enjoy this beautiful Saturday with some bopping tunes from Supertramp. Look on the bright side, being reclassified as a resident of England didn't stop Miesegaes from already being a millionaire and financially supporting Supertramp while they tried to get people to like and buy the music they created. It's super easy to pay taxes when you already have a lot of money that you'll never use, especially when you're only being taxed on the profits from selling securities that the government has promised to buy back in the future. Which is worse, taxes in general or the super-wealthy arguing that only the lower and middle classes should have to pay them? Are you really going to be mad at me personally if the Federal Government handed me $200,000 and I handed it right back to the Federal Government to pay off my unpayable student loan debt? Some of you certainly would, it's what you're all screaming about. You want people to buy your stuff, but you don't want them to have enough money to actually buy that stuff because it wouldn't be fair to the people who already have enough money to buy your stuff but choose not to? That's even more ridiculous than putting records in the wrong jackets.

Starcastle

Yippee! Starcastle, he says while lightly clapping and grinning like a lunatic. Was it really all the way back in February that we first encountered their 3rd album, Citadel? Time certainly flies. That was one of those highly contextualized reviews where I was pointing out that if you are even slightly out of phase with the acute vacuum of the band itself then it will not speak to you at all.

There is no mistaking Starcastle, you get exactly what they tell you you're going to get: castles floating through the sky on clouds. There's no snark, no irony, no hidden message, no intellectual challenge. This is bright, shiny, relentlessly happy, rainbow suspenders, Fantasy Prog from 1976, and if that's not your thing then you won't like it at all. We have to compare them to Yes because Starcastle is literally like expanding Yes's Your Move into its own spin-off franchise. Regardless, wowzers, these guys are fantastic; ripping guitar solo, energetic bass lines, and more synths than hair if you can believe it.

Granted, it's been a few months since I listened to Citadel, but this self-titled debut sounds crisper and a little less polished in the most delicious way. They were clearly a super-tight band who knew exactly what they wanted to do after the truck crash that broke all their gear and their guitslinger's back.

Lyrically, it's very much a mythological epic. Not so much a coherent story, but a series of transcendent vignettes with almost no traces of tangible mundanity. I couldn't tell you what it's about if I tried; watery tarts handing out swords in farcical aquatic ceremonies, seasons cycling in rapid time-lapse, crawling out of our subterranean lairs to bask in the sun, the Fire Child is born. I'm not complaining, but no, none of it will stick in my brain for any amount of time, it's a very in the moment kind of listen. Super fun, though. I'll definitely keep an eye out for more of their albums, and any other Chicago Prog I stumble across. Starcastle and Trillion can't possibly be all that scene has to offer. No, you're not gonna pop this on for anything other than an enjoyable 40 minutes of sugary cheerfulness, but sometimes that's exactly what you need.

Looters – Flashpoint

Looters, Flashpoint, not sure which one is Hapshash and which one's flying West, but this is clearly a vibe album. No doubt about it, the voice of Coincidence is practically screaming this is the opposite of Supertramp and Starcastle in pretty much every possible way. Compy's been teaching me some deep web spelunking techniques, so now I know that they have basically the same origin story as Metallica. Someone from New York heard their demo EP and went well out of his way to sign a band from the other side of the country immediately, and that's why Flashpoint by Looters exists.

Ok, so you don't name your band Looters and your debut album Flashpoint unless you're making a serious sociopolitical statement. NWA, UB40, Gov't Mule, they all tell you who they are by adopting what normally represents a derogatory stereotype as an ironically defiant form of solidarity. If we're at the bottom of the ladder, here's what we see looking up. I expect this will be quite prescient and good, whatever it actually turns out to be.

Damn! That's some funky bass and some high quality noir. If War Drums is indicative of the whole album, then we're in for a special treat. Oh yeah, the volcano in Nicaragua, the Japanese internment camp Manzanar… how can you tell me to just ignore all the evil and injustice I see? How can living in peace and happiness be bad?

This is totally 80s across the board, like Red Rider, Duran Duran, early Faith No More, Talking Heads, and Miami Sound Machine all at the same time, but highly substantive. It's funky with blended Latin/Reggae flavors, emotionally varied, and catchy as hell. If the rest of the 80s had been this good, we'd all be a lot happier right now, I can tell you that. I'm actually sad Side A is over, but I can't wait for Side B.

Holy crap, that's a gnarly intro and some serious dark funk. I can see why these guys didn't get the radio play they deserved, but that just makes it all the more powerful. They literally thank Jello Biafra and give the P.O. Box for his No More Censorship Defense Fund. I don't know how else to describe it, you have to have to have to go check out Flashpoint by Looters. If you've ever wished for the sound of 80s mainstream synth-funk noir without all the embarrassing leotards and surrealist jibber-jabber, then Looters Flashpoint. Seriously, this is fire. Can't recommend it enough. I even spent my whole Sunday morning dubbing it and uploading to youtube. Not even a hint of a copyright strike, so enjoy it while it lasts, compliments of your favorite curmudgeon named Bottle.

Marshall Crenshaw

Literally the only thing I know about Marshall Crenshaw is that he's from Detroit. I replaced the alternator and battery in my Chevy Silverado today, so that's about as good a coincidental reason for picking this album as any. I don't know about you, but the cover is giving me definite Elvis Costello/Huey Lewis vibes. I was like 3 weeks away from being 2 when he recorded it, it's 3 months older than my younger sister and 3 years older than Back to the Future, that's a fun coincidence. Is that an actual electric Ukulele on the back? I'm expecting the kind of 80s Pop-Rock where if there were music videos for all the songs, those videos would be him exactly as depicted here singing them at the waitress while she refills his coffee. Press play…

… yep, it's highly enjoyable singer/songwriter type Pop-Rock. There She Goes Again is totally And The News. Someday Someway is straight out of the 50s. It's all great, less Elvis Costello, more Buddy Holly. I can't believe for a second this is a random fluke record that went nowhere. He totally did a bunch of big stuff, I just don't personally know about any of it off the top of my head. A wikipeding we will go…

... exactly. He was literally Buddy Holly to Lou Diamond Phillips's Ritchie Valens. He helped finish the music for that Gin Blossoms song 'Til I Hear It From You. 9 more albums almost certainly as good. He looks really familiar. Gimme a moment to wander my mind palace...

... OHOHOHOHOHOH! [snap] I knew one of those pictures looked really familiar. He was the meter reader guy in The Adventures of Pete and Pete, and he played guitar in the episode where little Pete formed a garage band and they did a whole night of call in requests to earn enough money to pay the electric bill. Told you he was a big time superstar. Check the cast list to make sure I'm not totally crazy. I am totally crazy, but I'm also right. Man, I've got a lot of stuff in my head.

This is a perfect self-titled debut. Hi, I'm a dude named Marshall Crenshaw and here are some songs I wrote. Hope you like 'em. I do, Marshall, I like them a lot. Future you has a bit part in one of my favorite shows as a kid. Here's hoping future me stumbles across more of your records 'cause you're great.

One more record to go, Skip, but you're 0 for 4 on this attempt at intentional sabotage. Sure, every record could have dragged me down to Bruce's level, but this might be the most fun collection yet. I think the real question is why are my heartiest minions so much better at picking out random records than me? I truly don't know, so go check out Marshall Crenshaw, it's definitely already on youtube and if the awesome side of the 80s version of 50s Rock and Roll doesn't make you do a little office chair mambo, then you might want to check your own pulse and have the defibrillator close at hand.

Giant Crab

S: I'm sure I'll regret it, but what were your other favorite TV shows growing up, Bottle?

B: Hmmm, I mean I liked all sorts of TV shows as a kid. I watched everything, age appropriate or not, from Sesame Street to Quincy.

S: Sure, but what would you say right now were your all time favorite?

B: All time? Not contextual? Just favorite favorite?

S: Yes.

B: In that case, I guess, Fraggle Rock, Danger Mouse, You Can't Do That On Television, and The Adventures of Pete and Pete. Alanis Morissette was on YCDTOTV and said she was going to be a famous musician someday. There's tons of runners up, though. 3-2-1 Contact (that's where Bloodhound Gang got their name), Designing Women, The Golden Girls, Animaniacs, Wings, I even liked Full House and Family Matters, Fresh Prince of Bel-air, Welcome Back Kotter, Alf. I guess the top 4 are rightfully the top 4, though.

S: Interesting.

B: As interesting as this thing Skip found with a giant Crab on it? Stormy and the Glamulous Crabfishers would be ecstatic.

S: Too early to tell. I have a sneaking suspicion it will be stupid.

B: Of course it will be, this thing obviously only exists because of LSD and Marijuana. I bet the spoken story line is more interesting than the actual music. This is the absolte fringe of Psychedelic Rock, made by drugs for drugs on other drugs because they ran out of normal drugs. If albums were movies I'd introduce it with "you've seen Airplane!, Kentucky Fried Movie, Amazon Women On The Moon, Lobster Men From Mars, Killer Klowns from Outer Space, The Cars That Ate Paris (the Australian town, not the capital of France), Attack of the Killer Tomatoes, every Troma movie ever released, but I still don't think you're fully prepared to feast your earballs upon...."

Ernie and the Emperors woke up one morning and decided to change their name to Giant Crab, I assume because drugs. Hey, it worked for Head East. Supposedly this is a mix of Psychedelic Rock and Blue Eyed Soul, but it's obviously wackadoodle so who cares? Let's just sit down in our thinking chair and drink this only mildly intoxicating rum and coke. Fun fact, I detest the feeling of being drunk, so I really do keep it to the lightest possible simmer, just enough to let my charming personality do the talking. These are the jokes, son, if you can't laugh at yourself you're gonna be real upset when other people do it for you.

Lydia Purple? The Eleanor Rigby knock-off by The Collectors? Alrighty then, I guess we know exactly what we're in for. Imma be not so impressed if this turns out to be random crap and the giant crab does not in fact come forth. You all saw it, I was promised a giant crab. Don't make me go find that Harry Connick Jr. album about the space turtle for some sense of closure.

Well, I've got bad news and good news and better news. The bad news is that the songs aren't actually about a giant crab invading a suburban neighborhood and wreaking havoc, it's just a silly way to introduce themselves. The good news is that this album did not catapult Giant Crab into superstardom, so it's ironically apropos. The better news is that it really is a mish-mash of great hippie-trip cacophonousness and 60s Sunshine Pop, like your parents keep poking their heads down the stairs to see if you and your friends need some water or pizza rolls, then they head back up and you go back to spazzing out on the floor and staring at the imaginary light show.

So no, it's not exactly what I was expecting, but also no I don't feel any desire to hear the better of Harry Connick Jr.'s two funk albums. She was quite enough for this particular reluctant space cadet. As for listening to it, I'm not disappointed in the slightest. Traces of metallic butterflies, classic fab four adjacencies hiding behind every perceivable door, white guys attempting to woo their soul sisters, inviting your favorite local DJ to read all the song titles as a story about a giant crab invading Groovy Towne, winner of the Bottle of Beef Most Bizarre Concept for a Debut Album award. It honestly does deserve the renewed interest and elevated resale value. My copy is down in the VG- range 'cause it's been played a time or 30, but I'd sell it for $15 if you're just dying to pay too much.

We should really dissect the Goldmine Grading system some time, it's like a Master's course in intellectual BS. Bottle's Guide to Record Grading and Pricing, I like it. Anywho, thanks for listening to this bizarre adventure through the urban underground, say hi to the twinkle fairies for me. I'll brew a fresh pot of coffee for you in the morning when the acid wears off. Cheers.

Between the Buried and Me – Colors

… speaking of watching the pretty colors, it was insanely difficult to refrain from pre-ordering a copy of the sequel now that Between the Buried and Me have announced a second pressing.

I do however have other expenses on the horizon, and getting the trucky truck running for the garden gnomes again set me back a little more that I would have liked. So, we'll just pull out the original masterpiece and be content to enjoy it in all its wacky progressive death-metal goodness. I've got this 3rd book to work on and GREGORY's piano album to bottle up in the meantime, Compy's still doing an excellent job of avoiding the tedious hyperlinking of the blog, Skip and Sandra are off on their own adventure without my having to participate, time for my favorite pastime, enjoying my own aimless wandering through the hallways while we all just keep waiting and floating toward the sun. Fun fact, this album ends with a Picardy 3rd. Cheers.

Shadric Smith and Friends – Reflections

Walk with me. No, no, we aren't going anywhere in particular, just passing time. You know, I talk a big game, but I try to make it meaningful. You might not agree with me, you might be surprised that you actually do, that's not really my concern. We all have to contemplate our own mortality from time to time, but we should also take some time to chase away those blues.

We've all had a rough year or so, and it's tempting to try to will the world back to some simpler state of mind, but metaphorically speaking I dug my own grave long before they built fences like America is a gated community and people found any excuse to be as racist and mean as possible. Relax, it's just a metaphor. Not the racism part, that's terribly real and really terrible. I guess what I'm getting at is yes, obviously, you have to take care of yourself so that you can be in a position to help others, but you also have to actually go do the helping others part, not just say "I'm doing swell, everybody else can go jump off a cliff."

Then one day you wake up and feel old. You can't play all night like you used to, you get rusty, you feel like you're all alone with only the internet to keep you connected, but you know what? Your best friends are still there, you're still enjoying what you do, and there's a lot to be said for letting it bounce off you. Not ignoring it by any means, but also not letting the parts that don't involve you rule your life; tend your own garden, share the extra with your neighbors.

I see that look. You're thinking "Bottle hates Country, why are there banjoes and pedal steel coming over the intercom?" Simple, this isn't actually Country. This is Roots, modern Americana, and there's a world of difference between Redneck Rock and Americana. You're totally allowed to like the former, and I won't say a bad word about you. Not my thing, but to each their own. I just mean Country is a mythology, Americana is something quintessentially mundane. Oof, those eyebrows, they hurt my soul. Mundane is not a bad word at all. You think it means dull or humdrum, but it really means "of this earthly world"; the here and now, reality as we experience it, life as it is not life as we wish it would be.

Who better to provide the soundtrack to our little meander than some people I know? This is Shadric Smith's latest album, and Kris Karr plays drums on Route 20. I live in between the old and new versions of that particular highway, so we'll raise a toast to wherever we find ourselves at the moment, and enjoy Reflections by Shadric Smith and Friends like there's no tomorrow. Cheers.

Mind the Nevermind As We Promenade

I was gonna just mosey along with EL&P's version of Pictures at an Exhibition keeping us company, but Spencer Elden has gone where I didn't think he wanted to go.

This is a sensitive subject, and I'm known for being mildly insensitive to make a point, but not this time. My analysis is on facebook, my blog, in my second book and they were 100% honest interpretations at the time. Now, however, we stand on the precipice of a bifurcating reality. The opinions will be many, and range from coherent to ridiculously stupid. Here's mine.

Does Spencer deserve a shitload of money from the image? Yes, absolutely, an insane percentage of gross profits from Nevermind. Will that fix anything? No, probably not. Is this child pornography as the lawsuit claims? No, it's not. The lawsuit as defined will do more damage than good for everyone, including Spencer.

My argument as written says this is a gray area, and it very much is. The situation is unique unto itself, and it must be treated as such. In my analytical opinion, there was never nor is there now any intention to exploit Spencer Elden, and this situation would eventually arise had any other child been chosen for the cover.

Is he wrong for changing his opinion of the situation over time? Absolutely not. Should they remove it at his request? Absolutely yes. Should police raid our houses and prosecute consumers for buy millions of copies of Nevermind with his photo on it? No, that's ludicrous.

Is some pervert somewhere sexually aroused by the album cover? Probably, some people are really fucked up. Sorry for the swear words, but as you surely know by now, I use them for their actual meaning that no euphemistic language can accurately convey.

At its heart, this is a case of an individual battling a corporation for his personal rights, and Spencer Elden deserves to have his rights honored on this issue in the manner of his own choosing. The simplest solution is for Geffen to take the initiative and simply ask the plaintiff how he wishes to proceed with the assurance that they will comply. The worst possible way to go about it is to publicize the private proceedings in half-speculated garbage media reports like it's a tabloid goldmine; that is definitely exploitation.

The Union Underground – An education in Rebellion

… and we're walking, we're walking, watch your step as we enter this inauspicious folder called "music." Don/t worry, we aren't making a stop in all 73 subfolders, just most of them (some of them aren't full albums, some I've already written about, some aren't worth listening to or writing about at all). If you look to your right you'll see the second band John Moyer played Bass in, The Union Underground. This is a strange band, they only made this one album before John got called up to the majors, and it is somehow mistakenly labeled Nu-metal. It's actually much more Industrial and Groove motivated if you ask me, but that's not the strange part. You might remember their one big hit Turn Me On Mr. Deadman, but a lot of these songs got serious radio play in the early 2000s, all the ones with very few swear words in them, at least.

Lyrically this album is bizarre because most of it is either about drugs, Paul McCartney and John Lennon, or else uses lyrics from other famous songs as sort of writing prompts like they were taking a poetry workshop at the local community college (Soundgarden, Dire Straits, you name it). It's not bad in the sense that they failed to make a generic Industrial Metal album that speaks to their generic desire to be lifelong rockers, but did anyone actually need the South Texas version of Rob Zombie's little brother's Powerman 5000 borrowing Lane Staley's not wanting to be a heroin addict anymore MO?

Musically, it's also what I just described. Take Alice in Chains, Rob Zombie, Marilyn Manson, and the word motherfucker, put them all in a blender on puree for 2 minutes, then pour directly into the least used toilet in your house.

Ok, ok, that's too harsh. If you put it on at half volume while you're running power tools you could easily pretend it's a much better album with much better lyrics. That may not be particularly satisfying, but tons of bands are much worse. At least they aren't Finger 11.

If you don't want to go hear it for yourself, and I don't blame you, at least take a moment to contemplate one of the worst lyrics I've heard in a while"

> It's such a shame that it is this way,
> I'm a junkie, God is gay.

That obviously neither offends nor shocks me, but rather comes across like Andrew Dice Clay doing his best Dr. Seuss impression. I can't disagree with other critics who imply it's a "hey, we can do that too" kind of album, but there's also no follow up to prove me right or wrong.

I want you to know, this album sort of sets the bar for exploring this so called "music" folder. There is some great stuff in here, and some worse stuff. You all know I don't play favorites, so definitely bring a helmet for these next however many albums. It's gonna get weird.

Compy's Folder of Doom, Part 1

C: Are you rummaging through my secret stash, Bottle?

B: Yes, is that a problem? Gotta finish this book somehow, but I gotta stop splurging in the real world for a while.

C: No, no problem, just making sure there isn't some nefarious virus running around. I get notifications when weird stuff happens.

B: Op, sorry, no it was me. I made a copy that can walk around on its own, so I won't need to manhandle the Compcenter anymore. Sorry for the intrusion.

C: No worries. You did warn them it gets weird, right? Some of this stuff is a little family unfriendly, you know?

B: Of course I did, told 'em to bring helmets and everything.

C: Ok then. Just as long as it doesn't come back on me. No refunds, no warranty. Use at your own risk.

B: Goes without saying, you'd have to be daft to ride any bus I was driving unless you knew the consequences are your own problem.

Blink 182 – Enema of the State

Ah, Blink. They had to change their name because some other band named Blink half a world away menacingly said "change it now, or we'll come over there and change it for you." 182 is a perfectly lovely random number. If you're like me, you're slightly confused by the phase "toilet humor" because there's not one sing joke about toilets on this album. Who is expecting Enema of the State to be a probing look at the intricacies and nuances of the human condition? Actually, in a way that's exactly what it is, albeit from the peculiar perspective of middle-class suburban California 20 year old skater punks. They are, by their own admission, jackasses.

Long before Tom DeLong became a crazy guy who believes aliens exists, he was a guitar player who wondered if aliens exist. Long before Travis Barker was a famous guy with lots of tattoos on TV who might have played drums in a band at one time, he was the Drummer of Blink 182. Before that he was the Drummer of The Aquabats, who went on to be more famous for their Nick Jr. show Yo Gabba Gabba. Mark Hoppus had a TV show for a while, but mostly he's still known as the self deprecating bass player of Blink 182 because he's not insane enough to let a film crew document his actual pointless daily life.

First thing's first, this 3rd album is essentially the Pop-Punk standard. You must be this good to have your juvenile Pop-Punk humor broadcast on commercial radio. If you need a direct lineage, they just wanted to be like Descendents. Fine by me, I love Descendents. Blink 182 is a little too juvenile even for my low standards, but there is an interesting facet to their music. On casual listen, these songs sound absolutely horrifying, until you realize that's the joke. "I need a girl that I can train." He literally means a dog, the four legged kind with a tail that barks and stereotypically chases cats. Is this song about the legal age of consent? Oh, no, he's just mad she left him for another guy. Look at that loser and that whore, kinda sad how desperate they are for any sense of companionship. Half the songs include a line that actually says "I really was a jackass, wasn't I? Sorry about that."

Sure, there's plenty of room to argue with me on this, but I think this album is actually a sophisticated look at the reality of being a horny teenager in a world that has absolutely nothing of actual value or meaning. It also has Adam's Song on it, and we need to understand why. If the album as a whole means nothing more to you than toxic frat-boy masculinity on parade, then this song is like a brick wall and you're about to smash your face into it. If however, like I suggested, you take a more analytical approach and listen to it as an honest expression of what it feels like to live in that mentality, noting a sense of self-awareness and embarrassment along the way, then it becomes much easier to understand where this particular type of depression and suicidal ideation comes from. Waking up one morning to find out that life is actually really hard and the world actively wants you to fail is not a pleasant surprise for anyone. Some people get through it, some do not. There's not a moral there, it's just a multi-faceted look at the depression that comes with recognizing your own internal loneliness, Mark simply connects his own feelings of loneliness after coming home to no one but himself with an actual teenage suicide note. It was intended to be a song of support and an example of it gets better, but Columbine and the suicide of their friend made it too hard to play, so they stopped.

  Unlike Green Day, Blink 182 had no qualms about going straight to the majors, and no wishing to retreat afterward. Pennywise insisted they get a spot on the Warped Tour and there was no looking back. At the end of the day, you gotta call it like it is, Blink 182 write really catchy songs that are surprisingly cerebral despite their inherent juvenility. They know they are jackasses and to a large extent they accept the consequences of deciding to stay that way. I can respect that.

Sum 41 – All Killer No Filler

  Oh hey, Sum 41 rap old-school posse style on their hit single Fat Lip. Does that make them Nu-metal? All Killer No Filler certainly has metal bookends. It's also truth in advertising, this is a phenomenal Pop-Punk masterpiece about being a restless teenager who hates all the modern first-world problems he has to deal with on a daily basis. There's a lot more emotional nuance then Blink And You'll Miss It, that's for sure. They're also from Canada, and I apparently haven't met a band from Canada I don't in some way like more than their direct US competitors. No idea why.

In case you're wondering, yes, Nu-metal is very much among the 40-something genre tags listed on their wikipedia page. Ridiculous, even they say they are just a Rock band because Punk has too many rules to follow. They might be the youngest Rock band I've ever mentioned in relation to the 2008 Universal Fire. I'm totally biased, this is one of my top ten albums for pure enjoyment to listen to, I literally love every song and the whole album flows like a mountain stream left unmolested by an industrial waste chute. That of course means I have nothing but boring compliments for it, it speaks for itself, it's fantastic. This would be an album I'd recommend if you asked for an example of a good Pop-Punk album from 2001.

The Folder of Doom, Part 2

B: Alright, Compy. I gotta know, what the hell is going on with this folder? It's all over the place.

C: It's just a catch all folder, really. Things from over here, things from over there, copies of copies from one hard drive to another. Albums I lost the cases to, stuff from the internet, things other people let me borrow.

B: Oh, ok, good, I was worried you went out of you way to collect this stuff.

C: Oh gosh no! Yeah, if that were the case you'd definitely need to put me out of my misery. I pull things out of the trash, remember? Goes against my nature to put them back in a trash can.

B: Excellent. Should we try to be thematic?

C: Meh. Alphabetical order seems just as appropriate. Hills then valleys, you know?

B: Well, I kind of already ruined that, but a wise man once told me it's never too late to start all over again.

Welcome to the Folder of Doom

Sorry everybody, I made a real boner of this particular tour. I won't make you listen to the albums we already did, but if you'll all back up a little, we'll start from the top and do it the right way. Like I said, we won't peek inside every room, but I will at least tell you what they are and only expound upon the ones that strike my fancy. A real guided tour that lets you secretly linger on something that strikes your fancy even if it doesn't strike mine.

What do we have first? Alien Ant Farm? This one isn't the full album and I'm certainly not going to hunt the remaining tracks down for an easily forgettable actual Nu-metal album. Yes, they did that cover of Smooth Criminal, but the actual interesting thing they did is call their debut studio album Greatest Hits and their second album ANThology. Shocking no one thought of that before, but truth is stranger than fiction.

Moving right along, you'll see the American Pie soundtrack and An Education in Rebellion. The latter we already covered, and I don't even care enough to look which songs are actually on that soundtrack, so we'll just keep walking.

Ooh, The American Album by Anne Akiko Meyers. Sadly, she is not a particularly famous violinist. She doesn't have some weird thing to make her stand out. Perlmann had his vibrato, Heifetz had that weird hit every not wrong but correct it before anyone notices thing, André Rieu had the red Samson hair. This might shock you a little, but one thing America is not known for is giving a shit about Classical music. Hell, we're so bad at it we insist on naming the entire history of European Aristocratic music after one tiny portion of the 18th Century. We thought so little of Composers that they had to actually go study in France or else invite famous European composers to come over here to teach us. Interesting fact, quite a few of them said "that cultural heritage of the indigenous people you stole the continent from is really interesting, you might want to try to learn something from them."

Anywho, I won't bore you further with my wacko ramblings on the compositions of Walter Piston, Aaron Copland, Charles Ives, and David Baker, except to say that I really did perform those Copland and Ives Sonatas in front of actually people one time with my friend Marilyn accompanying me. Apologies for ruining your redneck utopia with my previous life of loving playing something other than Devil Went Down To Georgia. The good news is that all the heavy lifting has destroyed my body to the point where I just gave up, so yay sports team! Kick 'em in the used car sales. Oooh, Me First and the Gimme Gimmes is cued up for tomorrow! Punk versions of 50s Pop songs? You might hate that even more!

Me First and the Gimme Gimmes – Are a Drag

Do you like Musicals? Do you like Punk? Wanna hear Punk covers of songs from musicals? I thought so. Here's Me First and the Gimme Gimmes Are a Drag.

The band is a supergroup cover band. The core lineup is Fat Mike from NOFX, Spike Slawson from Swingin' Utters, and Joey Cape and Dave Raun from Lagwagon, but other big names from the California Punk scene fill in all the time. Matching costumes, themed albums with titles that refer to the band's name in a funny way, what's not to love?

Like I said, Are a Drag is all songs from musicals, and it's fantastic. No duds or bad arrangements, every track is top notch. I saw another of their albums in here somewhere, so that's something to look forward to. As the final cover of Stepping Out reminds us: no use permitting some prophet of doom to wipe every smile away, so go out and enjoy this lovely Saturday as much as I'm going to. Meet back here in 10 hours or so for another one of these album thingies I like so much.

Behind the Scenes

    B: I dunno, Compy. This alphabetical thing isn't working so well. It's the wrong shape for my brain to work in, and now there's this giant gap between the book version and the facebook version, and I'm starting to lose any sense of coincidental coherence.

    C: So? I thought you didn't care how it turned out. The point was to just do it.

    B: True, true, I guess when you're right you're right. Maybe I'll Missy Eliot the whole thing, write 'em in the book first and revise the facebook/blog posts.

    C: Go ahead.

    B: Ok, I will then.

Bloodhound Gang – Hooray for Boobies

    Alright, everybody. On we go. We'll pass by this subfolder of assorted stuff. Black Pumas is definitely a great album, but it already had its time to shine. Definitely go check it out if you didn't the first time. We already did Blink 182, so I guess that brings us to Bloodhound Gang. Everybody got their helmets?

    Bloodhound Gang got their name from one of the segments of an 80s PBS science show. I watched that show. Now we have to talk about genres. There's a strange disconnect between the genre of a song or album, and the genre of a band. Bloodhound Gang the band is a Hip-Hop band, mislabeled as a Rock band, who wrote songs in every conceivable genre. They are juvenile, crass, sometimes offensive, and meant to be the kind of completely inappropriate hilarity that could only exist in the 90s. I've touched on it a little in my reviews of Fugees, Beastie Boys, and other places, but to really get an understanding of what happened in that decade we need to talk about Lenny Bruce, enforced censorship, and the problem of reverse psychology.

First, I think we all to some extent recognize the antagonistic relationship between society and the individual. A tight-knit community appears highly discriminatory and squashes creativity in the mind of a free-thinking spirit, and a group of strangers picked to live in a loft usually try to find some common communal goal to help them navigate the hard parts of existence. It's a cycle that endlessly repeats, and all through your life you will find yourself on one side or the other arguing for the complete opposite of what you argued months or years ago. I don't think it's necessarily good or bad either way, but what's almost always missing from the battle itself is a clear understanding of context. Lenny Bruce was constantly being arrested and criticized for his unrelenting critical approach to oppressive social morality through comedy and satire. Why? Because he threatened the power of the establishment. He represented the breakdown not of actual American society, but of the mechanisms that structured that society for the benefit of the self-proclaimed elite. Throughout our history as a country there has been an unresolvable war between ethnicity and the mechanisms by which we discriminate in order to keep that ethnicity "pure." Science tells us that in spite of the real forces of geography, diet, and geneology, there is only one type of human. The tribal instinct and deep seated desire for self-preservation and happiness says "bugger that, different is scary, stay away from me."

I'm the exact opposite, different is awesome, how dare you tell me what I can or can't like, think, or do. If your motto is "don't tread on me," mine is don't stand in the middle blocking the path designated for walking. I'll move over if you want to walk faster, but don't forget that I was minding my own business and you're harassing me. Driving 6 miles over the posted speed limit like it's your religion makes you exactly as much a sheeple as you claim I am for matching that mostly reasonable number based on how long it takes to stop and how likely it is pedestrians will cross your path.

I could keep going, but this is a long hike to get to the point. If Bloodhound Gang's Hooray for Boobies offends you with their insensitive frat humor, poop jokes, naughty words, songs about porn stars, and general making fun of polite society, then they have succeeded, and I think that's hilarious.

As with anything, some people miss the context and adopt this form of confrontational humor as their default outlook on life, but the same is true for the inverse and everyone is forgetting that the whole experience is a coin toss. It's easy to forget which side of the coin you're on, and it's equally easy to wake up one morning and realize that you're the dirt bag. Ask yourself, am I right or am I defending my pile of garbage? By all means, enjoy your own pile of garbage, but don't be afraid to throw it away if it's stinking up the neighborhood. As Sum 41 reminded us, enforcing the politics of Punk is the complete opposite of Punk, so ask the Mirror of Doom if the mohawks and dog collars, truck nuts and beer goggles, are a sign of rebellion or a sign of conformity. I guarantee she'll be brutally honest.

Staind – Break the Cycle

Oof, Staind. Man this is a tough one. See, the problem with the early 2000s is that it's so hard to separate the good from the bad, and the reason is Nu-metal. What the hell does it mean? Is it Rap-Metal or is it Alternative Metal incorporated into some other genre? We have to dissect every word, and most of the time it still makes no sense. Add to that the fact that it was actually Mainstream at the time, and everyone is a gibbering moron by default.

Music is political. It doesn't want to be political, but people turn music into politics regardless. Luckily, there's a today test we can apply to some of this stuff to at least get a foundation for a coherent opinion. Does your music sound like Korn and/or Linkin Park? If it does, you're Nu-metal. If it doesn't, you're just a whiny puke acting like a narcissistic douche bag for attention. Aaron Lewis managed to fuck that whole thing up and be neither. I, Bottle, hereby christen Staind Bad Emo. It's certainly the Metal version of Bad Emo, but Bad Emo wins. Good Emo makes you say "oh, man, that sucks, I know how you feel, but I can't magic away the hurt. Just know I'm here for you, whatever you need." Bad Emo makes you say "you know you're being a whiny little puke, right? You're literally going down the checklist of Emotionally Abusive Boyfriend. I suggest you either shut up or go away. I take that back, just go away." Don't think Bottle is immune, I've been on that side of the tracks, and yes I kicked my own ass at least twice.

You might think to yourself, how did Aaron Lewis go from this to MAGA Country? The answer is that he didn't go anywhere. This is literally the whiny cry-baby, "give me back my America" mentality, and he never grew out of it. This is the reverse psychology on the other side of the coin, and the only place left that eats it up is Mainstream Country. Everyone else is to blame for your personal problems, so everyone else should feel guilty for invading your safe space. White middle-class suburban American business is the whiny, entitled, garbage side of America, ironically arguing that trees with edible fruit should be chopped down as fast as possible to make room for more hog-houses and industrial processing plants.

If that statement offends you, then I submit that you don't actually understand what I'm saying. Your value as a human being is not tied to whether or not people like you, or like what you do. Your value as a human being is determined by your ability to say "this is not the kind of person I want to be," and work as hard as possible to change that for yourself.

Sometimes it means standing your ground, sometimes it means compromising, sometimes it means telling people you love to fuck off, sometimes it means gritting your teeth and dealing with a load of bullshit, but if you choose the easy way out even though you know it's wrong, don't be surprised when I flush the toilet. At the time it was written, Staind's Break the Cycle was a decision point, 20 years later Aaron Lewis said sign me up for that ride to pander-town and keep that cycle spinning as fast as possible.

People are often confused when I point out that I'm a Bleeding-Heart Liberal, and I have to remind them that that phrase is a euphemism meant to keep them, not me, in a state of delusion. I'm thorny, I'm difficult, I'm wildly intolerant of hypocrisy, and I've had more experience with picking out the weeds of my own thoughts than most people twice my age. That phrase is designed to punish empathy, and insult the open acceptance of new ideas and cultures. The tricky part is that most people confuse basic human values for an opening they can exploit. That's the delusion, you as a fellow human being are equal in my eyes, but if you cross the line and try to take advantage of my generosity I will cut you off and tell you exactly where you can shove it.

Let's make it about race for a moment. Show me a time in our history where a Black mob burned down an entire White city in anger. Show me a time in our history where white men had to march for equal Civil Rights. Show me an actual self-made millionaire, a person who saved and scrimped and accumulated those millions without speculating on or devaluing the labor of others. You can't, and there's a very good reason why you can't. You are the recipient of a system of privilege and you're either too vicious or too naïve to acknowledge it. There are a thousand people more talented than you waiting for their shot at the big time. Competition is all fun and games for the winners, but when you're the perennial loser you end up faced with the choice of accepting your losing hand, or finding a winning team to bandwagon. I'm not a yay sports team kind of guy, but I respect your right to choose to be one. The real question is can you respect my right to wave bye-bye and move on. I'm not so sure Aaron Lewis can.

Let's talk about my student loan debt. We'll be generous and say you can garnish 50% of my salary. Still going to take 20 years of my full time salary to earn that money. Are you the type of person who wants to keep compounding the interest on that debt so that you'll keep taking 50% of my salary for 20 more years after that? If so, then you are a grifter and I have no respect for you. Yeah, if I do win the lottery I'll pay the full balance and Navient will make a huge profit because they won that wager, but that's the only way that debt is ever going to be paid off. You have to fully understand that my death is the only way that debt gets forgiven. You don't understand that at all, and I know you don't because you turn around and vote Republican. I've talked about this a lot, but we really do need to understand that the Democratic-Republican party split around the turn of the 20th-century, and that split is the basis of our current 2-party establishment, at the expense of all the other political philosophies. American politics in the 1800s looked a whole lot more like British politics does today, 5 or 6 special interests debating the best policy for moving forward. Essentially, in America, authoritarian big-government conservativism won. The only tangible difference between the Democrat and Republican parties is that the Democrats recognize that a large portion of American citizens are forcefully disenfranchised while the Republican Party intentionally uses language confusion to bolster its support among historical Republicans. I can't stress this enough, the Democrats are still very much a right-wing political party, but they take it upon themselves to represent the opposing view as much as possible and advocate for concessions. What I can't seem to get through to people in real life is that I am who you are criticizing when you say "Liberals are ruining this country." I am a hard-core Liberal, and that means that I tolerate your opinions as best as I possibly can in real life. I work very hard to not unfairly criticize people for beliefs that I strongly disagree with, and I wake up every morning and put on pants and live whatever stupidity life throws at me. Sometimes I don't do a good job and I call you a moron, then I apologize and try to find a better way to express my frustration. I understand your side of the argument, but I don't see any indication that you have the foggiest idea of what my side of the argument actually is, all I hear is regurgitated propagandist jargon and empty ideology that bears no resemblance to the real world I have physically lived in for 41 years. I have literally heard your "original" thought 3-dozen times over the loudspeaker, and when I present my opposing opinion your eyes glaze over like I'm speaking a foreign language. The most hilariously tragic part is that 20 times a day I literally point out that you think I'm a horrible person and you just buzz right along with that cognitive dissonance in your head thinking "Bottle is such a nice guy, I don't know how we'd stay in business without him, doop de doop doop." I'm terrified one day you'll wake up and actually figure it out, really realize that I'm being patient with you like you're a toddler who doesn't understand how complicated the learning process actually is. There is no such thing as talent, only spastically applied determination and laziness. You can do anything you want to do, you can learn anything you want to learn, you can be whoever you want to be, but you have to actually do the work to make it happen.

So, long story a little bit longer, Break the Cycle is a fantastic example of dramatic irony. If you detest it then congratulations you're a mature adult who outgrew this tragic phase of first-world adolescent self-importance, if you love it, you probably haven't broken the cycle at all and can't wait for Aaron Lewis's next single to hit KMGA, 'Merica's choice for shitty narcissistic douche-baggery. Sadly, the music part of the equation is phenomenal.

Tripping Daisy - I Am An Elastic Firecracker.

Yep, that's me. It's also Tripping Daisy's second album, and it's fantastic. Even Erlewine couldn't find anything bad to say about it, so really my review just has to be longer than two sentences.

I don't expect you to know Tripping Daisy, but you might have heard I Got A Girl one time. This is Alternative Rock bordering on Indie, but the band is probably best known for not being a band anymore. After Wes Breggren died of an overdose, Wes's dad helped finish their final album and they changed direction by becoming The Polyphonic Spree.

So, what kind of bang do you get for your buck? You get 90s Psychedelic Rock a lot like Flaming Lips. The Pop side not the long range noise-scapes kind of Psychedelic like Bardo Pond. It's quirky, it's strange, it basically says everything is a joke, but I don't really have much to complain about, it's all just stuff that gets in the way. Why try to fit in when there's no place for us in the first place? I may be a loser, but gosh darnit I'm gonna be a happy loser.

The real joy is that I don't have to equivocate and find some common ground to work from, this is who I am on the inside, this is the kind of band I wish I was in. Tell me where you practice, I'll show up for every rehearsal.

Crash Test Dummies – God Shuffled His Feet

What if God was one of us? Oh, wait, no, that was Joan Osborne not Brad Roberts, totally easy to mistake the two if you're not paying attention. God Shuffled His Feet by Crash Test Dummies is tonight's album. MMM, MMM, MMM, MMM, that's some deliciously weird Canadian Alternative Folk Rock. I've never been to Manitoba, so I have no idea if this is considered normal or weird there, but I do know that I love this album. Supposedly Brad says Andy Partridge's 2/3 of XTC is his primary influence. I can kind of see it in the humor of bringing absurd situations down to the level of matter-of-fact mundanity, but I don't sense any of the biting criticism. It's just good-naturedly funny to me.

Maybe my favorite thing about the whole album is how every single song has a completely bizarre way to express its idea. What do fingers really mean to me? Let's look in the dictionary and find out. How does a duck know what direction South is, and how to tell his wife from all the other ducks?

Wow, I forgot how much Rock they crammed in here without anyone noticing. The stank on the harmonica solos is outrageous. Like Mayall's USA Union violin nasty. Awesome.

Can the Psychic see me naked in her mind's eye? Erlewine says it's basically a lot like their first album, and Christgau pointedly didn't even bother. I agree, it's lovely, what else is there to say?

The secret is that it's really just one Columbo observation after another. Nothing is said condescendingly, but the overall impression is "guys, I'm not that bright, what's that say about the rest of you?"

Linkin Park – Hybrid Theory

Alright, we have to do it. We have to get a grip on Nu-metal. Every band can't be that, every band that lists Primus as their inspiration can't be Nu-metal. 7-strings and detuning do not Nu-metal make. Baggy clothes, white male rage, depression, no, no, no. All those things are there, but that's not what makes Nu-metal Nu-metal. Deftones were Deftones long before Nu-metal, you can't just retroactively include them to make your theory look good. You can't just say it's a thing Rick Rubin and Ross Robinson invented independently of each other. Sure, that's true if you squint just right, but what's the actual musical lineage, the Before – Nu-metal – After picture? I'll give you the deep cuts that Incubus isn't famous for and Sugar Ray's first album, but the very first band actually called Nu-metal was Coal Chamber, and those things are all so unalike it gives me a migraine. We need a better way to talk about genres, a better theory (have I dragged it out long enough?), a Hybrid Theory.

Bottle says Nu-metal is a pyramid, and at the top of the pyramid sit two bands: Korn and Linkin Park. We already talked about Korn, so we understand that there is a very real reason why life is not in any way peachy, unless you've already taken a giant bite and are now looking at the half of James and his insect friends that you aren't about to throw back up; that peach full of maggots from No Doubt's Don't Speak video (Shut it, Milton. I know it's an orange. Same difference). You get the idea. Tonight it's Linkin Park.

What else is definitely Nu-metal? Well, I think we can all agree that the second tier of this pyramid is Papa Roach, POD, Limp Bizkit, and because we don't have a choice, Kid Rock.

Hey Bottle, is Body Count Nu-metal?

No, that's just Ice-T and Ernie C making Thrash Metal. I see what you're saying though, Rap is a common component. But, if Nu-metal is just Rap, then it's Just Rap. You wouldn't call Beastie Boys Nu-metal, would you? Nu-metal isn't just rapping over a Metal band's music, that's Rap-Metal. Are we all convulsing because we know where this is headed? Yeah, there's a racial component to Nu-metal. We have to lay it out there, Nu-metal is an Alternative Metal band creating Hip-Hop. Not so much co-opting Hip-Hop itself, but very much connecting with the anger, one-upsmanship, and social criticism of Urban, predominantly Black and Latin communities, like a Mad-Frat Me Too movement. It takes some of the well understood frustrations and hopelessness of the stereotypical inner-city experience, and uses them as the primary means of expressing the repressed emotions of suburban, white 20-somethings. It's the suburban part that defines Nu-metal; these are not really inner-city kids of any ethnicity. As you might expect, you can do that in a meaningfully productive way, or you can really botch the surgery and be worthless, whiny man-bear-pigs.

So, yes, your Nu-metal band needs a rapper, a turntablist, and an emotional white guy who can both sing and scream effectively. That's a context in which I don't mind calling the first couple Slipknot albums Nu-metal. If you're lazy with measuring the ingredients you can quickly turn a lovely soufflé into Bad Emo like Staind and/or desperately regret taking part in the horrible atrocity that was Woodstock 1999.

We'll get to Linkin Park eventually, we just have to slog through the terrible side to get there. Kid Rock does not pass go or collect $200, he goes straight into the garbage can. Why? Because he's mostly shitty Rap-Rock and there's at least 7 layers of farcical irony between Kid Rock and actual Nu-metal. This beaver who is Bottle doesn't eat Taco bell.

The before part is Metal, then Rap-Metal (think Anthrax and Biohazard with Public Enemy and Onyx respectively; Run DMC with Aerosmith is technically an influence, but that's Rock), then fans of both Metal and Hip-Hop, then [dramatic popping of neck] Metalcore and Emo-Rap/Trap-Metal (which doesn't exist outside of a small Soundcloud community).

There are more tiers to the pyramid, but even I don't want to delve into Highly Suspect, Snot, Taproot, Hoobastank, or tread anywhere near Bring Me the Horizon, blech. Let's just contextualize Limp Bizkit and get to Hybrid Theory as quickly as possible.

Ask anyone and they will probably slightly miscategorize Limp Bizkit as the nexus of the Dark Side of Nu-metal. Certainly, the heart of the problem is taking Limp Bizkit very seriously, but there is some real truth to the notion that

Fred Durst really was that naïve and had no idea he was the official idol of misogynistic, frat-boy rapists. It was supposed to be a joke, he thought you knew that, it was intended merely as outrageous humor. Obnoxious sure, but not a serious statement about how life should actually be. Axl had a similar problem, remember? Fred Durst really didn't realize what was going on at the time, he just provided the soundtrack for it. The confusion here is the same confusion we always have when we let our brain thoughts out to play: some of you take it serious, personal, make these imaginary terrible things we all have in our brains real. You thoughts, feelings, emotions, etc. are valid and worth addressing for what they are, but half the things they might lead you to do are bad.

We'll swipe right to the conclusion, here's what makes Hybrid Theory good. After all the anger, depression, articulation of all his negative emotions, he says "… and I don't know what to do. I think I need to remove myself from this terrible situation." That's the key, the secret, the war is inside his own head and fighting that war is about to break/kill him.

I've talked about the distinction between artistic expression and wearing your heart on your sleeve, and we have to understand that Chester really does fall into the latter camp with Lane Staley, Cobain, Pretty Hate Machine Trent Reznor the actual studio janitor. The songs are of course much larger statements, but they were also deeply personal in their creation. They were not expressing healthy emotions, they were exorcizing the demons. That's much different from me, Bottle. I'm just the wee-little snarky class-clown part of Paul who couldn't exist without the help of all the other personalities.

Let's be frank, Chester hanged himself at 41, he lost his battle whether Linkin Park is great or not (they are great in my opinion). Is my finishing this 3rd book the ending process of Paul's mid-life crisis? Seems dumb, but why not? It started with his dad dying, and he was pretty freakin' bummed out. At the same time though, he seems genuinely more concerned for the people who have legitimately worse circumstances than his own, and he gets really frustrated that he can't physically do more to make a difference. I don't know that my loudmouthed calling it as I see it is much better, but some people tell me it is.

  I think I've tried more successfully than a lot of people to really contextualize the split between thought and action, but that doesn't mean I've actually succeeded. Lots of people are tired of my BS at this point, but since I was kind of being an asshole in the first place by saying if you're gonna throw your garbage on the floor for someone else to pick up, then whoo-ee am I good at that game. I haven't unfollowed a single person, but how on earth do you respond to me? It's tough, I know, these aren't the silly humor posts of pre-Trump Paul. Trump was Nu-metal 3.0. Not a good franchise in my opinion.

  I could be wrong, you might listen to Hybrid Theory and try to suss out what I'm trying to get at, but can you really write a letter to Linkin Park and tell them that 21 years later this guy you know put their breakthrough album in a perspective you never thought about before? I don't know any of them, it's just that I bought this album 2 decades ago and I happen to really like it. Same as any of the other 600 albums I really liked, hell same as the albums I detested. I may strongly disagree, but I haven't thrown them away. Seether, Finger 11, Sonny Bono, Petula Clark, Ten Years After, Gary Usher are all still here and I'll eventually gargle enough mouthwash to give them another chance. I couldn't eat a hamburger until I was in my mid 20s because I was repulsed by the combined flavor of ground beef and bread, plus it was either eat it or starve. Never said an intentionally mean thing about a real person in my life. Ideas though, let's just say if you're going to act out the worst of yours in public and/or nationally syndicate them for those sweet, sweet pander profits, then you should know I've got a nasty surprise of a rebuttal in my back pocket.

If your opinion demands my corroboration for its own validation, we'll butt heads. Conversely, you don't have to do anything with my opinion other than decide whether you want to hear them or not. I have no skin in that game, I don't need my opinions walking around, they are only a tiny portion of me. I just think you should know what they are before you try to corner them in a dark alley, that's all.

Kids See Ghosts

Sandra was the first to notice the screaming and thudding. She wasn't overly concerned. It's been a rough couple weeks for everyone, and none of it is the kind of problem a swift charge into uncertainty will solve. Generally that makes the problem itself worse and the fixing it comparatively ineffective. Bottle finally overfilled and she dare not touch Carl's mop. It takes more effort to corporealize the broom than it does to just eyebrow the problem into correcting itself anyway.

Skip, after several moments of staring at his desk and wobbling his head like he was having a serious psychic debate with said desk, turned to Compy. "Should we be worried?"

Compy, who did not appear outwardly flustered, simply replied "he knew what he was doing when he did it, and we warned the outside world."

E: Warned them about what?

C: He's been listening to the Folder of Doom. The highs are spectacular, the lows are, uh, concussion fuel?

E: Should we intervene?

C: Tough call, I'm gonna go with the fact that Sandra isn't here and say no, we wait.

Meep.

E: Sorry, didn't catch that last part, Compy.

C: I said "we wait."

E: No, after that.

C: nothing after that, that was the last thing I said.

MEEEEEP!

E: Oh, geez, you startled the bejeezus out of me. Sorry, what's up, Little Dude?

Meep meep meep

E: You got the stuff? What stuff?

Meep?

No, I don't think I technically qualify as new anymore. I assume you mean the stuff Bottle asked you to get?

Meep.

As Skip was formulating an appropriate response to what was unmistakably the phrase "don't defecate while the detective is around," Sandra appeared.

S: Hi, Little Dude, is that for Bottle? I'll make sure he gets it. Thank you very much.

Meep meep.

S: Me too, Little Dude, me too. Thank you again, toodles. I didn't know you were learning to speak Meepanese, Skip.

E: I'm not, I sort of just got the gist of it while I was lost in B-space. What's actually going on here?

C: Ok, ok, it's not just some random folder of stuff, it's stuff from Bottle's second life. It's the world as it was from the late 90s to the mid-2000s, before the cataclysm. Before you even ask, it was the last time the world went ape-shit. This folder is a microcosm of the world before 9/11, but more importantly at the precipice of "the war on terror," which as you may or may not realize has ended as our de facto foreign policy and now very much exists as our domestic policy. A whole lot of people are completely terrified by "Liberals: The

Enemy Within." Most people don't have any idea what "lliberal" actually means, so we're back to wagering our houses on making a hit cartoon like Disney did. Bottle's better at it than me, why don't we go bring him back to the now?

    S: Ok, Compy, Skip, let me do the talking.
    C&S: Yes Ma'am.

Slowly, Sandra opened the door to Bottle's office.

THUD. THUD. THUDTHUDTHUD.

    B: …stupid stupidstupidsonsofmorons … freakin' texas…
    S: Shut up, Bottle.
    B: Oh, hi Sandra … abuse of power … rewardfortattling ARETHEYFUCKINGNUTS!!!
    S: Yes, actually. Chocolate covered cashews to be exact.
    B: Ooooh, yumyumyum, did you thank the little dude?
    S: I did. Twice. It appears he brought you another surprise as well. Something called… Kid See Ghosts?
    B: Never heard of it. May I? What the hell *is* this? Sondtrack to an anime series? Titles…titles…nothing, nothing… Cudi? Like Kid Cudi? Seems odd for a Hip-hop album. Oh well, I certainly wasn't relishing the thought of listening to the Creed and Nickelback albums lurking in this folder, so why not? Gimme a few minutes to freshen up, then we'll explore this thing I know absolutely nothing about. Haven't even wikipedied it or nothin'….

… Kaay, that's certainly a translucent pink record. Oh, ok, Push T and Kanye West on the first track. This is from 2018. Ah, see? Everything is Kanye and Cudi, so this is like a producer's collab with friends? I expect weird. Ooh, that is different, let's just let Side A play out…

… holy hell. No words, right on to Side B, this needs dedicated attention…

… wow. Just wow. Musically this thing is amazing. It's super-duper short, but the compositions are astounding. I'm not really good at subgenres, but this is definitely the down-side of experimental Hip-Hop. Not negative by any means, but like chill psychedelic.

I feel like this thing got a lot of praise and/or awards. Not Pulitzer level, but standard industry "no complaints from us, good job guys" recognition. You can all go look it up and tell me, I'm happy liking it completely on its own terms. This is fun, genuinely wackadoodle at times, but not confrontational to my ears. You're clearly supposed to enjoy listening to it, and I certainly do.

I could say a lot of things about Kanye, but I probably have a very different impression of him than most people. I think he's obviously bipolar, the same way Lord Sutch was bipolar; untreated and trying to function as best as possible. Call him a jackass if you want, but you don't have any idea which Kanye you're seeing at any given moment, so it's kind of unfair to slap a label on the whole thing and walk away.

Lyrically I can't make much comment, it's going to take a few more listens to really get it in my head, but there's a lot of mental health type grappling going on. There are some really clever lyrics and some throw away garbage, but the vibe of the album is really nice. It's dark, but not frightening, a little bit loopy but not insane, it's a very minimalist but sample heavy Hip-Hop album, and the music is just as much a performance as the verses.

Color me impressed. I certainly don't feel like smashing my head against the desk anymore, so thumbs up to Kids See Ghosts. Go check it out some time.

OPM – Menace to Sobriety

Is OPM's first album really that terrible? It's just Alternative Rock/Hip-Hop above a foundation of Reggae. That was a pretty oversaturated market at the time, the Pop side of the Nu-metal equation. Remember Tripping Daisy a few albums ago? Happy losers. The sad and bitter losers didn't like them at all, but I think we can all agree that Heaven is a Half-pipe whether you're happy or sad, and if skateboards are banned from Heaven then it's clearly not Heaven at all, now is it? Oh, is it because it's all about smoking pot? That worked fine for Cypress Hill.

We need some personal perspective. If there was a metaphorical line to get into Club Gen-X, then I'm literally the last guy standing in it, and I know they'll reach capacity well before I get there. February, 1980. I missed being born in the 70s by less than 90 days, same as cash. Nope, 65% APR with points and penalties for Bottle; can't even get into the loser's club with my legit ID.

That's the story of my life. They thought about moving me up a grade when I was 8 or 9, but decided not to, my parents were renting a house and the landlord decided to give that house to his kids, so we had to move like half-a-mile away. We applied for a transfer but they said nope, too much paperwork, so I had to change schools for 5th and 6th grade. Get to High School and they take away off-campus lunches the year I get my driver's license, completely reorganize class time and scheduling such that I lose the ability to take Calculus and have to repeat Chemistry 1 just to meet the science requirements. Working on my PhD and all my committee members literally quit to go to other Universities, which is a minor nuisance compared to the magically disappearing tenured positions in the wake of the 2008 financial crisis. Same exact year as that Universal fire, that's a funny coincidence, har har.

I got great coaching, people saying "ok, your turn is coming up, here's my best advice for getting the most out of it," then I'm up to bat and the umpire cancels the game just after we reach the point where we can't reschedule, call it where it stands. Sorry we decided to eliminate you position 6 months after you would have already needed to submit applications at other Universities.

What has the world taught me? It taught me that the chain of command is more important than the objective. Those is a position of power and responsibility do not have my best interest in mind, they have their own best interest in mind and I am required to be thankful for the moments when those two things are indistinguishable from each other, but blindly forgive them when they aren't because it wasn't their decision to make.

I call shenanigans, you're lying, it was all BS from the beginning and you're cashing in your chips. That's fine, they're your chips. I just wanted to mind my own business and skate, but you came over and told me I was somehow ruining the world. You're the one who took opportunities away from me, but whatever.

I tell this story because Marco Rubio was all over the airwaves this morning saying "Biden doesn't get to apologize for his bungling of Afghanistan." This weekend we will be honoring the memory and service of people who died in the exit of that 20-year war, and I have not even the slightest shred of disrespect for their service and tragic sacrifice. Rubio on the other hand can kiss a grenade for all I care. I would love to hear his explanation of how he would have handled the situation different. Would he use a different color ink in his pen? Maybe pilot a better airplane that he bought himself? I'm not much of a fan of Joni "take away the Pacific Northwest's allowance" Ernst either.

My point is that none of these supposed representatives of the people are providing possible solutions to real, serious problems. They want to literally do nothing and say "them's the breaks." Rubio's goal is to set up his run for President in 2024 if he decides it will be profitable to run. Not profitable to win, profitable to run. He'll be spending Corporate donations and begging for your paycheck to do it. Ross Perot was a raging lunatic, but at least he had the decency to pay for his air time out of pocket.

So no, OPM's Menace to Sobriety really isn't that bad at all. The fact that their drug dealer is more friendly, honest, and dependable than anyone shouldn't be a surprise at all, that's an honest (if illicit) cash for crop trade, and business is business.

So what's really going on here? We all know my bias, and we watch me wake up in the morning and say "ok, time to investigate. I want to hear all the sides so I can actively interpret it without that bias getting in the way. I don't care if I'm right or wrong, I only care that I made a logical interpretation based on my actual experience."

Time and time again I keep reaching the same conclusion. Every bit of this stuff was a Republican championed project that fell to shit and their response is always "blame Democrats, they made us do it."

Horseshit.

Metallica – S&M

Today is a sad anniversary for me, so naturally my morbid sense of humor tries to help as best as possible by pointing out "when the soothing light at the end of your tunnel is just a freight train coming your way…."

The story goes that after attending a performance of Jesus Christ Superstar, Russian composer Dmitri Shostakovich expressed his regret that he never had the chance to create such a work of art. In that regard, British Oboist Michael Kamen was more fortunate. He got to arrange and conduct a

Metallica's Greatest Hits album, and perform it live as Jason Newstead's last Metallica album. You can even hear Jason play and sing backup vocals on it, that's like 9 giant steps forward and some tangible justice for him.

Some critics were all "yay! Metallica did a thing!" Others were like "ugh, Metallica did a thing." Some said "it's great if you wanted a live album with an orchestra, I guess." Others said "this seems kind of pretentious." Still others said "meh, whatever." Bottle says "shut your cake hole, I'm trying to listen to S&M, it's lovely."

3 Albums for Labor Day Weekend

We're doing 3 albums tonight because it's a labor of love. Not the first two albums, they suck just as much as the two halves of the day shift, but we close out the night on a hard-won victory. Plus, it's Labor Day Weekend, so the puzzle just assembles itself, really.

First up is Weathered by Creed. Don't let tracks 1, 2, and 4 fool you with their completely tolerable Alternative Metal anachronicity, the entire rest of the album of the album is tragically worse Creed than normal. They staged an ironic intervention for their Bass player and his response was "they tried to make me go to rehab, but I said no, no, no," so they fired him and Scott Stapp got a swimming pool full of liquor and dove in it (an Amy Winehouse and Kendrick Lamar reference in the same sentence? Is that even allowable?). Review over, the 3 tracks I mentioned are pretty good, but the rest of the album leaves you saying "why the hell did I listen to an entire Creed album?"

Bad news, Bottle, Nickelback's Silver Side Up is next. Ugh, ok, this is one of those albums you could like. You could. I don't like it at all because 1) that bass sounds like diarrhea. Not "oh god, I might die" diarrhea, but close enough to add pepto and pedialyte to tomorrow's shopping list. 2) Chad

Kroeger is a terrible lyricist. You can't tell who is he supposed to be as the narrator, and he mansplains his intended sentiments to a farcical extreme. Betelgeuse, Betelgeuse, Betelgeuse) he sounds unmistakably like Chad Kroeger. 2 out of 3 ain't bad, but 3 strikes and you're out. Make that 4 strikes because every successive song song gets progressively lazier as the album progresses, to the point where he's literally just singing the rhythm guitar part at times. I could give specific examples of all this stuff, but I feel like that's giving it too much credit. Like I said at the start, if none of that stuff bothers you, then enjoy.

So what's the good album? Oooh, Bring Your Own Stereo by Jimmy's Chicken Shack. This *is* a good one. Critics were genuinely thrilled by their first album, then said "I didn't hear myself ask for a second one, did you?" Bugger that, this album is full of hits. I told you that Alternative Rock with a splash of Reggae was oversaturated in 1999, and this is a lost in the shuffle gem. It's another one of those happy loser albums I enjoy so much.

I'm gonna let you in on a little secret. Come close, I don't want everybody to know, you know? They aren't actually losers. See, what happened was a bunch of prep-school trust-fund guys said "my dad worked hard so I could have all this money, I am not about to actually use it to pay people to work for me. If I did that then they would have money and I'd have to work too. Suck it, losers."

In response, the previously not actual losers said "so success is off the table for me no matter what I do? Ok, no gain baby no pain. We'll be fine."

That made the trust-fund kids even more mad because what they didn't realize was that their own self-esteem was tied to the power of material wealth, "…but if those losers are more happy than I am without all this money, then I'm the loser."

So, the formerly not losers turned ersatz losers said "yeah, you guys were the losers to begin with. Daddy didn't hand you the company, he handed you the money because you are completely unskilled at everything. We can at least change our own oil and mow the lawn."

So, the trust-fund losers got all competitive and said "we'll show you. We'll throw all that money away and be miserable just so you can't have it."

This naming convention is getting out of hand, so we'll just say the white guys with dreadlocks replied "that'll end up terrible for everybody, but you've already established that you're going to do the dumb thing and we can't stop you, so go back to the golf course or the race track or wherever it is you hang out with naked old guys and just leave us alone."

Yeah, I know it's a hard-core paraphrase, but that's basically 1999 and here we are in 2021, the billionaires with no actual money don't have a clue how anything works, but gosh darnit it's their inheritance so onward space cadets. May the Unexplained Aerial Phenomena that only Navy Pilots seem to experience have mercy on our quantumly immortal soul vibrations. Hey, if you come across a bath mat while you're dumpster diving for flower necklaces, I could use a new one. Cheers.

Lorde – Solar Power

Oh, Lorde. Alright, go ahead, give us the exit to eternal Summer slacking. Where are we going without even knowing the way? Here's Solar Power.

That was foreshadowing, by the way. Fallen Fruit sounds exactly like a Pharrell Williams reverse-engineering of Fastball's The Way, but that's not why we're here. We're here to stare at Lorde's crotch. No, that's not why. An album, yeah, that's it, she made an album 4 years after. She's like a prettier Jesus, or something. Oh, oh, sorry, now I remember, Royals made her a one-hit wonder, but what she really is is the

Alternative to something. Who or what, though? Billie Eilish and Phoebe Bridgers spring to mind. St. Vincent, maybe?

Note to retailers, placing a sticker over said crotch-shot actually makes it worse. Remember when they placed the parental advisory so that it looked like Kendrick Lamar was saying DAMN. and feeling dejected about the world warning you that his ideas and opinions are "dangerous"? Well, all this sticker does is say "lady parts are naughty. Buy this album so you can see what we're hiding."

One time my friends and I were lying down on the grass at a Rennaissance Festival and some of the lady cosplayers walked over us just like this cover. Somebody had a wax sculpture made of their middle finger. They taught us how to actually win that climb the rope ladder carnival game. Fun times. Oh, right, the Lorde's choir and happy loser songs in actual Pop format. I'm having trouble concentrating today.

I'm not gonna buy this album, we'll just fire up the old youtubulator and try to piece it together in between Geico, Aflac, and Mastercard commercials. What are the criteria for whether or not this is good? Well, Lorde's claim to the Pop Pantheon is the strength of her songwriting. Basically, as long as these things are multifaceted expressions of her thoughts and feelings about life without any cheesy or clichéd garbage, then she succeeded.

The world's on opioids, good lad off. She has run off to an island and doesn't want the outside world to contact her. We're all broken, maybe some Vitamin D will help.

Ooh, nice, these are just my thoughts from actual experience, take 'em or leave 'em. She's 22 now and starting to feel self-conscious about her earlier work, wait who's the Princess of Norway? Apparently she's a self-proclaimed clairvoyant. There's a fair amount of Des'ree style Goop lurking beneath the surface, but I think it's just a natural part of "the world is fake" subject matter, part of the problem so to speak.

Oh yeah, Leader of a New Regime is fantastic. Ok, ok, I think this is a sarcastic album, like hard-core sarcasm. Mood Ring is just vicious: actually begging your mood ring to tell you how to feel? Ouch.

This is all about the quarter-life crisis, nobody else has the solution for you, you have to go out and find it for yourself. My answer may not work for you, but you'll never find your answer if you don't actually go out and look for it.

Two thumbs up from Bottle, this is actually a fantastic album. I submit that the haters are the worst offenders in the "pigeon-hole Lorde into pleasing you" contest of Doom. Not a single doop-dee-doo or cheesy pre-packaged sentiment to be found anywhere on it. It sounds like a trippy lucid dream, what with the dark guitars, floating harmonies, breathy vocals, and choir verses. Yes, the verses are often in chorus like she's speaking for all of us, but not in a pretentious or underhanded way. She's saying this world you guys are trying to conserve is pretty terrible and we don't want to participate in it anymore, the party to mask the pain mentally hurts more than the pain itself. 6 out of 5 stars. I'm still not going to buy a copy of it, but I have nothing bad to say. This is a fantastic album. Go give it a listen and see how it strikes you.

It's a bird, it's a plane, it's a bottle, it's Breaking Benjamin – Phobia

Some days the hopelessness of the situation is too much. Today is one of those days. Today I am mentally and emotionally broken by the weight of $200,000. I'll be fine later once I reaarange some brain cells and shove it back in a bottle, but that doesn't make it go away, it doesn't make the next 20 years of trying to live on $900 a month any easier, it doesn't fix my falling apart car, it doesn't actually make anything better.

There's no reason for you to care, other than basic human kindness. I have to be in a position to give you something you want in exchange for your money. You have to be in a position to give me money for something I can give you. You are in the same situation. That's where the hopelessness rears its ugly head. I have to scrape and claw and worm my way into your brain, I have to beg and plead without begging and pleading. It rots my soul from the inside.

That's not a cry for sympathy or some passive aggressive guilt trip, it's simply an objective description of my reality as a human on this planet. It sucks 100% of the time, I just don't have the mental energy to ignore it today. So, on with the show.

I usually don't veto my brain when it tosses up an album, but tonight is an exception. The album my brain wanted was Offspring's Ignition, but 1) it's a convenient avoidance, and 2) I can literally listen to that album in my head any time I want.

No, Bottle says "hey, I'm Bottle, and if I know me, what I should really do is just lean into it and smile at the demons and say 'I'm better at this game than you. Choke on the melodrama.'"

So, here's Ben Burnley's album about his fear of flying/dying. You remember the last time we broke out Benjamin, right? It was Bottle's Butt-Rock Butstravaganza. This is a short-list, desert island with a solar powered CD player album. I made a human centipede joke and everything. This album is gorgeous. It also has one of those weird uber-specific but completely mundane memories attached to it. It came out the Summer of 2006 and I had just started that super awesome part of the story where I lived in Texas during the week and saw my wife and newborn son on the weekends. That's not the memory, just some context. The actual memory is the mailboxes and pebbled sidewalk of the apartment complex. Interesting addendum, Flyleaf is associated with the tree canopy surrounding the entrance to said apartment complex. No hidden message there, merely the literal brain path this album lives on. One of my actual students was my regular pizza delivery driver, so you know I tipped him like 60% every time.

What are we doing? We're shoving all that pain and depression from earlier today into this bottle of semi-adjacent misery. Track 9 and I already feel fantastic. You see, the trick is that I don't have to remember that garbage until I listen to this album again, but since this album is one of my all time favorite manual labor/demolition albums, Ben and whoever else he got to play on this album (he changed band members more often that Iron Butterfly or Lauryn Hill even) will just beat the crap out of that hurt. Yes, of course it's silly, but track 10 and there's not even a tinge of mope left, it works for me whether you understand it or not. You know what I'm talking about, synchronizing the garage doors, rematrixing the program, having Criscrosstopher Robin glue me back together? It's sort of like the Memory Palace thing, but in reverse. I put things in there to specifically forget about them.

Did your brain just cough and say "that kind of sounds like you're intentionally repressing memories"? Nope, I still know exactly where those memories are, I just don't have to deal with them until they ferment into something if not better, at least slightly more palatable. No idea how to teach you how to do it. Sorry. You can still go listen to Breaking Benjamin's Phobia anyway, it's great.

Mastodon – Blood Mountain

Mastodon is probably going to release a new single/video this Friday, so what better time to listen to the last one in my collection, the Earthy one, Blood Mountain? I really should find copies of the 3 albums I don't have. Anywho, story time about the wacky adventures of climbing a mountain in Georgia to put a crystal skull on top so you can kill the reptilian part of your brain and ascend to a new level of human consciousness.

I love Mastodon because the concepts for their albums are like Jeopardy answers for "Things Marijuana Might Say." Then they actually go do it, and the only possible response is "that could have turned out really stupid, but somehow it didn't. Great job, guys." Really, you say it out loud and it's laugh out loud ridiculous, but then you pop in the CD and it's like Homer drooling and saying "doughnuts."

Kay, we got a hero. He's looking for a crystal skull. Hello, mountain, you sound a lot like what the next album is going to sound like, guess I'm supposed to climb you now. If I know our hero, he's got moxy, all heart no quit. Oh crap, I was not expecting all these one-eyed sasquatch things. No talky-talk, I've got some sword fighting to do. Whew, glad that's overHOLY HELL THE TREE ARE ALIVE! I take it back, I don't need enlightenment. Run Away! No, seriously, it's a freakin' sharknado! Maybe eating those berries was a bad idea 'cause now I'm inside the trees and that Huntress lady is probably going to chop my head off. No, wait, now I'm like on the tundra and an avalanche is going to bury me. Oh, wait, still got the skull, I must still be high from those berries. Huh? Did I win? No, I think I really am running away. No next step of evolution for us humans, sorry I guess.

Yep, that's Blood Mountain. Josh Homme does the chorus for Colony of Birchmen. Scott Kelly sings something on every album, so he doesn't get special mention. There are some not great parts, like the speaking, but they do something cool right after and the whole album is so all over the place that it doesn't really matter anyway.

I know people like to call Mastodon Prog-Sludge, but c'mon can't we just say Prog-Metal and be happy? The best part of Mastodon is that you never feel like they're doing it just for the sake of the theatrics (like some Maidens made of Iron), nothing is ever a gimmick, it all just rocks in various and head-bobbingly enjoyable ways. Sure, sometimes it sounds like Troy and Brent are singing two completely different songs at the same time, but that's part of the charm if you ask me. Like Supertramp and Steppenwolf and Nirvana, I can't help the fact that I adore every second of it, even the least sensical parts. Give us the new album already!

Bottle Visits the Trash Heap

I usually avoid this hallway. So much garbage, so little value. Still though, plenty of quiet for thinking. Maybe the Lady of the Heap has some good advice. Hey, Lady? You in here?

L: Bottle? It has been a long time. How are things progressing?

B: Up and down. It's a wacky ride out there. Not sure the end is ever going to materialize. The Auditors are really pushing and warping the boundaries of reality, you know?

L: Yes, yes, I know. Doesn't help that they aren't real enough to punch in the gut.

B: Exactly! Hard enough to conceptualize real people, let alone the imaginary consequences of their actions.

L: Well, you know me, I like a good tirade as much as anyone. Go on, pour it out.

B: Ok, you asked for it.

One of the biggest problems I keep running into is that there are no actual billionaires the way people think there are. They get this glazed look in their eyes when you tell them those Lords and Ladies don't have any actual money the way regular people have a jar of quarters, or even $10,000 in a savings account. All they have is some level of control over a localized economy. They are literal Kings and Queens, like you, guarding their piles of garbage. No offense.

L: None taken, go on.

They own corporations, they are literally the government of an economic State, and for the most part they live their lives on the ledger of those corporations. If/when they need physical money, they sell some portion of their assets to pay for it. It might be 5% of some stock, it might be selling a mansion or a rare sports car, it might be firing 500 employees from some underperforming factory.

Yes, of course there are standard commericial bank accounts and all the normal stuff, but for the most part all of that money exists only in the process of exchange, it's all earmarked into the foreseeable future in the form of a contract or in the form of taxes. The only money that exists in tangible form is the money that walks in the front door and leaps out of our pockets, a process in which they literally do not participate.

It's easy for people to misunderstand that because the roles are reversed down here on the hot pavement. Down here, money is what you need in order to do whatever it is you want to do, but up there, money is merely the result of what you do. In the minds of Musk, or Bezos, or Buffett, or any of them they do not work for money, they steer the ship that trickles that money down to you. They literally divide their assets and slosh them around to keep up the appearance of progress and growth.

Where does that difference come from? It comes from the liability shelter of the corporation itself. I like to pick on Musk (he's an easy target), so we need to understand that Musk is neither financially responsible for the 5 or 6 companies that form the economic bubble he lives in, nor is he responsible to the American economy beyond paying taxes on any portion of revenue that exceeds deductible business expenses. Musk the person neither makes nor spends any actual money, he simply manages the balance between income and expense for that corporate network which includes his personal cost of living. All he actually does is trade assets and occasionally take a nap at Grimes's house.

I'm not picking on him just to be mean, and I'm not saying what he does is right or wrong, I'm simply trying to point out that his reality is very different from yours and mine. His actual goal is to send human beings to Mars. Silly or not, that's all he really cares about. Whether he consciously thinks about it or not, he doesn't actually care about anything on its own terms, if it doesn't help accomplish acquiring the money, technology, or protections for his own personal brand of manned interplanetary space flight, then Musk doesn't give a crap.

Let's shift to Warren Buffet. Buffet is the owner and CEO of Birkshire-Hathaway. His salary is only $100,000 a year (compared to Musk, whose salary is basically $0.00). The rest of his net worth is completely invested in his subsidiary holdings. Buffett is a lot more complicated than Musk, because Buffet is basically his own investment firm.

The BH Economy, for lack of a better term, is fueled entirely by a 6-7% royalty on profits, as opposed to Musk's Government contracts and intellectual property. What does that really mean? It means that Buffett, as an objectively successful investor, personally insures BH. BH then provides corporate services to their subsidiary companies (GEICO, Kroeger, etc., you can go look up the list for yourself, it's public knowledge), and reinvests its profits at Buffett's direction. The way you should think of it is that Warren Buffett himself is giving you a business loan for 6% of your net profits. If your company makes 2-million in profit, Buffett gets $200,000 of it, and reinvests the profit from that wherever he thinks it should go. That's a paraphrase, obviously, but mostly accurate. It sounds very similar to Federal/State income tax because it is, the only structural difference is that Warren Buffett is King, he is the government of the State of BH.

The proof is in the pudding, so to speak, his track record speaks for itself. What we really need to understand is that this exact scenario is what the Economic Right says is 100% better 100% of the time than any form of Federal Government intervention or regulation of the US economy. Is that true? I mean, BH lost 11-billion in 2020 from buying Precision Castparts in 2016 because PC folded. What happens when he dies? He is 90, you know?

To be clear, yes, that 11-billion vanished into thin air as far as BH is concerned. Buffett paid 32-billion to buy it, but liquidation only returned 21-billion to his portfolio. Remember, Buffet only makes 100k a year, every bit of the rest is in the little black box we call "the stock market." That 11-billion was part of the working capital of PC, and it has conceptually diffused across the entire money supply. It's not really true, but you can start to conceptualize that 11-billion loss by saying it inflated the money supply by $33 per person in the US. All things being equal, the government should expect an aggregate increase in consumer spending, say about half, of 5-billion. People will spend $5-billion more than they would have if PC was still in business. That spending could go to paying off credit card debt, or buying a new toaster, or whatever. What I'm trying to get at is if I hand you $30, you are highly likely to immediately spend $15 on something you would not have before. Not everyone will react that way, but a lot of people do in the real world, half of a windfall is a completely justifiable splurge.

The tricky question is how much of that 5-billion will walk right back through the front door of a BH subsidiary every year? We'll just divide BH's 245-billion in revenue by total GDP: 245-billion/22-trillion is a little over 1%. So, 50-million. Pretend that's pure profit, BH gets its 6%, we're feeding BH 3-million a year that they just keep reinvesting. Actual math says it will take 3,700 years to make up that 11-billion loss, but actual math isn't the same as corporate math.

BH 's reported net profit was 26-billion, let's say they devote 10% of it to recouping that loss, how long to absorb that 11-billion? 10% is still 2.6-billion, so they basically recoup that loss in 4 years. Does that matter to BH? I don't think so. Does it matter from the ground up? Yes, absolutely. Think of it as 4 years of stagnation inside the BH economy, basically half a decade of real, everyday people treading water. Where does that put us? Oh, look, a Presidential election. Warren Buffet did a stupid thing when Trump was elected, and we could easily be at the break-even point around the time of the next election.

    L: So, what does that mean for you, Bottle?
    B: Well, it's really just one possible way Buffett might compensate for that loss. If your money comes from what Buffett does, you might expect to feel stagnant for the next 4 years and get really conservative with your own spending. The point is that it doesn't matter very much to him personally, he has no reason to care. The manager of a Kroeger store might care a lot, though. It could mean having to fire 2 cashiers, and those 2 cashiers very much care about not having a job anymore.
    I don't like net worth as a measure of value, especially when it acts as the Auditor of what regular people can and can't do. Narzon is back behind the curtain whispering "Mars, Mars, blast humans off to Mars," and Musk just relies "Yes Ma'am, nothing else really matters to me." Buffett's sitting there saying "What do I care? I'm going to die soon, even if I live to 104."Down here on earth, though, people are getting sick and dying, even Rupert Murdoch and his son are foregoing their salaries this year, which by the way is the exact opposite of Milton Friedman's intentions and a whole lot like Communism, States are literally taking rights away from their citizens and blocking access to Federal appeal, and I'm still trying to find $200,000 in the couch cushions. For what? Just so

we can leave more human garbage in space? So we don't have to drive our own cars anymore? So Iowa can feed the whole world's appetite for pork, and soy beans, and $0.20 cheaper gasoline? I can do or quickly learn to do anything, but no one with money has any interest in anything except turning their competition into their employees. We the people are an annoyance to the wealthy, but the other side of that coin is that the wealthy are an incredible hindrance to everyone else.

   The only way to pay off my debt is to be in more debt, and I think we can all agree that's stupid. The only thing I'm failing at is convincing people to give me enough money to pay back my student loan debt. At a certain point you have to say it's not my fault, it's Corporate America's fault because they refuse to let money they don't need circulate outside their control. I need $3,000 a month in my pocket just to get back to 0, but I'm stuck in the under 2k club. The real problem is that there isn't any way for the business sector to recoup that extra money, once you hand it to me it's gone forever because I don't have the collateral necessary to promise to give you more in return. I'm willing to admit that we're both being greedy, but I'm not willing to admit that our motivations are equal when you have the ability to help me but refuse to admit that you just don't care. Honestly, I'd have more respect for you if you did. I wouldn't necessarily want to hang out with you, but at least I could say "at least he's honest."Buffett can eat an 11-billion mistake, but I can't even write him a letter asking for a quarter-mil.

   L: It doesn't sound like there's any conclusion there, Bottle.

   B: There is, I just haven't arrived there yet. At the end of the day, a self driving car and a passenger ticket to Marvin's planet don't help me in any way, because all I'm hearing from the outside world is that the faster I legitimately work myself to death to shore up someone else's bottom line, the better off financially my friends and family will be because that's the only way my debt goes away without begging for their money, and that's the only proper, fair, and morally righteous way the world should be.

L: That's sounds pretty morbid.

B: That's because it is. Extremely morbid, and extremely real. I choose to keep putting it back in a bottle, but some of my actual friends made that choice in the other direction. I don't blame them, it's pure mental torture out here.

L: So what are you going to do?

B: Well, I'm going to keep being me, and I'm going to have Compy throw together a GoFundMe fundraiser. All I lose is a little bit of egotistical pride, and there's at least a possibility that someone might help. Possible is better than nothing.

L: Sounds like you didn't really need my help at all.

B: Au contraire, I needed you most of all, Garbage Lady. Like I always say, I have no idea how it will turn out until I actually do it, and I literally have nothing to lose; couldn't have put it into words if you weren't here to listen.

Soul Asylum

B: In case I don't say it enough, thanks for sticking with me everybody.

E: We can't exactly leave, what with the one-way escalator.

C: Captive audience.

S: Badum, clank.

B: Excellent repartee, my friends. No, I can't do much about the fact that you're stuck in my head, but you're totally free within that context. Skip, you got to see Minion City, and it sounded like you had fun.

E: Yes, I suppose that's true. Ok, what kind of horror show have you got for us tonight?

B: Glad you asked, it's a real doozy. Before we start, though, we have to remind ourselves of some reality. I didn't force any of you to be here, did I? Granted, that Marvin guy didn't really know what he was getting himself into, but we're making the best of it, right?

E: Fair enough.

B: I waffled a bit on Compy, even asked Sandra for advice, but you said it yourself, being a Beefette is more fun than you were having on your own.

C: I did, and it's still true. Garbage Lady is the best friend I've ever had. No offense, Bottle.

B: None taken. I'm crap compared to her. I didn't make Sandra choose castles, did I?

S: No, no you didn't.

B: There you go. I can't make the universe better, but I can try to find some agreeable perspective. Everybody suitably primed? Ok, here we go.

You all know I'm not trying to play on your sympathies or force you to do anything other that really think about how you feel. I know that's extremely confrontational for a lot of people, but this segment of Bottle's Life is all about the not lying part. I like to think I understand me pretty well, so I'm trying to show you all of me.

The honest truth is if you expect me to say that working hard, getting along with everyone, being punctual and reliable, helping others, etc. is the secret to success, then you might want to brace for the impact of the shovel I'm going to smack you across the face with, you know, like the 2x4 in Tommy Boy. How many of the "get a job" crowd are perfectly happy with their own jobs and wouldn't rather be at home sitting on the couch? I'm perfectly happy with my day-job, and I could flick off the lights forever and live completely within my means if it weren't for the fact that it's not enough to pay for my education that people told me to my face makes me too well educated to work for them. Take those words to heart, me Bottle, I'm too well educated to be allowed to work for whatever money is available. Do you not see how insane that is considering that I am long past the point of being able to teach Music Theory at a major University? I got nothing but praise the whole way along. I've tried to find some reason why I was terrible, why I deserved to get fired, honestly it would make the whole thing make so much more sense. Show me how I'm a moron, I will actually say thank you. I love being wrong, it means I learn something, and I LOVE that feeling. Now, if it turns out that I'm not wrong then you have to trust me that I won't hold it against you, but at the end of most real-life arguments people usually say "no, Bottle is basically right." Me being wrong is the first place I look for a solution to any problem, it's always possible.

The point is that I'm trying to follow 'Merica's terribly confusing rule book, but it is some serious work and I'm lost at sea. All of which is merely the prelude to tonight's topic, that video for Soul Asylum's Runaway Train.

You remember, they used photos of actual runaway kids, and many of them were reunited with their families because of it. Bottle wonders "is that good or bad?" Well, statistically speaking, kids with loving stable family situations don't often run away to be intentionally homeless. Sure, some of those kids had legitimate psychological problems, some of those kids were what we might call melodramatic whiny brats, but some of those kids were running away from the very real effects of violent alcoholism and drug abuse, sexual molestation, other forms of physical and psychological abuse, and they very much did not want to be "found." I have no percentages, my point is that it isn't one thing *or* the other, it's both at the same time. That video helped some people, but it hurt others. You can interpret it however you want, but even newly teenaged Bottle was wondering how many of those kids were being sent back to the hell they thought they had finally escaped.

I like my day-job, I'm perfectly happy with my $16.50 an hour, but it's so far below good enough that it's a coin flip whether or not to throw it in the dumpster and light it on fire.

Arrested Development

Special treat tonight, Arrested Development. Unbeknownst to Lindsay, I don't mean the TV show. Don't get me wrong, it was a good show, but I am for lack of a better term a curmudgeonly music critic. Forget Michael and George Michael, let's hear Speech and Baba Oje and the rest of the crew talk about why problems got them pessimistic. Maybe not literally 99 of them like JAY-Z, they are the positive conscious alternative to Gangsta Rap, after all. Tangent: I do have Snoop Dog's debut album in the Folder of Doom, but the story arc just isn't giving me a good entry wound, I mean point. So, G-Funk on the back burner, the representatives from Tennessee have the floor (they're actually from Atlanta, but the song's not called "Georgia." Coincidence isn't omnipotent. Regardless, oblique Green Day reference, for anyone who still has their Bottle Bingo cards at the ready).

3 Years, 5 Months, and 2 Days in the Life of… a band that spent that exact amount of time looking for a record deal. Pretty speedy considering southern Hip-Hop hadn't blown up yet (pretty hard to argue that Arrested Development didn't jump-start Atlanta Hip-Hop considering Outkast formed the year they won a freakin' Grammy). They formed in '88, so Bottle math says there's very little room to argue about the accuracy of the title.

Intro over, now we get to the juicy stuff. there's a standard critical description of Arrested Development, and it goes like this: that first album is phenomenal, but there's this faint aftertaste of preachiness we're not fond of… they did an Unplugged (which we don't really count in either direction)…

oof, the preach-tentiousness of that that second album is too much, put 'em back in the cocoon (Chysalis was their label, get it?). They made quite a few more albums after EMI took them on board in 2000, but their mainstream career was completely over by 1994. I have their debut album, let's give it a spin.

Golden age Hip-Hop has a truly wonderful structure, and it comes from the interludes that literally put the songs in a real-life context, a group of people/friends/enemies actually interacting with the world around them. For an unashamed Mundaninite like myself, that's delicious no matter what they are actually talking about. In this case, it's all about how they feel like they have to fight the whole world just to be their best selves.

Some people are going to press play and immediately key in on the antagonism between Afro- and Euro-centrism, some people will find this album really dated from a sonic perspective, some people will get downright angry. From a certain perspective this album is incredibly confrontational, for example they are not overly enthusiastic about Southern Baptist mentalities. On the other hand, of course it's confrontational, social critique is an integral part of Hip-Hop. I metaphorically threatened you all with a shovel yesterday, how could I have any argue? I listen to it and ask myself "can I relate to how I think they feel, and what they are trying to say?" Yep, sure can. Not the same circumstances or scenarios, obviously, but the underlying dynamics at play, for sure. Stop blindly coping with the horrible (that's what people tell victims to do), and actually try to change things for the better, or as I like to say, get up and do do it.

Relax, they aren't getting all Diogenes on you by saying that Mr. Wendel is a better human in the eyes of whatever God is, it's more like Michael Stipe examining the bums down the alley and recognizing that we are often extremely wasteful instead of generous for no good reason. If you're only going to eat half that sandwich anyway, maybe try sharing it instead of being disgusted when he fishes it back out of the trash can because he's homeless and starving. They're really just saying that they feel like actual people are more important and valuable that the name of the college on your resume. I have no argue with that one either, I just happen to be dangling from the cliff from only 3 or 4 fingers.

Increased attention to spiritual stuffy stuff? That one's not going to do it for me. I think the absurd is as real as it gets, but we don't have to agree on the whys when we clearly agree on the whatsits. I don't mind the rain at all unless it's a euphemism for bullets. I like to think that I am also everyday people, and we definitely don't like getting shot and murdered, or having our girlfriends harassed and assaulted. What's that stupid joke? Punch a pacifist hard enough and he'll quickly find out he's not actually a pacifist? Something like that. Not important.

What is important is that this is a fantastic album. The old-school happy drums and scratch-and-sniff turntables might feel a bit corny for those of us who lived through the era of Grime and feel trapped inside the trap of Trap, but if you remember that what we're really trying to do is stand up for peace and love and self-respect in the face of a world that sneers at things like that, it's not hard to get back into that 80s mindset of party with a purpose. As Ella Eyre reminds us, we don't have to take our clothes off to have a good time, especially considering we're trying to support women who chose to keep their babies like Madonna did, and raise those future kings in the knowledge that community love and support is what really matters. I'll second that emotion (Smoky Robinson? This review might be more allusion than content).

Anywho, on the next Arrested Development, Aerlee Taree challenges Headliner to a game of horseshoes, A GAME OF HORSESHOOOOOOES!

No Doubt

I don't want to scare you guys, but we're on page 313 and getting down to the wire. Not gonna lie, I'm lost. How the hell do we end it? I mean, I'm down to a few really weird things that even I don't want to listen to and it's all European Aristocratic party improv after that. I feel guilty splurging given my aforementioned existential dread. However, none of that compares to the night terrors of another round of Halloween, Thanksgiving, and [shudder] Christmas albums.

I thought about making GREGORY's album the end, but I'm in this nasty "want it to sound really good" headspace. I miss not caring if it sucked. I have to close out Bridbrad's ridiculaous Auditor subplot, something about Communism vs Planned Obsolescence, we have to decide whether or not to stick our forks in the toasters and become a real media empire. I'm applying for closed-captioning transcription jobs and seriously considering looking into alternate teaching certification. It's a freakin' mess in here. This imaginary world is getting way too crazy and complicated for one little bottle to contain, and I'm about to inherit the entire day-shift next May if we don't materialize some minions out there STAT. I know I say I'm every woman, but I'm really just a girl in the world, that's all that you'll let me be....

You've no doubt figured out what tonight's album will be, but I didn't figure it out any quicker, just magically happened at the end of the last paragraph. I know I came in on the breeze, but we've all changed since yesterday. Possum, no that's not right, tragic? Yeah, Tragic Kingdom. Not at all like the Toadies, I'm losing it. It was really sad when Gwen Ifill died, damnit wrong person... snap... aintnohollabackgirl... snap snap... I had a dream once where I was playing tennis with Gwen Stefani on an aircraft carrier, no context or anything, I give up. Enjoy.

Butthole Surfers – Weird Revolution

Kay, so we're back in the Folder of Doom, and I guess I have to point out that the last time Butthole Surfers made a studio album was 2001. They were originally making an album titled After the Astronaut in 1998, but they stopped giving a crap for 3 years. Released in August of 2001, so yeah. You remember their one weird hit song Pepper, and you probably remember being really sorry you checked out anything from their back catalogue. Good. They didn't want you to like their music. They truly did not care. I adore them. So, yeah, the baby shooting laser beams at fighter jets was total coincidence. What's not a coincidence is that they didn't really like this album at all. I could pull out all my Bottle Battle cards and go to town on behind the scenes stuff, but all the drums are made to sound sampled even if they aren't, there's very little actual guitar work of Butthole Surfers "quality," and if I didn't know any better I'd say someone who thought they were important repeatedly screaming that Gibby wasn't being Beck enough for his liking. They were really hyping up a new album in 2018, but that never materialized. Fans of Butthole Surfers tend to like the first album they heard and nothing else. Partly that's because the albums are so random, but it's mostly because the band is the exact opposite of consistent and they literally only do what's fun at the moment. Ironic considering they completely hated making albums and would have rather just played random shows and light hotel rooms and RVs on fire. You know how Primus is bizarre, but you never feel like Les Claypool is going to go to jail after the show? Well, it's the exact opposite here, how did these guys make bail in time to actually get to the show at all? Or like GG Allen, how was that psycho allowed to freely wander around in public? They aren't technically broken up, but I wouldn't hold your breath for much more than a random solo album every few years.

Regardless, Weird Revolution. Is it good, is it bad, does it matter? I think they'd tell you it's pretty terrible, and critics get al non-dairy creamer about it (that's a half-and-half joke), but down here at Crazy Bottle's we ask the important questions: is it confusing? Is it logical? Am I glad I listened to the whole thing? Did I wince at least once, and laugh at least twice? Gimme an hour…

… protecting our women from the bow-legged, bug-eyed normal man… squirrels smoking crack… had to get a bike, had to paint it red… the people in the window are the victims of the sky… Shit Like That is pretty normal for Butthole Surfers… Bob Dylan on a motor scooter… if it weren't for all the people I'd be all alone… get down get down get down get down get… his dog drank gasoline… jet fighters never die… absolutely no ambulances… foreign languages are totally normal for Butthole Surfers… and cried my tears through an eye without a face at all…

Kay, first of all, this is a fantastic album. We have to check the score card, though. Confusing? Yes. Logical? No. Happy Bottle? Indubitably. Wincing? No, actually, this is decidedly tame for Butthole Surfers, but Mexico was borderline. Laughing? A little, but mostly I just enjoyed it.

Final verdict: this album is like if Violent Femmes hired Beck to produce a Revolting Cocks album. It has the flavors of Hip-Hop, Industrial, like a strange Len Steal My Sunshine vibe on Dracula from Houston, and I guess that's technically rap if you're not allowed to just say that's just normal Gibby Haynes. Now, this is by far the most radio friendly album they ever made, I'll give you that. Everything on here is a pop song, albeit filtered through a full sheet of LSD blotters. Unlike their classic albums which veer from pure Noise Rock to Country to

Avant Sludge all in the space of 5 minutes, this one is insanely consistent. If your Butthole Surfers is the ADD exacerbated by cocaine and cheap beer Butthole Surfers, then you will hate it. I however kinda feel like yeah, this *is* the weirdest Butthole Surfers album. It's approachable. By that I mean you could play it for a friend and be like "ok, this really isn't that bad at all. Were they a whole lot weirder before this?," to which you might reply "you have no idea."

To be fair, Independent Worm Saloon is probably my favorite, but Butthole Surfers is not a discography band at all. You should just be glad that any of their albums exist.

Coldplay – Parachutes

Coldplay was super-famous, right? Not a joke, I have this notion that everyone but me followed their entire career. I literally only remember Yellow. Butthole Surfers told us Jet Fighters never die, so I'm just gonna go ahead and say it's because their Parachutes work properly.

I do remember that Coldplay were hailed as the new Radiohead because tons of people detested Kid A, and threw their copies out the window like my friend Stephen did. I honestly didn't know Post-Britpop was a genre. I do know that Chris Martin grew sour on Gwyneth Paltrow's Goop, and started not being a vegetarian after they separated. I have no interest in anyone's dietary proclivities (not by choice, but I've eaten quite a few animals on the list of things people think are off-limits).

Somber, slow music with happy-ish lyrics is a pretty solid recipe in my book, but none of this stuff is actually in my head at the moment. I do know the band actually thinks this album is complete crap, they actually call it "bad music." I have a hard time calling any music bad, the ideas and motivations behind it are what make for a happy or perturbed Bottle. I get to decide that, not you. Press play.

First of all, that's a pretty gorgeous clean tone. Shiver is in 6/8, that's a breath of fresh air. Who honestly hates Chris Martin's half crooner, half sensitive hipster voice? I don't. I like Spies a lot, which is weird considering that siren wail is objectively annoying and my least favorite falsetto for no reason is on full display, but goodness gracious how pertinent is it right now? Yellow is way more Indie-Noise than I remember. It'll get old really quick, but here in the middle of the album it's a nice pick-me-up.

One thing I will say is this album feels a whole lot longer that it really is, it's a completely proper 42-minute LP. Mostly that's because the songs are slow. It also has a very distinct vibe: a black and white hipster montage of early morning housework in your lonely apartment while it's 40-degrees outside (4.4 repeating for you Celsius aficionados). Maybe that's just me, but my brain says this is the opposite of Summer night-time music. It sounds bleak.

OP, I just realized I'm going to have to call myself out. I am totally guilty of saying "you win, crowning achievement as a rookie, have fun with all that fame and success in your future, this is my stop." I've actually done that a lot (Green Day, Megadeth, My Chemical Romance, Cake, Offspring, you name it), but never with a debut album, unless you count Godsmack, which I don't. In my defense, I also said I don't think you have to be consistent in what you do or don't like. Heads, tails, same difference, I guess.

It also now occurs to me that this is a chemtrail album, there are 4 or 5 albums we could do next. Also, the obvious influence of OK Computer is ridiculously center stage. High Speed is the most blatant. No, really, like plagiarism level obvious. That song is a total Abidas, Sunbucks, Michaelsoft Binbows. Still, haters gonna hate, but not me. This is a lovely album whether Coldplay likes it or not. Who cares what their opinion is?

Third Eye Blind

Speaking of Alternative hipster Rock, am I the last person on earth who still remembers all the lyrics to Semi-Charmed Life? Remember when Michael Stipe needed someone to transcribe It's The End Of The World As We Know It and physically hold up the sheet of paper in their Unplugged? As far as I recall, third Eye Blind never did an unplugged, but I have referenced them several times over the last 2 years. Let's not jump off the skyscraper and instead listen to their self-titled debut.

My fellow discerning drugs in music listeners will know that Alcohol and his Vice-President Marijuana obviously sit at the top of the pyramid. Below that we have the Twilight tandem of Heroin and Cocaine. Bit of a free-for-all below that, but basically you have Amphetimines, Hallucinagenics, and Barbiturates. Third Eye Blind fall under the influence of cleaning your entire bathroom with a toothbrush, because "Ooh-woo, Meth."

We have to put the question of Stephan Jenkins's real-life narcissism and business douchebaggery aside, because at the time they made it they thought they were still a group of friends. Filing articles of incorporation and trademark in his own name, and relegating the rest of the band to contract employees came after he realized just how much money he was going to pay them instead of himself. Some people turn into monsters when they win the lottery. It just happened to turn out that Stephan was team Edward (a vampire, if you missed that Twilight set-up). You can be a jerk if you own up to the consequences, but not telling your cofounding co-writer that you cut him our of your verbal 50/50 is pretty terrible. More on that later.

The album itself is about loss, or rather trying to avoid/deal with loss that stems from relationship problems, addiction, suicide, and splitting royalties evenly among all those annoying co-writers. There's more than a whiff of delusional self-victimization going on here.

Unlike Chris Martin, Jenkins's borderline obnoxious California nasal voice with an occasional lisp makes my knuckles itch from time to time. I'm not going to compare Third eye Blind to Dave Matthews Band, except to say that this album is very much like Crash in that you have to decide how you're going to listen to it. If you mistakenly think the feelings and perspectives are normal and totally justified, then I'm gonna squint and make the paper-machet in my mouth face. This is wholeheartedly narcissistic douche-bag type stuff, but the question is if it's serious or sarcastic. Is he saying these are the inner demons he needs to work on, or is he saying everyone else makes bad choices that hurt his feelings? Hard to decide since he never clarifies.

Not everything misses the mark, but there are some big moments when I'm not sure how to take that. Don't think I'm being overly fussy, that's a pretty well-documented reaction to most everything he's done over the last 25 years. No one knows if he's being subtly introspective, or if he's just being a self-important jerk-wad. I have a feeling his heart is in the right place, but he always seems to create his own fork in the road and end up taking the wrong tine. Consolidating stakeholder shares to a single person isn't inherently a bad thing, it definitely helps cut out the direct influence of industry goons from the decision making process, but Cadogan eventually realized that he didn't own his own songs, Jenkins did. We all remember that didn't work out too well for John Lennon, and even though the settlement is private I can assure you Cadogan walked away with ownership of the songs he wrote. Splitting the money evenly inside the band (if that was Jenkins's intent) wasn't what Cadogan cared about, and he flat out refused to sign a million-dollar advance on an EP if he didn't own the songs he wrote or get production credit on it. That EP never got made, by the way.

More white-guy almost rap; it was a really popular, now slightly embarrassing, tend at the time. "Singing with rhythm" as Tommy Lee vainly tried to defend his own abysmal attempt at it. The Tarot cards are all stacked against this album. That's where the "falling man" logo actually came from, we're way back in 1997, remember.

But is it a good album? Only one way to find out... Man, this is fun. It goes by a lot faster than Coldplay's first album even though it's 15 minutes longer.

So, I think the tricky thing about this album is that these are all reaction songs; he's responding to a situation that negatively affects him. Him, he's playing the victim here. If I've taught you anything it's that those reactions are 100% selfish and whiny 100% of the time. What's actually important is working through which ones are valid and which ones go in the dumpster. This album doesn't have a Sorting Hat moment like at Hogwarts, so it's a bit heavy-handed to force Stephan's shittily adolescent business decisions on it.

The real conundrum: is this Alternative Rock? It's Rock, obviously, but is it Alternative? Spoiler alert, no not even freaking close, this is total Mainstream for 1997. I know you're confused, but I think we cnan agree that Foo Fighters were Alternative in the mid to late 90s, but they won the battle of the bands and are now the platinum standard of vanilla Rock. This though, whether good or secretly ironic or not, is total Mainstream "other people are cramping my style" garbage. Yet, I kind of think it's dramatic irony; what he's really trying to say is that this mentality is the source of our own misery.

It's a coin flip. I mean, it sort of ends with the revelation that he can't fix the world, but what does that do to the previous 12 tracks? It's a "you can't go back, only move forward" statement, and in that respect I can say it's great, but you can still hear even that sentiment as a passive-aggressive "if you would only listen to me" kind of thing. I'm just gonna have to assume it feels like what reading my drivel feels like if you didn't know that I'm laying it out there to decide if the way I feel is fair or justifiable. Lots of times it is, but sometimes it's not. I really like this album, but I could be wrong. It could be straight-forward garbage and I'm giving it credit it doesn't deserve. Stephan seems like a total douche-bag, but I'm not totally convinced he's actually trying to be that guy, maybe he's just naturally and tragically believable at it. All I can say is that if I were out on the ledge about to jump and he said that song to me, I'd probably respond "fuck you, you tool" and jump. Clear as mud?

Compulsory license fees

Let's talk compulsory license fees. First, we need to understand what they are. In general, copyright law says that once a song has been published it belogs to the general public, but the owner of the copyright (the composer/songwriter by default, but sale/transfer of copyright is often a mandatory requirement of commercial publication) has the right to collect royalties from its use. We'll ignore all the complications that brought us to where we are today and simply say that the compulsory fee for doing a "cover version" of a song is the greater of 9.1 cents or 1.75 cents per minute. Most songs are under 5 minutes, so we all kind of agree that it's just 9.1 cents per unit.

Let's say I want to put p(nmi)t's cover of Radiohead's No Surprises on an album. As far as I know they are still BMI artists, so I need to obtain BMI's compulsory license for that song. If I'm going to publish 100 copies on CD, then the fee is only $9.10. If Thom York or somebody got mad at me, I'd just whip out my license and say "I paid the fee in good faith, and my version does not alter the song in any significant way. Sorry you're mad about it, but I haven't broken any laws." His lawyers would say "Bottle's right, he doesn't need your permission to do that."

Obviously, my $9 doesn't matter much, but if I were to actually sell 100,000 CDs they might be a little testy about the $9,000 I technically owe them. Scale is important.

You might wonder how how Spotify, Youtube, or even the Major Labels themselves get around this. The answer is that they don't. you can negotiate directly with rights societies and artists for a lower rate, and that's what they do. It's not unfair or evil, business is a 2-way street. On one hand, copyright holders deserve fair compensation, but on the other up front fees can result in huge losses for publishers if revenue is far below the expense of licensing.

Say I'm a real label and one of my artists wants to cover a song. We're going to do a 20,000 unit run because we think this album has real potential. $1,800 is the compulsory fee for that song, and that expense is completely unrefundable. Say we're wrong, it's a total flop, I'm stuck with 15,000 copies of this thing returned by retailers. From a certain perspective it might seem a little unfair that the copyright holder profits from my misfortune.

I look at this whole scenario and I go to the copyright holder and say "look, I'm willing to lose $900 on this thing but that's it. I'll write you a $900 check right now, or I'll tell my artist no. can we make that deal work? It could still flop, but I have accepted that risk and everybody is ok with it, and we move on.

With streaming revenue, this can get out of hand real quick. Spotify has negotiate their license down to half a penny or whatever (because there's not way to predict whether a song will get 12 plays of a million plays, and they can't just write a billion dollar check tomorrow because they are limited by their own subscription rates and payroll). The down side is that these a Spotifies terms, and they apply thaier rate across the board, whether you like it or belong to a PRO or not. Say you're song legitimately blows up, it's getting 100,000 streams a month. The math says you're losing, yes actually losing, $8,600 a month in revenue. Is that a fair windfall for Spotify, or are they raking in the millions by exploiting their negotiated rate?

We can't answer that question inside my hypothetical numbers, but we can get a better understanding of the whole scenario by wandering out into the real world. For 2020, Spotify reports an operating loss of 581-million Euros. Revenue was 7.88-billion Euros, but it cost Spotify over 8-billion to keep their platform alive.

We have to take that at face value. Spotify, as a business, is still a commercial failure. That's bad for the owners of Spotify, but good for everyone who got some portion of that 581-million, but bad because that 581-million is actual inflation, but good because we can use Spotify's loss to buy other stuff. That coin just keeps flipping forever, but the real question becomes which is worse? Is it worse for the music industry itself to lose money because Spotify isn't profitable, is it worse to lose even more revenue by giving Spotify an even lower licensing fee, or is it worse for the industry as a whole to drive Spotify out of business altogether? Adam Smith says "the invisible hand" should decide, Marx would say "either way, you're exploiting artists," actual Marxian Communism says "none of this would have been a real problem if you had just sat at the table and really hashed out a plan for all contingencies."

Rob Zombie – Hellbilly Deluxe...

B: I really should save it for this year's Beefoween, but I need it today. Ow! What was that for?

S: I told you last year.

B: Oh, right. "I hereby outlaw…." I was hoping you weren't serious, but a boot to the head rings loud and clear. May I proceed?

S: Of course. I still have one more boot, though.
B: Understood.

I've got good news and bad news. The good news is tonight we're listening to Rob Zombie's first solo album after White Zombie broke up. Maybe we'll save La Sexorcisto: Devil Music, Vol. 1for actual Halloween. The bad news is we have to navigate this "ethical vegan," PETA award thing. We are Sex-bob-omb, and we're here to sing about demons and living dead girls and rescue farm animals in our spare time!

I'm joking, I hate the industrial food complex too, possibly more than most vegans, ethical or otherwise. I disagree with PETA in terms of their approach to living living people, and their eagerness to treat them in a decidedly unethical manner. PETA very much condones espionage, violence, arson, lying, and blackmail.

What we need to understand is that ethical vegan" is not simply a denotative syntagm. It doesn't merely mean that someone eschews all animals and animal byproducts for ethical reasons. It could mean that, it probably did mean that at some point, but not now. I have many friends who are just vegan, and conversely I don't demand anyone cook their petsif I come over for dinner.

Not everything Ingrid Newkirk says is wrong, by the way. Her logic, however, leads to some pretty terrible places, like publicly saying of course PETA would vehemently oppose a cure for AIDS if it involved animal testing of any kind. She has been directly compared to Che Guevara (born 45 years after Marx became a dead dead girl) by multiple people who aren't me. No, this isn't one of Bottle's famous tangents, it's all extremely relevant. You know how Glen Danzig didn't actually kill your baby or rape your mom? That's because he isn't actually a psychopath. To the best of my knowledge, Rob Zombie is not a psychopath either. Ingrid and Che Guevara, though? Not gonna sugar-coat it, bat-shit insane, murderous psychopaths. To be fair, Ingrid does at least seem to understand that going to prison for killing people is extremely counterproductive to her larger goal of mercy-killing all animals.

I know this is a difficult subject for most people, but I'd like to think that my sharing of things Marx actually wrote is a giant leap toward showing you that there is a huge difference between saying that violent uprising is inevitable given the internal cognitive dissonance of enforced Capitalism and saying "I volunteer, and I brought enough ammo for everyone! Be a good Comrade or I'll put a bullet in your head too."

My point is that Ingrid would rather euthanize a thousand objectively happy and healthy animals a day than let them be "tortured." Torture in this case very much includes adopting them out to new "forever homes."PETA euthanizes 99% of all animals brought to their shelters faster than you can get a pizza delivered to your house.

I personally subscribe to only killing animals if A) you intend to eat them, B) they are dying a painful death in front of you, or C) they are legitimately devastating your resources (like all the damned rabbits around here). Hunting for sport very much offends me, but I'm not going to burn your house down or refuse to eat your sandwiches over it. I refuse to eat Liautaud's sandwiches because they aren't good. Then again, I also adamantly defend assisted suicide and I don't want to be artificially kept alive, so maybe I'm the crazy one.

Next on the list, not all animal research is equal. Yes, there are terrible places and animals are subjected to disease and certain types of physical trauma, but all legitimate research facilities have a care and use committee, and they are regularly audited and inspected. No, I'm not an immortality kind of guy, and no I'm not a humans are special guy either, but knowledge doesn't grow on trees. Sadly, less and less food seems to grow on trees these days as well.

Enough of my silliness, on to my other silliness. I adore Industrial Metal, and Rob Zombie has cornered the market on mixing it with horror. Hellbilly Deluxe: 13 Tales of CadaverousCavorting inside the Spookshow International, now that my friends is a title that just might make Dwight yokum vomit. B-movie samples, necrophilia, the car from the Munsters, all things you should definitely censor and hide from impressionable teenage minds, lest they grow up to be unpatriotic, depraved losers like me and Rob. You could argue Rob is significantly less of a loser than me, but I think I made my point. This album isn't real.

And now for the dismount, the ending of the end, just when you thought it was safe to go back into the water...

E: Bottle, I'm really lost here. I sort of get the coin flip metaphor, but I don't understand the point.
B: Oh, ok, that's sort of the easy part. We're stuck. Instead of doing anything, we're just flipping a coin without calling it in the air. The point if that we are literally ignoring the choice because we're somehow dissatisfied wirh 50/50. I don't know why, I mean statistics says 50/50 is better than 0/100. Still, that's not the real answr to your question. The real answer is that we're afraid of all the consequences, even the good ones.
E:Huh?
B: Let's look at the binary logic, but with goods and bads. Good + good = good, bad + bad = bad, right?
E: Yes?
B: But that's not the whole story. A good thing that turns out bad is bad, but a bad thing that turns out good is also bad, a different kind of bad, but not eberyone has such a discerning palate. The end result is that ¾ of the possibilities are some form of bad. 75% of the time, everything sucks. We tell a lot of stories to make the suck less terrible and/or inflate

how much more awesome that 25% good is, but every once in a while we all pretend to sneeze while saying "horseshit." It's better to keep a mental scorecard and shuffle the burden around appropriately.

E: That looks like favoritism.

B: Dude looks like a lady, doesn't mean it's true. You have to either figure it out, or make it not an issue.

E: But people are unfair, they just are.

B: No, they aren't. they want to be fair, they want their lives to matter. They're unfair because they don't have good choices available to them. Even if they did, they have so much experience getting shafted by making good choices that they eventually give up. Making a game out of life is the real unfairness, in my opinion.

E: But that's still not fair.

B: Nothing is magically fair. You can't make it vanish, but you can recognize that unfair and compensate in a meaningful way. Reward the work, not just split the prize money.

100 times a day people hand me choices that don't actually affect me either way. Sometimes I refuse to make those choices, sometimes I flip a coin, mostly is say "you suck it up today and I'll make it up to you because he's done more than his fair share." Then I remember that, and the next time it happens I go the other way if I can. Now, if you don't like the choices I make, stop bringing me garbage that doesn't affect me. I'm not your mom or your dad. I'm not afraid to make to choose wrong, but I take the consequences into consideration and try to mitigate them. Context is everything.

C: Bottle, do you remember that conversation from Aug. 12?

B: Not by date, no, was that about the time of Skip's little adventure in B-space?

C: Yes, and more importantly, are you sure you're not psychic?

B: Like 99.2%, why? Oh yeah, his wireless adapter crashed and I joked about being the Transcriptionist of Doom. What's your point?

C: Well, now all of a sudden you've pushed us earlier in the evening, and you're moonlighting as a moonlighting transcriptionist afterward. That's a bit iffy, don't you think?

B: Nah, total coincidence. I don't mean the two things are unconnected, I just mean it isn't voodoo magic. There's a logical series of actions that unfolded behind the scenes.

C: Ok, this time I'd love to hear it because I am befuddled.

B: Sure, there are a few not at all supernatural forces at work. 1) I've had years of practice manipulating what jumps to the top of my feed tomorrow, 2) facebook is filtering out a fair bit more garbage than they were evn 6 months ago, and 3) There are only so many sponsored ads to go around. Writing "transcriptionist" obviously gives those things a bump in relevance. I also read comments, so I had names of a couple prominent sites that do first pass speech recognition, but need actual brains to correct them. I also need money and hate gibberish computer generated closed-captioning, so I thought it should only take a month or so to decide if I can really make part time job money at it, what's there to lose except a little more time? The fact that all those things coalesced, not to mention the fact that Bottle's mom was a medical transcriptionist, just means I was predisposed to key in on the possibility. See? Not magic, totally mundane human psychology.

C: Oh. I guess that makes sense. Not exciting, though.

B: Who said life was supposed to be exciting all the time? Not me. In fact, I often imply I'd like it to be even less exciting than it actually is. I don't get bored, remember?

Cabaret Voltaire

S: Sorry I'm late, I had some business to attend to. This earlier than normal stuff is hard to make happen.

B: No worries, but now that you're all here, are you ready for the real terrifyingly clairvoyant coincidence?

C: I think I see where this is going. How morbid are you going to get?

B: Only the minimum. Skip, what did we talk about this morning?

E: Uh, the way we perceive the coin flip.

B: Exactly. Then Compy asked about coincidence, and I talked about how the behind the scenes of facebook play into it.

C: Yes?

B: Ok, so last night I just felt like I needed some Industrial from my dwindling supply of albums, and Rob Zombie came to play. Well, sadly Richard H. Kirk died today. I can't lie, I like Coil better than Cabaret Voltaire, but they are better than Atari Teenage Riot, so we're just going to randomly pick their 3rd album. Read 'em and weep.

C: Wowzers.

B: Save that for a moment, because I'm not done yet. Cabaret Voltaire's 3rd album, Red Mecca, is very explicitly a 50/50 split about the rise of televangelism and the Christian Right on one hand, and the Soviet-Afghan War and the Iranian Hostage Crisis on the other. See the difference between coincidence and Coincidence?

Chorus: Woooowzeerrrrs.

B: Yeah, that's the kind of spook-show Coincidence that keeps me up at night. 1981, if you're keeping an historical checklist. Here it is 40 years later and it's like a recurring theme. Good news, Cabaret Voltaire has that covered with those twisted Henry Mancini bookends. Same dress, different window, as I like to say.

Cabaret Voltaire was pretty out there, more public happening than band at first, but they played a lot of shows with Joy Division and it was the Punk scene itself that made Cabaret Voltaire shows musically legitimate rather than just an evening of fist fights and bottle throwing between the band and the audience. Throbbing Gristle was very interested in signing them to Industrial Records, but Rough Trade offered to give them a tape machine instead of an advance, so the rest is history.

Chis Watson left the band after this album, and they followed New Order into a more commercial direction after Ian Curtis's suicide. So, this is kind of their last proper Experimental Industrial album, and it's really good. You aren't going to have any idea what he's singing when he's singing, but it's probably not optimistic. Instead, what you should focus on is that some kids from Sheffield are trying to make music with found sounds, random pieces of electronic equipment, and only the crappy reality of being teenagers in Sheffield in the 70s, Sheffield being an a significant epicenter of innovation during the Industrial revolution. By the 1970s though, international competition was destroying the iron, steel, and coal mining industries. When Thatcher became Prime Minister in 1979, the bottom fully dropped out and cities themselves became an "economic problem."No secret I'm not a fan of Thatcherism and it's because right-wing economic policies turn human life into a game of numbers. Larger numbers get larger, smaller numbers get smaller, and only abject stupidity can make that reality different. That's great for people who already have enough money to buy their own life raft, terrible for the working class and their children and grandchildren.

Now, you might be under the impression that I hate cities altogether. I don't. The problem is that economic theories cannot translate from one scenario to another. The economic systems of a city are fundamentally different from those of suburbs and rural areas, in large part because each scenario places unique restrictions on the psychology and physical reality of its inhabitants. Add to that the fact that all 3 interact with each other in logistically unchangeable ways, and it should be obvious that a blanket definition of economics is deranged.

We have this strange idea that Urban, Suburban, and Rural areas are naturally separate from each other, that all the businesses should be here, all the houses over there, and the fields and animal poop way out yonder so we never have to think about them. We have trucks and trains and boats to move all that stuff around, so we don't have to think about that either. Everything we need just exists in some warehouse until we're ready to buy it, and someone will bring it over to my house whenever I want. That's a delusion, and it's the actual source of most modern problems. We forget that right now is a unique time in human history. Right now is the living with our choices stage, and we see all of the expected coping strategies: yelling at people to work harder, complaining about the cost of dumb things like education and healthcare, ignoring the actual work, being afraid to get dirty. I'm rambling. We were listening to some kids from Sheffield express their lives at the epicenter of a schism between right and left socio-economic ideologies at a 40-year later schism between right and left socio-political ideologies. Rest in Peace, Richard H. Kirk. You earned it.

Bottle rummages through empty rooms until he finds what he's looking for

Is business as we understand it really the best compromise between individual greed and the public good? If so, to what extent does it require regulation so as not to infringe upon the liberty of those who do not wish to participate?

It feels like we're past the point of no return. China, Russia, even most of Europe is mocking us, or looking at us thinking "what a bunch of morons." In terms of trade, there's a strong argument that most of the world is playing by the WTO rules we helped draft at its founding. I'm giving Trump the benefit of the doubt here, I think he really was trying to force corporations to reinvest in our economy instead of turning us into a nation of importing couch potatoes, but his strategy of raising tariffs was completely nonsensical. Tariffs are not a penalty to foreign trade. Tariffs are a bizarre penalty on ourselves meant to discourage buying imports over domestic products that we end up paying anyway because we have no choice. Corporations don't care what the price is because they deduct any current operating loss from previous profits. The Federal government ends up paying those tariffs as a corporate tax refund. Instead, they won't do either, they won't pay their workers, they won't go pick up anything at the dock, they'll just sit on their hands and wait. Sadly, our short attention spans won't realize this, and when 2022 really sucks they'll blame Biden for shutting down our 20-year military campaign in Afghanistan. In what bizarro reality does that have anything to do with the fact that thousands of people are dying from nasty free-evolving respiratory virus, or the fact that no one wants or is physically capable to work at a meaningless job for a company that doesn't care about them as a human being?

It's not about money, it's not about wealth, it's to the point where I think it's just bullheaded ego. No one has the balls to stand up and say "it's our fault. We were wrong."

In my experience, the more unstable, risky, and desperate a financial situation, the worse people treat each other. That's one of the few correlations that directly translate to all level of structure. Bosses, spouses, friends, rival businesses, when money is crazy they all act like garbage. A lot of it has to do with the way we think about money.

The way we estimate how much money we make or spend can have a huge impact on our outlook. When we compare income to expenses we round, we omit expenses that seem trivial, we project into the future. It seems like it should be obvious, but the reality is that if err in thinking we have more money than we actually do, it feels like we "lost" money, or that it has somehow been "stolen" from us. Conversely, if we underestimate it feels good, we're happy that we have more money and we tend to say "everything is going great." That situation changes so rapidly that we end up justifying our miscalculations and adjusting them in even worse ways.

The most common strategy is to simply ignore expenses altogether, add up income, and expect some metaphorical bill for a portion of it. We all do that with income tax, but we mistakenly summarize it as "I make x-amount, but the government steals 15% of it." First of all, a few minutes with a calculator will tell you your entire tax liability to the penny, but even I don't sit down and do it. I'll freely admit that's dumb. Instead, typical math goes like this:

I make 16.50 an hour, so 8 hours a day equals 132, 5 days a week equals 660, 52 weeks a year equals 34,000. Already I'm several hundred dollars short of the actual number. That's fine if I end up having more money than I expected, but bad because I'm actually being taxed on the 300 I rounded out of my total salary, not to mention any overtime pay I might have earned. The point is that even though I know 34k is a bad estimate, the quality of that estimate changes depending on how I use it in further calculations. We all know there won't be 34k in my checking account at the end of the year, I spend money every day. So, we need to go back to that 16.50 and try to bring it down to something closer to the truth.

As a starting point, let's take that 132 a day and deduct some actual spending. 5% goes into my 401k, so we'll round that up to 7. Pretend taxes are 15%, so 125-19=106. I basically use that 6 in gas every day, so we're at a more realistic $100 a day. Now, I only work 8 hours a day, but it takes up 10 hours of my time. As far as money in my actual bank account, I get to keep $10 an hour.

$100 a day, 500 a week, 26k a year. That's still an overestimate, but it's much closer to reality. That 8,000-dollar difference didn't actually go anywhere, it never really existed. It's simply the difference between the ways I think about money. It's the difference between think I make 16.50 an hour, and acknowledging the cost of making 16.50 an hour. It's also a more accurate gauge of whether or not some one-off gig is worth the extra time. If it's worth 10/hr then it's comparable to my full time job, so something I can do in my spare time without spending any more money needs to be worth at least 5/hr to be worthwhile.

Now the important question. How wrong is my 100/day estimate compared to actual reality? 10 days should be 1,000, but reality says 900. So, my estimate is much closer, but still wrong in the wrong direction. I end up with $100 less than I expected. It's better than my first estimate, -100 as opposed to -300, but it's a serious problem if I already spent that 100 I don't have.

How big of a deal is that 100? The answer depends on how much money I have in my checking account. If my balance hovers around 1,000 then it's fairly insignificant in the short term. Sure, I might be shocked to find 200 less than I expected, but I'm not in any danger of overdraft and I just ease off of doing extra stuff next month. On the other hand, if I'm hovering around 300 or 400 because of unexpected expenses, then it could be a serious problem.

You could do all sorts of things with this thought experiment, but all I'm trying to show you is the real world consequence of sloppy thinking. If you start talking like I actually make 34k a year, I'm going to say "no, I only actually get to use 26k of that." on paper yes, in reality no. 8,000 of that simply doesn't exist. I might get to use it in the future, but then again I might not. By the way, you'd be flabbergasted how different the situation looks from the employer side.

The question I want you to ask is "how sloppy is my own thinking, and how much of my stress am I responsible for creating?"

Forget Capital, forget retail vs. wholesale, forget real or intellectual property, forget the government, forget specialized knowledge, forget all of it. What really distinguishes Capitalism from Communism? The answer is that they represent opposing philosophies of the nature of value. Capitalism posits cost as a measurable balance between want and scarcity and that measured quantity is determined only in the moment of exchange. Communism inverts that relationship and considers value only in terms of the equivalence that results from the exchange. This is very different from our modern conception of market vs. command economy, and for good reason: there is no instruction manual for translating these philosophical orientations into real-world systems, relationships, or governance, and people have done a terrible job of it.

So, even though it's difficult, we have to throw away our preconceived notions and think about things from a hypothetical point of view. Regardless of what your high-school history books told you, the USSR, Maoist China, Castro's Cuba, none of it is actually what Marx called Communism. There's a good reason for that, too. Marx died long before anyone started claiming political power in his name, so he wasn't there to point out that a government with an authoritarian leader shouting "work or die!" is the opposite of his ideas. His idea is just a bizarro version of ours, or rather we are the reverse-psychology version of Marx's materialist history of human society.

Marx's theories were essentially happy little descriptive theories that said "look, the history of Europe is nothing but an endless loop of oppression, revolt, and usurpation. Humanity at large is doomed to be enslaved by that peculiar European hegemony because it can only survive by growing larger and larger, stealing your resources, and enslaving people in an arbitrarily ignorant system of wage labor. Their political and economic theories have no regard for human life or intelligence save for the profits that can be exploited from them, and they use religion to brainwash you into believing that you are unworthy and undeserving of a meaningful existence. The worst part is that they are so smooth, delicious, and highly addictive that you won't even realize until it's too late. Then you'll have a civil war, but even that will be pointless because you'll just end up being the ruling class and oppressing some other group of people."

Enter the 20th century, and the light bulb flicks on over everyone's head. "He's right! All we have to do is start a war and elect our own political dynamos and presto change-o we're the ruling class. Glad he's not here to tell us we're doing it wrong."

Yes, he did say bloody war was inevitable, but he followed that by saying you can't just replace it with your own political representatives, you have to actually do it yourselves. You have to agree on a plan together, work toward it without adult supervision, actually prevent the cheats and liars from stealing it again.

Everybody has to participate and everybody needs to get the reward. Get rid of this money garbage, stop thinking in terms of winning the lottery because 99% of the human population by definition can't win the lottery. Think in terms of what you can do, what you want to do, and what everyone around you actually needs. Food, water, a place to live, and a proper education are a good place to start.

Now, I should mention that none of this actually requires the absence of a monetary system, but it does require removing the political power of money, and accommodating the varying desires and abilities of the people around you.

You have to be willing to accept what others have to give, and allow them the freedom to learn and apply both old and new skills. Nobody sets out to be a terrible doctor, nobody wants to be bad at math, but placing them at the mercy of those who devalue their work for personal gain is barbaric. In other words, you have to both treat people fairly and prevent them from taking advantage of you. That's actual compromise.

How might Marx encapsulate that in a quip? The free development of each is the condition for the free development of all? You know what? Screw it. I give up. Somewhere around here there's someone who can say it better...where did I leave it...aha! We'll just read a speech by James Ikerd. He's a retired professor of Agriculture and Applied Economics, here's a link (yes, I know you're reading a book and I just told you to switch to a computer and type, just go freakin' read it because I can't republish it here):

http://web.missouri.edu/~ikerdj/papers/OhioCorporatization1.html

He sounds like he's sitting at the table with me.

      C: Are you about to do what I think you're going to do?
      B: Finish this stupid book? Yep, sure am.
      S: This is a dangerous game you're playing, Bottle.
      B: Please, Hammer. Don't hurt 'em. Sorry, that was crude. I've been doing it for 2 years now. Intentional or not, Marx was a madmaniacle genius.
      E: What are you guys talking about?
      B: Didn't read it, did you Skip?
      E: No. Why should I? It'll just be more of your confusing confusions.
      B: Exactly! That's the fun part.
      E: Not gonna do it.

B: Even if I point out you're doing exactly what John Ikerd says is the problem?

E: Nope, not even then.

B: Suit yourself. Don't say I didn't warn you.

E: Grrr. Fine. Fine. I'll go read it… you utter bastard!

B: Great News! Skip's here everybody. Now we can pro…

E: You're not seriously going to end this project by arguing that-

B: Shhhh. Don't spoil it. Where was I? Oh, yeah, proceed to the recapitulation and end with my own Shosti5 hammer to the noggin. Unlike Micky-D's, I'm legitimately lovin' it.

Recapitulation

It started with the unassuming intention to listen to my dad's record collection. It became a poorly-tethered carnival ride through life. Now here we are, how's it gonna be? The Capitalists are Communists, the Communists are Capitalists, the working class is just reacting to being exploited, none of it makes any sense.

But, as I like to say, of course it makes perfect sense. Ikerd just told us we need to be Communo-capitalists like the good old days (coincidentally right around the time Marx was trying to finish all those books before he died, but died before he could finish all of those books), and it's pretty impossible to say I don't agree. The secret is all in the rhetoric. I'm sure I wrote the phrase "the words you use matter," and I've been talking about looking at the problem from both directions. People matter, ideologies are garbage. Mutual benefit, not winners and losers. The corporatism Ikerd talked about is the Capitalism Marx was talking about, the Capitalism Ikerd talked about is the Communism Marx was talking about. What took me 2 years to tease out in my own bumbling way, he did in a single freakin' speech. Sure, you could argue my version was more nuanced, more entertaining, more creative, but he's even got the Auditors in there. AND I'VE NEVER READ IT UNTIL TODAY!!!

You can argue if you want, but I've given you all the material I'm drawing from. All I can do is implore you to read more, question everything, and stop electing other people to be in charge of you. Life is hard, stop trying to make it harder. There's no prize at the end of that tournament.

My coworker quit at lunch-time today, and it's pretty impossible to find anyone to work at the moment, let alone replace him at the sales counter. All I can really do is summarize the situation by mocking the people at the top of the pyramid. "Waaa, why do all the poor people hate me?" Because you're the one making them poor, but you're telling them it's their own fault. We aren't stupid, but we're pretty sure you are.

Coda

E: You know what this is like? It's like the end of The Dark Tower series.

B: Is it?

E: Yes. The whole thing. You did a cool thing, went off and did something different, kept telling everybody you had no idea if you would ever actually finish it, then did finish it but said "you're not gonna like how this turns out. You even said you were going to do it somewhere in the middle. You suck.

B: Thanks, man. That means a lot.

E: What is wrong with you?!

B: Nothing. I look at problems from the other direction. Everybody's screaming "get off my lawn," but I couldn't hear them very well, so they came over to my lawn to scream it at me. They mistakenly thought I screamed it back at them, but all I did was point out that their lawn was over there and it appears their own kids are lighting it on fire. I've tried to light my own lawn on fire dozens of times, but I'm apparently terrible at it.

I don't need permission to do what I want because nothing I want to do hurts people. My little 3-foot radius is a no bullshit zone, and even people who say they hate me enjoy being there. I'm plenty confusing, but I like to think the results speak for themselves. I love people, but I hate their stupid ideas. I blame the ideas for that one.

E: So you're, and I say this against all logic, a Communo-capitalist?

B: Nope, just a part of a person I've never actually met. I was born inside an idea, and though it's very tempting to grow my wealth and power into a proper Empire of Doom, I think what I'd really like is to take a proper nap. Wake me up when you guys finish making the book suck less. Or more, it belongs to you now. When you're done I'll publish it proper and we'll find something else mutually beneficial to work on. Cheers.

And now a word from our befuddled narrator

I, um, I guess, no…. Welp, hi everybody. Bridbrad here. That certainly qualifies as an ending. I mean, I think the moral of the story was that we're all confused because Marx didn't just invent Communism for the fun of it. He also invented our concept of Capitalism so that Communism could be its enemy while being the same thing at the same time, but all he was really doing was pointing out that either way you look at it, you're being exploited and in turn exploiting others, so what ridiculous non-sequiter way would Bottle put it? Gimme a moment… something about an album… Compy, can you help me out here?

C: Ha! Ha ha, ha ha ha ha!
BB: What? What's so funny?
C: Spirit animal.
BB: What?

C: Lord Sutch. He said Lord Sutch just might be his spirit animal, and everybody had fun right up until they realized he wasn't actually joking.

BB: I'm not following.

C: No reason you would. He buried it in his off-hand dismissal of Adam Smith next to "Hitler's garbage prison diary."

BB: Yeah, I remember that part. So what?

C: Ok. Do you know anything about L. Ron Hubbard?

BB: The science fiction writer?

C: Yes, but he also invented an intentionally fake religion for the purpose of demonstrating the power of Religion. The whole kit and caboodle: aliens, a pyramid scheme, only famous people can afford to join, and the only real rule is that you have to actually trick yourself into believing that it's real, then go crazy.

BB: So?

C: "He was basically Alice Cooper before Alice Cooper," but he was really just copying Screaming Jay Hawkins. I think what Bottle's trying to say is that we're all just living in the imagination of Karl Marx. We can't help it. We're doomed to destroy everything like the first half of Nevermind, then rebuild it because it's the only structure we understand.

BB: Damnit, Bottle!

B: Shhhhh. I'm trying to take a nap.

Epilogue

... and just like that, I'm done writing this 3rd book. It's a fair bit shorter than I expected, but I got that M. Night Shipoopie twist in there, so that's cool. Skip still has some major editing to do, but with any luck I'll be puking it out into the real world in time for my friends to gift their enemies a doozy of a trilogy for Christmas.

B: Ready to finish this piano album, Mr. Bones?

WHENEVER YOU'RE READY TO TAKE THIS TOP HAT BACK.

B: You are like a bizarro Frosty the Snowman, aren't you? How delightful. I can't see nothing, you gotta open my eye. Index me Compy.

C: But I don't wanna do it.

B: Go ahead, index me….

So said-eth Bottle,
Sept. 9, 2021.

Artsist Being Reviewed

A Perfect Circle, 62
Arrested Development, 310
Art Garfunkel, 159
Astrud Gilberto, 107
B52's, 149
Beastie Boys, 142
Better Than Ezra, 85
Between the Buried and Me, 262
Blink 182, 267
Bloodhound Gang, 273
Bob James, 129, 130
Boney James, 133
Bram Tchaikovsky, 83
Breaking Benjamin, 297
Bush, 185
Butthole Surfers, 314
Cabaret Voltaire, 328
Cloudkicker, 196
Coldplay, 316
Crash Test Dummies, 280
Creed, 293
Deltron 3030, 15
Des'ree, 135
Detective, 227
Dethklok, 74
EL&P, 91
El-P, 12
Flora Purim, 134
FM, 228
Fugees, 50
Genesis, 96

Gentle Giant, 229
Gerard Smith, 208, 234
Giant Crab, 259
Greta van Fleet, 52
Greta Van Fleet, 47
Griot Galaxy, 219
Guiffria, 89
Guns 'N Roses, 32
Hillary James, 129
Intergalactic Touring Band, 98
James Horner, 18
Jazz Crusaders, 138
Jimmy's Chicken Shack, 294
Kansas, 8
Kendrick Lamar, 210
Kids See Ghosts, 286
Krokus, 161
Lee Greenwood, 165
Lightning, 232
Linkin Park, 281
Looters, 256
Lorde, 295
Marianne Faithful, 11
Mastodon, 13, 169, 299
Me First and the Gimme Gimmes, 272
Metallica, 72, 110, 292
Molly's Yes, 242
Moody Blues, 29
Najee, 140
Neil Diamond, 63

Nickelback, 293
No Doubt, 313
Noonish Moon, 65
Oasis, 85
OPM, 289
p(nmi)t, 116, 149
Pearl Jam, 145
Pointer Sisters, 158
Red Hot Chili Peppers, 30, 70
Red Rider, 6
Rob Zombie, 323
Shadric Smith, 262
Sheriff, 225
Shostokovich, 19
Snarky Puppy, 199
Staind, 275
Starcastle, 255

Steve Miller Band, 161
Sting, 68
Sum 41, 269
Supertramp, 10, 253
System of a Down, 24
The Cars, 80
The Fireman, 218
The Interrupters, 206
The Union Underground, 265
The Vandals, 16
Third Eye Blind, 317
Trillion, 7
Tripping Daisy, 280
TV on the Radio, 209
U2, 204
Weather Report, 163
Yes, 5

www.ingramcontent.com/pod-product-compliance
Lightning Source LLC
Chambersburg PA
CBHW031232290426
44109CB00012B/264